PRINCE ALBERT

PRINCE ALBERT

The Life and Lies of Al Gore

**DAVID N. BOSSIE &
FLOYD G. BROWN**

Foreword by Robert D. Novak

Merril Press
Bellevue, Washington

Prince Albert

First Edition
Published by Merril Press
June 2000

Merril Press
Merril Mail Marketing, Inc.
P.O. Box 1682
Bellevue, Washington 98005
Telephone: 425-454-7009
Visit us at our website for additional copies ($9.95 each) of this title and others at www.merrilpress.com

Library of Congress Cataloging-In-Publication Data

Bossie, David N., 1965-
   Prince Albert: the life and lies of Al Gore / David N. Bossie & Floyd
   G. Brown ; foreword by Robert D. Novak.
        p. cm.
   Includes bibliographical references and index.
   ISBN 0-936783-28-1
      1. Gore, Albert, 1948- 2. Gore, ALbert, 1948---Ethics. 3. Vice-
Presidents--United States--Biography. 4. Legislators--United States--
Biography. 5. United States. Congress. Senate--Biography. 6. United
States--Politics and government--1993- I. Brown, Floyd G., 1961-
II. Title.

   E840.8.G65 B67 2000
   973.929'092--dc21
   [B]
                                                            00-032862

PRINTED IN THE UNITED STATES OF AMERICA

DEDICATION

To my parents,
Norman and Marie Bossie,
whose love and encouragement know
no bounds and whose values
showed me the right path.

D.N.B.

To my children,
Peter, Patrick and Olivia,
because I want you to know
the value of truth.

F.G.B.

TABLE OF CONTENTS

FOREWORD

By Robert D. Novak

In the summer of 1994, David Bossie and Floyd Brown arrived at my Washington, D.C. office on Pennsylvania Avenue, one block from the White House, in a visit arranged by my daughter Zelda, who then was working for me as a reporter. It was a remarkable experience.

It was the first time I had ever met either of them, and the first time I ever heard of Dave Bossie. Like everybody else who follows politics, of course I knew about Floyd Brown. He had become famous-though most mainstream journalists would call him notorious-for his memorable Willie Horton television commercial ("Weekend Passes") directed against Democratic presidential candidate Michael Dukakis in the 1988 campaign. But most journalists had never met him, and neither had I.

Bossie and Brown did not arrive at my office alone-or unarmed. They brought with them a huge evidence stash: documents, letters, transcripts and clippings. Their common purpose was to condemn William Jefferson Clinton as so morally and ethically challenged that he could not serve as President of the United States.

The pattern of making maximum accusations that sound outrageous to many people but backing them up with fastidious documentation is the Bossie-Brown style. It has characterized their political endeavors, jointly and individually, that has helped shape the politics of the past decade. It is also the method employed in producing Prince Albert.

That hoard of irrefutable evidence that they brought me in 1994 provided the raw materials for several future columns in addition to providing fascinating details about manifold scandals or potential scandals that I did not have time to explore. Not long after our meeting, Brown moved to Seattle. But in the intervening six years, I have worked with Bossie on many projects and found him to be an invariably accurate source. He and Brown make no pretence at objectivity or even fairness, but accuracy is their watchword.

At the time of their meeting in my office, Bossie and Brown since 1992 had been running Citizens United--Brown as chairman, Bossie as director of political affairs and communications. Citizens United was described as a "conservative grassroots lobby," but it was really a fact machine directed against Bill Clinton. Brown still heads Citizens United, and Bossie now owns and edits a monthly newsletter packed with new information called The Dave Bossie Investigative Report.

Both have functioned for the most part outside the political mainstream, but they are also Republican activists who have been deeply involved in regular election campaigns. They occasionally appear smack in the middle of that mainstream-leaving behind them a wake of disturbed politicians. I shall never forget the look on the face of the platform committee at the 1996 Republican national convention in San Diego when Floyd Brown, as a Washington State delegate, showed up as one of their number. Much the same attitude was held by some members of the House Committee on Government and Reform and Oversight (the Burton committee) when Dave Bossie served as its chief investigator in 1997-98 (after duty as an investigator in the Senate Whitewater probe).

Why do Bossie and Brown so frighten their own allies? Are they not fighting on the same side in the same war?

They are, but they use different weapons. To forestall a Clinton-Gore hegemony in American politics, they do not deal in euphemisms or drawing-room language. Considering the implacable nature of an enemy typified by James Carville, they return fire with fire. That is because they consider the stakes so high. "Al Gore, Jr. wants to be President," they write, "so he can run our lives, not run the family farm in Carthage."

They take no prisoners, contending that financial support from polluters is not an aberration by environmental champion Gore: "Like his friend and boss Bill Clinton, Al Gore combines the worst attributes of socialism and capitalism, bureaucracy and bribes. Their DLC [Democratic Leadership Council] 'centrist' liberalism prefers influence peddling to free market competition. Clinton and Gore like to sell government favors to big business for a price."

Albert Gore, Jr. has been the subject of an ample supply of biographies, some of them quite objective and quite thorough. But there is nothing like Prince Albert. Indeed, it is less a biography than a multiple-count indictment. It is the full dossier on the Vice President. Such a dossier is required to counter the image of Gore as a southern centrist, occupying the middle of the road in contrast to "far right" Republicans. As conventional biographers do, Bossie and Brown begin with Sen. Albert Gore, Sr., but in much greater detail and without dwelling in psychobabble about the demands on Prince Albert to attain the presidential heights that his father had sought unsuccessfully. Moreover, they reject the portrait painted by the son of a courageous southern liberal who lost his Senate seat in 1970 because of his stands. Rather, the Vice President inherited a tendency to hide his liberalism-in the case of the senior Gore with strategically placed votes.

While "pompously and piously" condemning Judge Robert Bork for opposition to the 1964 civil rights act, "Gore neglected to mention his father had voted against the bill." The old Senator also joined the majority during the Republican 80th Congress in voting for the Taft-Hartley Act, designated by unions as a "slave labor" bill. "Al Gore has created a retrospective myth that hails his father as a brave civil rights crusader. Albert Gore spent far more time crusading for Armand Hammer than he did crusading for oppressed black people." The late Armand Hammer, the oil tycoon who has now been revealed as a Soviet agent, is only briefly mentioned in conventional Gore biographies. But not in this one. Hammer was the source of the Gore family fortune, and the two Alberts "both ran errands" for him. To Bossie and Brown, the two Gores "adopted an equally cautious attitude toward the USSR during the Cold War. Both father and son usually shied away from boldly confronting the big issues of their respective eras." Gore's sponsorship of the ludicrous Midgetman missile, the basis of his reputations as an arms control expert, is correctly derided here. "Like his appeasing father, Gore never thought of overthrowing the USSR, only of co-existing with it." As a Senator, the younger Gore consistently opposed anti-Soviet initiatives: in Angola, in Cambodia and, most notably, in Nicaragua. The arguments for support of the Contras by his mentor and patron, New Republic owner Martin Peretz, "failed to overcome Al Gore's moral cowardice and political calculation."

The "shining exception" cited here for Gore in foreign policy was his vote, against the urgent wishes of the Senate Democratic leadership, for the Gulf War in 1991. But even here, he is shown as a calculating politician. Bossie and Brown report the never denied story, ignored by conventional biographers, of the Senator bargaining with Senate Republican and Democratic leaders to find out how much speaking time on the Senate floor each would give him if he came out for attacking Iraq (Republican) or, instead, for not going to war (Democratic).

The image for Gore asserted by the authors is as a "liberal wolf in sheep's clothing," repeating the Clinton pattern. "Contrary to his DLC image, Gore, like Clinton, is a big spender and thus a big taxer." The authors do not depict Gore slowly evolving as a liberal but rather exposing what he previously had hidden on controversial social issues. "Apparently, Gore opposed homosexuality in his early years only to appease his conservative constituents in Tennessee. He told Tennessee voters what they wanted to hear only in order to get elected. His true opinion on the subject finally emerged."

Gore is actually seen as less deceptive than Clinton, as in his astonishing 2000 campaign position "to completely overturn the ban on gays and lesbians in the military, even if Gen. Colin Powell opposed him. Gore said he would only appoint members of the Joint Chiefs of Staff who share his absolute views on gay liberation. Clinton would never say anything that direct, forthright and fanatical on a controversial issue." Indeed, Bossie and Brown paint a Gore who in the White House would govern to Clinton's left. They predict Gore would "genuflect more to the needs of Mother Earth than Clinton," would be more aggressive in using military force around the world and would "work much harder to remake the country to his technocratic specifications than lazy, frivolous Bill Clinton." They see "self-righteousness" replacing "self-pity" in a Gore White House.

It's all footnoted. There is much more to the Al Gore story than the Buddhist temple escapade and telling all those tall stories, though that is recounted as well. But will Republicans try to strip the sheep's clothing from this liberal wolf? The facts have been provided for them by Dave Bossie and Floyd Brown.

INTRODUCTION

The cold night of January 24, 2000, Al Gore was on fire. Surrounded by trade union activists and democratic party loyalists, the stiff Ivy Leaguer was transformed into a bar room brawler. It was the first caucus night of 2000 in Iowa, and the Vice President trounced his opponent for the democratic nomination, former Senator Bill Bradley. He moved quickly across the stage that night. His arms waved at hyper-speed. His words were fluid and tough.

Gore's target that night was the Republicans, and their heir apparent George W. Bush, and he attacked him without mercy. Gore was the nominee and he was no longer the wooden statue. Sweat poured from his brow as he heated up the invective against what he called reckless tax cuts that would end America's prosperity. "Are you better off today than you were eight years ago?" he asked. The Iowa crowd screamed in sweet chorus: "Yes."

How did this transformation take place? Weeks before this night, the media was pronouncing the Gore campaign dead. This rapid change in the campaign's dynamics brought memories flooding back into our minds: memories of other campaigns and other similar nights. The year was 1992. The candidate was Bill Clinton. His campaign was pronounced dead nearly eight years earlier to the day. Clinton's career had been on the ropes as a result of the Gennifer Flowers' tapes. Little did we know at the time, Clinton's handling of that controversy is what would cement his relationship with the American people.

Americans love an underdog and Gore had effectively gone from front-runner to winning underdog. Al Gore had morphed himself again, and this process of always being willing to change and adapt is what he shares with his mentor Bill Clinton. It is also the reason Gore is a very successful politician.

Al Gore has completely revised himself many times in his life: from tobacco farmer to tobacco fighter, from southern conservative democrat to southern liberal, from friend of business to friend of the earth, from private school scion of a wealthy family to dirt poor country farmer, from Ivy League war protestor to war hero, from internationalist foreign policy wonk to defender of his native Tennessee, from reformer of politics to defender of the *status quo*, from pro-life congressman to pro-abortion Senator. Transitions, morphing, changes, revisions and adjustments come easy to Al Gore.

This is why he caught our attention, and why we knew his whole story needed to be told. This is the story of the life and lies of Al Gore. As President, you will never be sure of what he may do because change is the only constant in Al Gore's life.

We start with a history of his family. To understand Al Gore you must understand his roots. His father, disappointed that he didn't achieve the Vice Presidency raised Prince Albert to be President. Al Gore's life has been building toward this campaign. Each move has taken him closer to this final goal. To understand Prince Albert you must understand his progression.

Gore is a street fighter. We believe he has an advantage against George W. Bush. The purpose of this book is to help you, your friends and family make an informed decision on Election Day.

We know that much of what we share in this book will never be told to the voters. Ironically, as in 1992, the media is again protecting the liberal candidate. Please don't keep the information you learn in this book a secret. Pass it along.

We want to say thanks. First, without Chris Gray this book would not have been possible. Thank you for your months spent working on this project. Chris, you did a masterful job.

Second, we wish to thank our families. We do what we do because we love our families, and we love our country. And their support allows us to do so. To Joseph Ingrisano, Mary Beth Brown, Barbara Comstock, and Katrina Haag, we offer our gratitude for suggestions to the manuscript. To the dean of investigative journalism, Robert Novak, thanks for honoring us by authoring the foreword. And, thanks to John Mastranadi and Jim Schumann for their encyclopedic memories.

We hope that after reading this book you will understand why we believe Al Gore to be more dangerous than Bill Clinton.

Clinton's effectiveness as president was undermined by his character weaknesses and lack of self-control. Al Gore has purpose of mind, self-control, and passion.

Al Gore will be much more dangerous than Clinton to our liberty and freedom if he is elected president.

Sincerely,

Dave Bossie and Floyd Brown

ONE

The Gores: A Southern Ruling Class Family

The Tennessee Gores

Al Gore, Jr. often refers to his humble rural Tennessee roots in speeches. Gore likes to paint himself as a self-made man tilling the soil. The occupant of the Vice President's mansion claims: "I live on a farm today." [1] To listen to him, only overwhelming popular demand forced Gore to leave the family farm. Gore rarely, if ever, mentions how his relatives distinguished themselves in politics, law, medicine, business, and literature since the seventeenth century. One Thomas Gore, Gentleman, helped to found the first English colony at Jamestown, Virginia in 1607. He was the first of many Gores to assume leading roles in the American South. [2]

After this first Gore settled in Virginia, many cousins followed him there or immigrated to nearby Maryland. Like most early settlers, the Gores moved south and west seeking virgin land so many of them moved to the Tennessee and Mississippi territories.

During the War for Independence, two Gore brothers, both privates in the Virginia Line of the Continental Army, fought well enough to earn large grants of land in the Tennessee territory. Their land grants located in what is now Overton County, Tennessee, next to Smith County, where the Vice President's current estate sits.

The Tennessee Gores did not prosper as much as their cousins who settled in Mississippi did. The Mississippi Gores became landed gentry and members of the learned professions of law and medicine. The crops and cattle suited for Middle Tennessee did not return the rich profits enabled by Mississippi cotton. Like their Virginia ancestors, the Tennessee Gores grew and harvested tobacco. But tobacco did not return the profits cotton did. So, the Tennessee Gores were unable to purchase slaves for labor. They also were unable to become as educated and powerful as their Mississippi cousins. Yet, their more affluent Mississippi relatives chose not to purchase slaves, although they certainly could afford them.

The Mississippi Gores also tended to oppose secession after Lincoln's election in 1860. However, although the Tennessee Gores were poorer than the Mississippi branch, they were more ardent supporters of the Confederacy. Even then, the Tennessee Gores were more partisan Democrats than their Mississippi cousins were. Many of the latter owed allegiance to the Whig party. When war broke out in April 1861, most Tennessee and Mississippi Gores joined up to fight for the Confederacy. At least one of Al Gore, Jr.'s great-grandfathers wore the gray and served in America's bloodiest war.

Gore's paternal grandfather, Allen Gore, was a farmer of modest means. However, Allen Gore shared a lifelong friendship with Cordell Hull. Hull (1871-1955) was an internationally renowned Tennessee politician from the town of Carthage in Overton County. Allen Gore, like Hull, a Baptist farm boy, lived in the neighboring hamlet of Possum Hollow. In their boyhood days, Allen Gore and Cordell Hull would "run the river" together during the 1880s, rafting down the Cumberland River to Nashville, the state capital, and then hitch a ride back on a steamboat.

Hull was more ambitious than his friend was. By studying hard, Cordell Hull managed to graduate from Cumberland Law School. Hull then politicked hard in the Democratic Party to win elections for the offices of state legislator and circuit judge. Judge Hull, as he was known back home in Tennessee, rose to become U.S. Congressman for Tennessee's Fourth District in 1907, Democratic National Committee Chairman in 1921, U.S. Senator in 1931, and finally, Franklin Roosevelt's longtime Secretary of State, 1933-1944. Hull still holds the record for longest tenure at the State Department, over eleven years. Historians also reckon him among the most incompetent leaders of the State Department. Hull was a bungling diplomat who was utterly ignorant of foreign languages and cultures. He was retained because FDR chose to be his own Secretary of State, and needed a front man to screen his devious maneuvers.

Hull became renowned for not knowing what his own President was doing in foreign affairs. Hull's pronounced lisp also made him a butt of ridicule among the Washington press corps and diplomatic community. Hull was ashamed because his wife's father was Jewish. So he went out of his way to avoid getting involved with any foreign policy matters dealing with Jews. During the late 1930s, when European Jews were clamoring to enter the United States to escape Hitler, Hull delegated immigrant decisions to State Department official Breckinridge Long, a notorious anti-Semite. Long simply turned a deaf ear to the entreaties of the Jewish refugees. After the U.S. entered World War II, Long pretended the Holocaust was not occurring. Hull defended Long's policy toward Jews in his memoirs.[3]

Besides being a pompous advocate of reciprocal trade agreements, Hull's big claim to fame consists of being the "Father of the United Nations." He was awarded the Nobel Peace Prize for helping to found this Parliament of Man. Hull believed deeply, along with FDR, that the United Nations would end war and the struggle for power between nations. No individual better symbolized this disastrous monument of utopian delusions than Cordell Hull.[4]

But although Hull flopped at foreign policy, he left a lasting legacy in domestic politics. The Gore family shared Hull's devout faith in progressive taxes that soaked the rich. They also cherished his hostile attitude toward private business corporations. By assisting Albert Gore, Sr. to win his former job as Tennessee's Fourth District Congressman in 1938, Hull did much to found the Tennessee Gore political dynasty. During the 1938 campaign, Albert Gore, Sr. repeatedly traded in on his family's association with Hull. Posing with campaign posters showing Hull's picture, Albert Gore, Sr. asserted on the stump, "He (Hull) is my ideal in public life. I will seek the advice and guidance of Judge Hull." [5] Gore did just that. Critics of Vice President Gore's pompous, humorless manner may not realize it traces back to Cordell Hull. David Maraniss and Ellen Nakashima of the *Washington Post* observe: "Hull's public manner was invariably formal and correct, as if to insist that he never be taken for a hillbilly from the hollows of middle Tennessee. Gore, Sr. consciously modeled himself after Hull, adopting the same formal bearing for the same reason, but then slightly exaggerating it: always in dark suit, white shirt, and tie; courtly, but rarely relaxed in public, little small talk or informality, always on, speaking in complete sentences full of Latin-rooted words, as if his thoughts were being recorded for history.[6]"

The stiff manner adopted by Cordell Hull and Albert Gore, Sr. bespoke a deep sense of inferiority about their backgrounds. Unlike say, Harry Truman or Ronald Reagan, they could not joke about themselves and put audiences at ease. They were unable to charm or make small talk. They could only grimly drone out their prepared texts. These two Tennessee social climbers inflicted their painful pomposity upon Al Gore, Jr.

Despite his droning speaking style, Gore, Sr.'s close identification with Hull allowed him to easily win the Democratic primary. The primary win automatically handed Gore the general election for the latter's House seat in 1938. Albert Gore, Sr. emulated Hull's deep faith in the United Nations during his House and Senate career. Both Gore, Sr. and his wife Pauline served as longtime delegates to the United Nations. They impressed the value of UN activities upon their children. It was fitting that Vice President Gore, grandson of Hull's longtime friend, became a cheerleader for the UN. After several American military personnel died in a helicopter crash over Iraq in 1994, Al Gore, Jr. intoned solemnly "that they died in the service of the United Nations."[7] Dying in the service of the United States is trivial by comparison?

The Mississippi Gores

The Tennessee Gores needed a boost from Cordell Hull, their Carthage neighbor, to rise to power. The Mississippi Gores already boasted national political influence in Thomas Pryor Gore (1870-1949). This Mississippi Gore cousin, although totally blind from accidents in his youth, graduated from Cumberland Law School in Lebanon, Tennessee a year after Hull did in 1891. After migrating to Texas and the Oklahoma territory, Thomas Gore became Oklahoma's first U.S. Senator in 1907, the same year Hull was first elected to Congress. He also became the U.S. Senate's first blind member.

Thomas P. Gore served in the U.S. Senate 1907-1921 and from 1931-1937. A stern follower of the Progressive movement, he became renowned for outspokenly opposing big business, especially the railroads, utilities, and investment banking houses. Thomas P. Gore ardently supported regulating these big business concerns. He also devoted much time and effort to securing compensation for the Indian tribes of Oklahoma. Although usually anti-big business, Thomas Gore did favor oil companies since Oklahoma was rich with petroleum. He designed and legislated the oil depletion allowance for petroleum producers. The oil depletion law is still in force today.[8]

But Thomas Gore became best known for attacking and condemning the foreign policies of both Woodrow Wilson and

Franklin Roosevelt. Thomas Gore was an ardent isolationist and American nationalist. He condemned the involvement of the U.S. in both World Wars. Thomas Gore voted against American involvement in both World War I and the League of Nations. He lost his Senate seat in the 1920 election for his isolationist stance. After being re-elected in 1930, Thomas Gore continued to eschew overseas involvement. Thomas Gore also resisted many New Deal financial policies. Roosevelt's abandonment of the gold standard especially excited his disgust. Senator Gore confronted FDR personally with his disagreement and contempt. He refused to allow Roosevelt to call him "Tom."

Gore especially despised FDR for praising the "common man." Thomas Gore was a paternalist and elitist who disdained public opinion and popularity. The arrogance of the Gore family, so obvious in the current Vice President, showed itself in the blind Oklahoma Senator's character. Roosevelt found Gore such an irritant that he gave New Deal challenger Joshua Lee enough help to beat the Senator in the 1936 Oklahoma Senate primary.

Although Thomas Gore bravely resisted FDR and "the age of the common man," he was guilty of grave sin himself. In 1892, while already blind, he raped a blind teenage girl in Texas and impregnated her. His parents used their influence to buy the raped girl's silence. Like Vice President Gore's boss Bill Clinton a century later, Thomas Gore committed perjury to save himself from prosecution. The future Senator's mother raised the child conceived in the rape as her own daughter back in Mississippi.[9] Since Thomas Gore was an atheist, he did not let shame or guilt over this rape retard his political progress upward. He just went along with the myth of innocence his powerful parents created for him.

Senator Thomas P. Gore's most lasting legacy does not consist of legislation, speeches, or even sexual assault. Instead, his arrogant legacy lives on in his beloved grandson, writer Gore Vidal. Vidal is internationally celebrated for his novels, essays, and blatant espousal of gay liberation, sexual promiscuity, and atheism. Vidal idolized his grandfather Gore. He used to read to him for hours while a child. Vidal modeled his elitism, his isolationist foreign policy, his contempt for business, and his atheism after his grandfather Gore's practices. Vidal even jettisoned his first name Eugene in favor of his middle name Gore, in order to honor the blind old Senator.[10]

Gore Vidal follows his grandfather Gore in disdaining the Tennessee Gores as social and intellectual inferiors. He mentions how the old Senator ranked socially higher in Washington than Albert Gore, Sr. during the 1940s and 1950s. The Tennessee Gores were Southern Baptists, unlike the Mississippi Gores who were either Episcopalians or atheists. Vidal usually conceals this disdain since he actively assisted and defended the Clinton Administration, especially during the impeachment crisis. But Gore Vidal sometimes jokes openly about Vice President Gore's robotic personality, Baptist piety, and lack of humor.[11]

Despite Al Gore, Jr.'s constant sermons about farm life in Tennessee, the Gores excel at playing hardball in Washington, D.C. Al Gore, Jr. wants to be President so he can run our lives, not run the family farm in Carthage.

TWO

The Sins of the Father: Albert Gore, Sr.'s Political Career

The Hardscrabble Years

Albert Arnold Gore, Sr. (1907-1998) cast a giant shadow over his son's life. It is impossible to understand the son without understanding his father. Al Gore, Jr. still lives according to the values and habits imposed upon him by his late father and still living mother.

Education offered Albert Gore, Sr. escape from his father's farm in Possum Hollow. Gore, Sr., as noted, modeled himself upon his father's famous friend Cordell Hull. By studying hard and acquiring a law degree, Gore, Sr. hoped to become powerful and famous. After graduating from high school, Albert Gore, Sr. taught in the one-room schools of Smith and Overton County. This experience colored his entire life. Albert Gore came across as a righteous, condescending schoolmaster, bringing civilization to unwilling teenage savages. He always knew what was best for his charges. Both his public speeches and personal conversations resembled classroom lectures. Al Gore, Jr.'s speaking style follows his father's stern schoolmaster approach. Teaching in these rural schools also enabled him to attend Middle Tennessee State Teacher's College. It made him familiar to the voters of the Middle Tennessee region. After finally working his way to a B.S. in 1932, Gore, Sr. was elected Superintendent of Education in Smith County. Ever since 1932, the year of FDR's first Presidential election, at least one member of Albert Gore's nuclear family has subsisted on a public payroll. Gore held this school superintendent's office until 1936.[12]

While serving as Superintendent of Education during the day, Albert Gore, Sr. commuted by car to Nashville to attend a YMCA law school at night. While drinking coffee at the Andrew Jackson Hotel in Nashville, he met Pauline LaFon, a law student working there as a waitress. She worked to pay her tuition at Vanderbilt Law School. Pauline's father was a once prosperous merchant whose business failed in the depression. Her family's ordeal only made her a more driven feminist. She tried to better herself with a marriage in her late teens, but ended up divorcing her husband. Although warm and patient with people, Pauline was totally lacking in a sense of humor. Her character resembles Hillary Clinton's in many ways. Like Mrs. Clinton, Pauline LaFon idolized feminist First Lady Eleanor Roosevelt. Only the tenth woman to graduate from Vanderbilt Law, Pauline was even more eager than her future husband was to pursue power was. Pauline disdained some of Albert's country habits, such as playing the fiddle. She was also more intellectually gifted than Albert Gore, Sr. But unlike Hillary Clinton, Pauline LaFon possessed keen political antennae. She recognizes and patiently caters to people's needs and desires to get her way. She will refuse to press a point in order to achieve victory at a more favorable time. Her people skills endeared her to the stiff young school superintendent. Albert and Pauline courted, passed the Tennessee bar together in 1936, and married the next year.

Passing the bar did not mean entering the private sector. Albert Gore gave up the school superintendent's job to become Tennessee State Commissioner of Labor in January 1937. He then began campaigning and raising money to win Cordell Hull's old seat in the Fourth District. Gore played lead fiddle in his hillbilly band while campaigning through the district. A flowery stump speaker, Gore frequently spoke 10-15 times a day in the villages of the Fourth District. Hull helped him behind the scenes from Washington, while pretending to be neutral. Cousin Grady Gore, who also grew up in Possum Hollow, donated $40,000 to the campaign from his base in Washington, D.C.[13]

In the Depression year of 1938, when 18% of the labor force was unemployed, $40,000 was a huge sum. It was equivalent to roughly $1,000,000 in today's dollars. Both Albert Gore, Sr. and his son claimed to be the champions of the poor and oppressed. Albert Gore, Sr. even told the press he mortgaged his family farm in Carthage to borrow money for the 1938 primary campaign. This story reflects the standard Gore poor mouthing about money.

The New Dealer: The Early Years in the House

1938 represented a double triumph for Albert and Pauline Gore. Albert won the Fourth Congressional District seat and Pauline gave birth to a beautiful baby girl, Nancy. The ambitious young power couple moved to Washington, D.C., where they lived at reduced rates in cousin Grady's Fairfax Hotel. Pauline Gore "retired" from her brief private law practice to a job answering correspondence for her heroine, Eleanor Roosevelt. She was then employed on her husband's Congressional staff. Members of the Gore family learned early how to get on the public payroll.

While his wife drew a staff salary, young Albert Gore, Sr. learned the arcane customs and rules of the House. He sought advice from Judge Hull on how to conduct himself. Young Congressman Gore became renowned early for his fierce partisanship. He perceived the Democratic Party as a path to eternal salvation, not just as a political instrument. Political analyst Michael Barone points out how excessively partisan Al Gore, Jr. is.[14] He fervently believes, without irony, that Democrats are truly virtuous and Republicans are truly evil. The Vice President learned this Manichean article of faith from his parents.

Albert and Pauline differed from most southern Democrats serving in Congress. Most southern Democrats supported the New Deal as an emergency measure to relieve the Depression but fiercely opposed labor unions and federal regulation of race relations. The Gores, by contrast, were dedicated liberals well to the left of most Tennesseans. Al and Pauline recognized the truth of historian John Lukacs' observation: The United States is the only Western country where one climbs socially by moving Left.[15] The young power couple fervently followed Franklin Roosevelt as both a religious and political leader. Al Gore, Jr.'s parents wanted the Federal government to constantly regulate people's lives in order to improve them. Albert and Pauline both believed in progressive taxes that soaked the rich. Taxation and government spending represented the path to progress in their minds. They even covertly supported some civil rights measures during an era of segregation. While sitting on the House Banking and Appropriations Committees, Albert Gore put this liberal faith into practice.

The Gore faith in regulation led Albert to zealously support the Tennessee Valley Authority, or TVA. This New Deal socialistic federal authority built power plants and dams to enhance navigation, control floods, and generate public power from the Tennessee River and its tributaries. The Cumberland River, which flowed through Gore's Fourth Congressional

District, was a tributary of the Tennessee. Gore took credit for the dams and the Cordell Hull Lake created by the TVA's intervention in his district. He also condemned the conservationists who opposed the TVA for damaging the natural beauty and resources of the region: "Ecology is now a household word, but many of those who use it do not seem aware of the fact that by definition ecology is tied to economics, that man's *well-being* is tied to his *being*; that although preservation of an unsullied crystal stream, a purer atmosphere, a virgin tract of forest, or an unblemished landscape are noble goals, they are not the noblest: the noblest is to provide man with the basic stuff of his existence-food and housing, and meaningful work. Before we can recreate we must create."[16]

His son later wrote a long book a half century later, Albert Gore, Jr. warned mankind to serve nature's needs. Mankind should worship Mother Earth. Gore, Jr. pointedly ignored his father's reminder that man's well-being came before nature's.

During the 1939-1941 period, Albert Gore, Sr. fought in the House for the TVA, federal aid for farmers, federal regulation of big business, and war measures against Germany and Japan. Although Gore worked hard to bring the U.S. into World War II, he chose to avoid doing any fighting himself. Although some Congressmen of military age, such as House Democrat Lyndon Johnson and Senate Republican Henry Cabot Lodge Jr., immediately enlisted for combat duty, Gore stayed put in Washington. He preferred fighting on the House floor to fighting on European battlefields. Unlike most southern men, who are traditionally eager to prove their honor during wartime, Albert Gore, Sr. was gun shy. Finally, though, he realized his political future would suffer if he did not enlist.

So, Gore used his Washington insider status to have his cake and eat it too. He knew FDR was to issue an executive order in January 1944 forbidding members of Congress to retain their seats while serving in the armed forces. Therefore, Gore gave himself a Christmas present in late December 1943. He waived his Congressional immunity from the draft and joined the Army as a private on December 29, 1943. Then he waited a few days until Roosevelt issued his order, and "allowed" the President to shift him to the enlisted reserves. Gore then resumed his seat in Congress and sat out the bloodiest year of the war for American soldiers. Gore waited until December 4, 1944, a month after his re-election, to finally resign his seat. The Army ordered him to

Europe as a replacement soldier, but before he shipped out, the Pentagon changed his orders and made him an Allied Military Government prosecutor and observer. Therefore, he spent five months in Europe serving in a non-combatant role much like his son years later. Gore then returned to Congress after Germany surrendered on May 7, 1945. Like his son's boss, Bill Clinton, Albert Gore, Sr. preserved both his life and his "political viability" during a bloody war.

After this "strenuous" wartime duty, Albert Gore returned to make war against Republicans. Gore maintained his reputation for excessive partisanship. He continually accused the Republicans, who won back both houses of Congress in November 1946, of being incompetent, wasteful, and cruel. His son would sound the same litany in the future. He voted against both Republican tax cut bills of 1947 and 1948, supported Truman's tax increase bills, and loudly condemned Republican "greed." His son would follow his tax and spend ways. But Gore joined with the Republicans on one important measure. In order to preserve his political viability back home, since Tennesseans were angered by the recent strikes ordered by big labor, Gore voted for the 1947 Taft-Hartley Act. This Republican bill curbed the unions' ability to both organize and strike. It is probably the most successful anti-labor statue ever enacted. His son, by contrast, never met a union he didn't like. Al Gore, Jr., so much like his father in many ways, always courts big labor unions and does their bidding, no matter what scandal it involves.[17]

Roused by the passage of the Taft-Hartley Act, big labor flexed its muscle in the 1948 elections. It flooded Harry Truman's long-shot campaign with campaign funds and get out the vote drives. Big labor did much to win the White House and both Houses of Congress for the Democrats. Although Albert Gore, Sr. voted against big labor, he reaped the benefits of its lobbying. He was now a rising House member in the majority. But Providence blessed Albert Gore, Sr. further in 1948. Pauline Gore gave birth to the son she and her husband yearned for on March 31, 1948. The baby was christened Albert Arnold Gore, Jr. He became a major focus of his parents' ambition. Al Jr. was raised to become President.

In Armand Hammer's Back Pocket

Like his son a half century later, Albert Gore played an enthusiastic and expansive role in foreign affairs. Despite his own shameful conduct during World War II, he voted for the 1946 draft extension, 1948 Selective Service bill, and the 1951 Universal Military Training bill. Gore, Sr. also backed every foreign aid or assistance bill the Truman Administration requested. He blasted Republicans who opposed these measures as "isolationists." Gore and his wife also continued their fervent support for the United Nations as the best means of resolving foreign policy problems. But Gore's most consequential Congressional act in the late 1940s involved his decision to become an advocate for Dr. Armand Hammer.

Hammer (1898-1990) was the Soviet Union's favorite American businessman. From Lenin's coup in 1917 until his death in 1990, Hammer and his father did sweetheart deals for the world's most powerful Communist dictatorship. Hammer became famous in business circles as the Chairman of Occidental Petroleum. But before he acquired Occidental in 1957, Hammer trafficked in less respectable commerce. As a medical student in 1920, he killed a woman while performing an illegal abortion on her. Hammer's father, who was a licensed doctor, took the rap for his son and was sent to Sing Sing prison.[18]

Armand traveled to Russia to take over his father's rackets. During the 1920s and 1930s, Hammer lived in Moscow and served the business needs of both Lenin and Stalin. He supervised and expanded his father's fledgling operations with the Soviets. He successfully lobbied the Roosevelt Administration to officially recognize the U.S.S.R. and establish normal trade relations with it. For a time Hammer had a contract with the KGB to train its guard dogs. Hammer also acted as a fence and money launderer for the U.S.S.R. Hammer helped the Politburo to obtain American high technology for military uses. He also helped to place Soviet espionage agents in the U.S. government. These various activities won Hammer the nickname "the Godfather of American corporate corruption."[19]

Hammer became *persona non grata* at the White House once Harry Truman became President. Under Truman, the U.S. finally realized it was engaged in a cold war with the Soviet Union. FDR's lax security practices were discarded. J. Edgar Hoover and his FBI had kept Hammer under close surveillance since the

1920s. Hoover wanted Hammer prosecuted, but Hammer's powerful friends in the Roosevelt White House had always prevented the FBI Director from getting the goods on Hammer. Now Hoover hoped he could finally nail Hammer.

Since the White House now refused to protect him from the FBI, Hammer turned to make friends in Congress. In 1949, he began a close alliance with Albert Gore, Sr., Republican Senator Styles Bridges, and Congressman James Roosevelt, FDR's eldest son. Under Gore's lead, these three became Armand Hammer's protectors on Capitol Hill. Whenever one of Hammer's shady or subversive schemes with the Iron Curtain came under attack, Gore would loudly defend Hammer's patriotism. Gore worked closely with Bridges and Roosevelt to protect Hammer's operations from harassment by the executive branch or congressional committees. Gore once took the House floor to defend Hammer against an accusation of bribery for government contracts. Much later, the accusation was proven true. Hammer bragged openly that he had Gore "in my back pocket."[20] Since Gore's hero Cordell Hull had appeased the Soviet Union on diplomatic and trade matters, Gore saw no problem with this relationship. While the U.S. and its allies pledged themselves to a struggle to the death with the Soviet Union, Albert Gore, Sr. labored to help the U.S.S.R.'s favorite American businessman. Al Jr. later emulated his father by also helping Hammer.[21]

Hammer rewarded his Tennessee ally with financial favors. In 1950, while the Korean War raged, Hammer made Gore a partner in his cattle breeding business. Albert already owned a large farm in Carthage where he raised tobacco and cattle. Hammer gave Gore bulls and heifers to enrich the Tennessee Congressman's herd of Angus cattle. For some mysterious reason after 1948, rich and powerful figures regularly appeared at the Gore livestock auctions to pay outrageously high prices for cattle.[22] Sometimes they purchased the cattle and did not even bother to pick the animals up. Hammer also plied Gore with expensive gifts of silver. He aided Gore with campaign funds.

A Southern Liberal: The Senate Years, 1953-1970

Armand Hammer's rewards assisted Albert Gore's increasing ambition. Thanks to Hammer's help, Gore was able to unseat incumbent octogenarian Senator Kenneth McKellar in the 1952 Democratic primary. In the one-party Democratic South before the late 1960s, winning the Democratic primary was tantamount to winning the election.

In the Senate, Gore, Sr. played a large role in pushing through the interstate highway system. He held many hearings on the issue in 1955 and 1956. His efforts paid off with the interstate highway bill's passage. But like his son, a half-century later claiming he created the Internet, Gore gave himself far too much credit for the bill's enactment. President Eisenhower played the primary role. But father, like son, usually claimed more credit than his due.

Gore certainly thought about seeking the White House, but several obstacles blocked his way. First, the South before 1964 still suffered the evils of racial segregation. Blacks were not permitted to mingle with whites in schools, public transportation, or public accommodations. They were also unable to vote in many southern localities. This racial situation made it difficult, if not impossible, for a southerner to be nominated for President in a national Democratic Party dominated by northern liberals. A southern presidential candidate risked alienating his regional base if he supported black aspirations. He risked alienating the nation if he clung to white supremacy. It was almost impossible to be both a liberal and a successful southern politician. After the Supreme Court's integration decisions from Brown vs. Topeka in 1954 onwards, the dilemma of the few southern liberal politicians intensified.

Second, even if Albert Gore, Sr. continued his liberal legislative record in the Senate, three other southern Senators already commanded superior liberal reputations. These three Senators, Lyndon Johnson (1908-1973) and Ralph Yarborough (1903-1996), both of Texas, and Estes Kefauver (1903-1963) of Tennessee, were better known than Gore. They were also better at communicating to voters. Along with Gore, these three Senators also opposed the March, 1956 "Declaration of Constitutional Principles" manifesto condemning the Supreme Court's integration decisions. The manifesto was supported by over 90% of all southern Senate and House members. Kefauver, Tennessee's senior U.S. Senator, had run for President in 1952. Kefauver possessed the common touch and charm Albert Gore, Sr. conspicuously lacked. Kefauver came from a prominent gentry family and had earned a Yale law degree. Voters, especially women voters, cherished his character so much they even overlooked his alcoholism.[23] Kefauver also earned a national reputation for his battle against organized crime. Johnson, the Senate majority leader, was the most powerful, ambitious, and ruthless of southern liberals.[24] These attributes may explain why he eventually secured the White House. Yarborough was the bravest and brightest, but also the least ambitious, of the southern liberal Senators. He was also the least senior, not having been elected until March 1957. All three of the Senate's other southern liberals surpassed Gore in sociability, nerve, talent, and electability. To use the language of Al Gore, Jr.'s adviser Naomi Wolf, Albert Gore, Sr. was the "beta male" trailing behind the "alpha male" southern liberal Senators Kefauver, Johnson, and Yarbrorough.

Albert Gore, Sr.'s "beta male" characteristics were well known during his Senatorial tenure. However, thanks to his son's tireless proselytizing, today's historians forgot what a timid legislative record Albert Gore, Sr. compiled in the Senate. These historians retroactively transformed Gore, Sr. into a brave liberal selflessly pursuing racial justice. Numan Bartley, leading scholar of the post-World War II South, offers a prime example of this Gore family propaganda: "Senator Albert Gore, who after the death of Estes Kefauver in 1963 was perhaps the most prominent progressive member of the southern Senate delegation."[25]

Bartley, a close associate of certain Gore family allies, [26] wrote these false words in 1995. Albert Gore, Sr. himself admitted he followed a cautious course on civil rights: "There may have been some political 'heroes' in this cause, but few, if any, were to be found among white southern politicians. I know I cannot include myself. …[I concentrated on economic issues] and let the sleeping dogs of racism lie as best I could."[27]

Al Gore has created a retrospective myth that hails his father as a brave civil rights crusader defeated by racist reactionaries. The actual historical record contradicts Gore's comforting myth. Albert Gore spent far more time crusading for Armand Hammer than he did crusading for oppressed black people. He did let sleeping dogs lie. His son adopted an equally cautious attitude toward the U.S.S.R. during the Cold War. Both father and son usually shied away from boldly confronting the big issues of their respective eras.

Albert Gore, Sr.'s timidity, though, did not help him to rise above the Senate. The turmoil affecting the U.S. between 1954-1970 proved inhospitable to a cautious, calculating, politician like Albert Gore, Sr. When Adlai Stevenson was again nominated the Democratic Presidential candidate in 1956, Albert Gore resolved to be his Vice Presidential running mate. Gore yearned for this chance to be near the ultimate prize. Observers at the 1956 convention were astounded to see unemotional, tight lipped Albert Gore work himself into a frenzy. George Reedy, an aide to Lyndon Johnson, remembers: "A man came running up to us, his face absolutely distorted...His eyes were glimmering. He was mumbling something that sounded like 'Where is Lyndon? Where is Lyndon? Adlai's thrown this open, and I think I've got a chance for it if I can only get Texas. Where is Lyndon?' And we suddenly realized we were talking to Senator Albert Gore of Tennessee," Reedy recalled. "I have never seen before or since such a complete, total example of a man so completely and absolutely wild with ambition, it had literally changed his features."[28]

This incident illuminates the quest for power animating both Albert Gores. Despite their cultivated images of self-control and rectitude, both father and son lusted for power. Gore, Sr. backed out of the 1956 Vice Presidential nomination only after the publisher of the Nashville *Tennessean*, the state's leading liberal newspaper, threatened to destroy his career if he did not withdraw in favor of Estes Kefauver. Instead of fighting for his dream, Gore surrendered to a powerful threat. He made a show of endorsing Kefauver on the third convention ballot. Kefauver was not grateful for Gore's charade of support. Kefauver's daughter, Diane Kefauver Rubin, bitterly observed four decades later: "He (Gore) tried to snatch the vice presidency from my father, but played along as though he were a friend." [29]

The 1956 convention was the closest Gore, Sr. came to the White House. Stevenson and Kefauver lost to Eisenhower in a landslide. Then LBJ became Kennedy's Vice Presidential choice in 1960. Gore, Sr. realized his chance was gone. He and Pauline raised Albert Jr. to be their great White House hope.[30]

Armand Hammer's financial favors helped relieve Gore, Sr.'s Vice Presidential disappointment. Dr. Hammer remained a close ally of Gore through the 1950s and 1960s. Anti-communism lost respectability after Senator Joseph McCarthy's censure in 1954. The liberal American media assumed an attitude of indifference to Hammer's treasonable activity. Only J. Edgar Hoover and the FBI kept Hammer under close watch. Senator Gore kept running interference for this "capitalist selling the hangman the rope" (Lenin's phrase). He defended Hammer on the Senate floor after the latter was attacked by the anti-Communist magazine *The Reporter*. The journal criticized Hammer, a security risk, for leasing a U.S. Army ordnance base in Morgantown, West Virginia for his fertilizer manufacturing business. Gore also introduced Hammer to his friend, Senator John F. Kennedy of Massachusetts, in the late 1950s. Kennedy hit it off with Hammer and willingly accepted his lucrative campaign donations for his 1960 Presidential campaign. Kennedy was so grateful for Hammer's help he allowed Gore to bring him as an honored guest to the 1961 Inauguration.

Gore used his influence with Kennedy to lobby for Hammer's use as an Administration go-between to the Soviet Union. Kennedy responded by putting Hammer in charge of a mission to investigate the Soviet crabmeat controversy. Evidence indicated the Soviets were using slave labor to manufacture crabmeat. If the evidence was true, Kennedy would maintain the ban on this export from entering the United States. Commerce Secretary Luther Hodges, much like his successor Ron Brown 35 years later, believed in cordial trading with America's enemies. Hodges named Hammer his official emissary to make a long trade mission. The February-March 1961 trade mission itinerary included Western Europe, the Soviet bloc countries, and the Third World.

While on this trade mission, Hammer willfully ignored the evidence of slave labor.[31] He accepted the Soviets' assurance that wage workers manufactured the crabmeat. Hammer also gave Hodges a bullish report about the wonderful trade opportunities the U.S.S.R. offered. The Kennedy Administration not only lifted the crabmeat ban but allowed trade with the Soviets to expand. Albert Gore, Sr. lauded his friend Hammer for thawing relations between the two superpowers with his trade mission.

On March 17, 1961, Gore wrote to Hammer: "In the broad spectrum of the struggle for East and West to live in peace on one planet, this may not appear to some as a major item, but when one considers the dangers to mankind involved in war today, any step that moves toward better understanding and peaceful relations is important."[32]

Gore's son was to use the same congratulatory rhetoric to justify the Clinton Administration's refusal to enforce Congress' ban on slave labor imports whenever Red Chinese trade was concerned. Hammer gloated because the crabmeat investigation enabled him to expand his Occidental fertilizer business with the

Soviets. Seven years later in 1968, Senator Gore accompanied Hammer to Libya, where Hammer had bribed King Idris into giving Occidental a contract for oil fields. Albert Gore, Sr. always enabled Armand Hammer to get richer. Hammer reciprocated by continuing to pay exorbitant prices for Gore's livestock.[33]

While Gore's foreign policy involvements paid off lucratively, his domestic policy stands were becoming politically dangerous. He coasted to re-election in 1958, but the 1964 contest loomed as a tougher contest. His good friend President Kennedy was assassinated on November 22, 1963 and Vice President Lyndon Johnson, a fellow southern liberal, succeeded him. Because of Johnson's ascent to the White House and Kefauver's death in early 1963, Gore and Yarborough were now the only two southern pro-civil rights liberals in the Senate.

These changes in the Senate put both men behind the political eight ball. Johnson took advantage of the national mourning to push through the Kennedy Administration's Civil Rights Bill in 1964, an election year for both Gore and Yarborough. Both Senators believed in the legislation, which abolished "Jim Crow" segregation once and for all. But Gore feared for his political viability in Tennessee if he voted for the bill.

So, he voted against it. Yarborough bravely chose to be the only Senator from the former Confederacy to support this landmark act. Given Lyndon Johnson's landslide against Goldwater in 1964, which only failed to win the Deep South and Arizona, Gore could have voted yea and survived in a very close race. Johnson's winning margin was 145,000, while Gore's was 51,000. In 1965, after safely being re-elected, Gore did support the Voting Rights Act enabling minorities in the South to register to vote. Gore, also, began to consult his son's views on difficult and controversial issues like civil rights and gun control.

Gore, Sr. became arrogant toward his Tennessee constituents after the 1964 election. He became besotted with his news media image as a lonely southern liberal. Despite his relationship with Armand Hammer and cowardly vote on the Civil Rights Act, the news media covered him quite favorably, probably because he was a Kennedy intimate. After voting for the Tonkin Gulf Resolution to make war in Vietnam in 1964, a vote only two Senators dissented from, Gore became disenchanted with LBJ. Gore and Johnson were never close anyway because Johnson had prevented

Gore, Sr. from rising higher than the Senate. After things went sour in Vietnam, Gore began moving well to the left of Johnson.

In a demagogic speech at the 1968 Democratic convention in Chicago, Gore accused Johnson of enacting Goldwater's foreign policy in Vietnam: "Mr. Chairman, fellow delegates, four years ago our party and the nominee of our party promised the people that American boys would not be sent to fight in a land war in Asia. The people made an overwhelming commitment to peace. They voted for our distinguished leader, President Lyndon B. Johnson, but they got the policies of Senator Goldwater."[34]

This speech, which Al Jr. helped him draft, libeled Goldwater. During the 1964 Presidential race, the Arizona Senator forcefully critiqued what he called "Johnson's no-win policy" in Vietnam. Goldwater candidly called for a win or withdrawal approach to Vietnam. Johnson, by contrast, hewed to the devious escalation policy begun by his vague 1964 Gulf of Tonkin resolution. The escalation policy offered at best only an indecisive no-lose policy. Blinded by partisanship, Albert Gore, Sr. and his son, both refused to admit that the Vietnam War was directed by liberal Democrats, not conservative Republicans.

Gore, Sr. hated having to share blame with Johnson for the war's disastrous effects. Like his treasonable crony, Armand Hammer, Gore wanted to appease Communist countries. He wanted to trade with Communist dictatorships, not make war on them. In hawkish Tennessee, Johnson became decidedly unpopular with his Hamlet approach to Southeast Asia. Gore damaged his standing with Tennesseans by attacking LBJ from the peacenik left instead of the hawkish right.

Albert Gore, Sr. compounded his own problems by forgetting where he came from. In the late 1960s, he began to vote the *The New York Times* line on hot-button moral issues. Gore voted for gun control. He voted against an amendment permitting prayer in the public schools. He voted against a bill banning the busing of public school students. Gore also voted against Nixon's two southern nominees to the Supreme Court, Clement G. Haynsworth, Jr. and G. Harold Carswell. Al, Jr. encouraged his father to take all of these left-wing positions.[35]

Then Gore endangered his re-election hopes further. In the past, he chose to quietly support a policy of appeasing the Soviet Union and its Communist allies. From 1965-1970, he loudly championed an anti-American foreign policy. He voted for the Cooper-Church amendment declaring a definite date for withdrawal from Vietnam. The Cooper-Church amendment notified the North Vietnamese Politburo when it could begin its final, all-out offensive to conquer South Vietnam and Cambodia. In a move reminiscent of his son's foolish opposition to ballistic missile defense, Albert Gore, Sr. voted against developing an anti-ballistic missile defense system, or ABM, in early 1970. After all, his crony Armand Hammer constantly assured him that the Russians wanted only peace and profits, not world domination..[36]

Tennessee Republicans licked their chops over Gore's controversial votes. Polling indicated Gore's liberal votes rendered him vulnerable. In 1970, the Republicans fielded Congressman Bill Brock of Chattanooga to run against Gore. The August 1970 Democratic Senate primary in the Volunteer State indicated Gore had become unpopular in his own party. Gore beat segregationist Hudley Crockett by only 30,000 votes. Gore was ripe for scalping. Therefore, Brock hammered him with the nationalistic southern strategy developed by the Nixon White House.

The Republican southern strategy appealed to the frustration of southerners and northern ethnics fed up with the moral disarray of the liberal sixties. They abhorred urban rioters, welfare cheats, drug abusing hippies, the liberal no-win policy in Vietnam, antiwar protesters and draft dodgers, and activist Federal judges striking down school prayer and decreeing forced busing.

Senator Barry Goldwater and California Governor Ronald Reagan took these themes and transformed them into Republican conservatism. Albert Gore, Sr., by contrast, ardently defended Northeast Corridor Federal liberalism to his Tennessee constituents. To his credit, the beta male finally went down fighting like an alpha male. Gore, Sr. battled bravely for his bad liberal causes. He boasted of his liberal stands and defied the popular protests of gunowners and school prayer advocates. Gore scolded Brock for running a dirty campaign. This attack was simply political posturing, since Brock never brought up Armand Hammer, Gore's chief *Achilles' heel*. One wonders why he did not mention Gore's friendship with Hammer. Perhaps the Nixon Administration needed Hammer for its own foreign policy uses.[37] Al Gore, Jr., who had recently graduated from Harvard and enlisted in the Army, campaigned strenuously for his father across Tennessee. Al, Jr. always wore his uniform during the campaign. He wore it to demonstrate to voters his father opposed the Vietnam War, not the soldiers serving in it.

Albert Gore, Sr. ran hard during his last and most difficult campaign. He lectured the voters in his stiff schoolteacher's manner to do their duty. Duty as Gore, Sr. defined it consisted of bowing down to unelected liberal Federal judges and bureaucrats. Duty also demanded deference to *The New York Times*, *The Washington Post*, and *CBS News*. He appealed to Tennessee's traditional Democratic loyalties. But his slavish loyalty to northeast corridor secular liberalism finished him. Brock fired a barrage of tough ads late in the campaign accurately accusing Gore of supporting gun control and opposing the Anti-Ballistic Missile System and school prayer. But Brock did not attack Gore for supporting civil rights, despite his son Al's later lie to that effect. Brock, Howard Baker, and most East Tennessee Republicans traditionally supported civil rights legislation. East Tennessee Republicans stayed loyal to the Union during the Civil War and Reconstruction.[38] In fact, Gore himself admitted: "Some blacks, too, refused to vote for me because of my views on the 1964 Civil Rights Bill."[39] The challenger's well-timed ads enabled him to beat Gore, Sr., who tasted defeat for the first time in his life. The final vote was Gore, Sr.: 48%, Brock: 52%. 43,000 votes separated the loser from the winner.

Albert Gore, Sr. turned 63 a month after the election. He briefly considered a comeback in 1976, but decided to let his son pick up the mantle of the Gore political dynasty. Gore, Sr. first accepted Armand Hammer's offer to do lobbying work. Then he took up Hammer's offer of a 1972 offer of a $500,000 a year salary (over ten times the then salary of a U.S. Senator) as Chairman of the Island Coal Creek Company, an Occidental subsidiary. The Island Coal Creek Company constantly came under attack for its violation of pollution laws in Kentucky. Al Gore the earth-worshipper never mentions that his father chaired a polluting company from 1972 to 1983.[40] Hammer also gave Gore a seat on Occidental's Board of Directors. These subsidies made the onetime poor boy from Possum Hollow a very rich man.

THREE

The View from The Fairfax Hotel:
Al Gore, Jr.'s Childhood and Adolescence.

"People who have no weaknesses are terrible."
Anatole France

Al Gore, Jr. often tries to play the Tennessee country boy in public. He loves to reminisce about bucolic days on the Gore farm in Carthage. Gore usually lavishes numbing detail on the arduous chores he performed on the family farm. Many bored journalists lampoon his pompous speechifying about feeding the cattle, nurturing tobacco, and chopping up tree stumps. However, what Gore claims about his farm chores is true enough. He did perform all those arduous tasks on the family farm in Carthage. He discharged all the character-building duties his father assigned to him. But he neglects to mention he only spent summers on the Tennessee farm while growing up. Three quarters of his youth actually occurred in Washington, D.C.[41]

Gore dislikes discussing his D.C. upbringing. He knows it distances him from ordinary voters. Over 99% of Americans are not raised by a U.S. Senator father and United Nations delegate mother in Washington, D.C. Few Americans are also deliberately raised from birth by powerful parents to be President. When reporters asked Albert Gore, Sr. in 1992 if his son was presidential material, the former replied proudly "We raised him for it."[42]

Albert and Pauline Gore's project to make Al Jr. President caused the son to become a wooden figure from his earliest years. The Gore parents warped Al by insisting he develop according to their own future specifications instead of allowing him to find his own way.

Al grew up a lonely boy thirsting for attention. Gore admitted to his Vietnam buddy Mike O'Hara how his upbringing made him different: "He [Al Gore] told me one time his way of getting attention was by being very polite. He said, "I was a real little politician."[43]

Al struggled especially to please his father. Asked to describe the relationship between father and son, Tipper Gore answered: "You remember Oedipus? ....You had a very powerful father—a hero to many people—and a son coming to maturity and finding his own dignity." [44]

The Gore family lived on the top floor of D.C.'s elegant Fairfax Hotel in Suite 809. The Gores lived there for a reduced rent thanks to a blood relation's generosity. Albert Gore's cousin from Possum Hollow, Grady, had made good and now owned both the hotel and its famous restaurant, the Jockey Club. Now a Republican, Grady was not too partisan to favor his Democratic Senator kin with reduced-rate lodging. The Fairfax sits at the corner of 21st Street and Massachusetts Avenue N.W. in the exclusive neighborhood known as Embassy Row. The neighborhood derives its name from the fact that most foreign embassies are located there. Just across Massachusetts Avenue lies the exclusive Cosmos Club. The Cosmos boasts among its members the most powerful and prestigious members of the Washington Establishment. During the school year, young Al Jr. caught the bus that stopped at the Cosmos Club in the morning at 7:55 A.M. The bus took him to St. Albans School.

St. Albans, an elitist school for the American ruling class, is an exclusive Episcopalian primary and secondary school. It is regarded as the most prestigious boys prep school in the D.C. area. St. Albans tries to emulate the model of an Anglican English public school by calling its classes "forms" and its headmaster "Canon." When Gore attended it, its yearly class sizes averaged roughly 50 pupils. Located 1.9 miles up Massachusetts Avenue from the Fairfax Hotel, St. Albans resides in a neighborhood considered more plush than Embassy Row. It ranks as one of the most expensive private schools in the country. Most of the boys there are sons of politicians, diplomats, socialites, and journalists. Many Roosevelts and Kennedys are graduates. Gore cousin Gore Vidal also attended it two decades before Al Jr. did.

Al's older sister, Nancy, was enrolled in the equally exclusive Holton Arms School for Girls, then located near DuPont Circle. St. Albans and Holton Arms did not resemble at all the one room schoolhouse where Albert Gore, Sr. studied and taught. Al Gore, Jr.'s parents pretended to be egalitarian Democrats looking out for the little people. In reality, like most liberals, they were social climbing elitists seeking to ingratiate themselves with the best people. Albert Gore, Sr. once explained why he sent both of his children to expensive private schools: "What I sought to do was compensate them for my own inadequacies...to provide for my children a better education than I had had."[45]

Al Gore, Jr. studied at St. Albans from the fourth grade until graduation, 1957-1965. Despite summers spent on the Carthage farm working and playing with ordinary Tennesseans, Al always oriented his outlook to the power elite of D.C. His Tennessee friends observed with amusement how he compartmentalized his different lives in Carthage and D.C. He shed his Tennessee accent and country way of walking as soon as he returned Inside the Beltway. His one-time Carthage girlfriend, Donna Armistead, observed it took him two weeks to stop walking like a city boy once he returned from Washington.[46] In the 1980s, Al's children giggled about how their dad turned on his Tennessee accent when visiting the Volunteer State. Al Gore's ability to act liberal in Washington and talk conservative in Tennessee was learned at an early age.

Al Gore stood out at St. Albans as a calculating social climber. Many of the teachers, not just the students, resented his relentless efforts to ingratiate himself with powerful people. Although St. Albans existed as an indoctrination center for the globalist elite, the school's headmaster, Canon Charles Martin, did believe the students should live Christianity, not just mouth it. Canon Martin, a Mr. Chips character who captained St. Albans from 1949-1977, emphasized doing what he called the "hard right" over the easy wrong. He prized moral excellence over academic or political achievement, and made a point of praising morally courageous students.

Always eager to succeed, Al Gore went along outwardly with Canon Martin's program. Gore worked hard in class, on the playing field, and in extracurricular activities. He usually ranked academically in the middle of his class. Charles Saltzman, who taught English, Gore's favorite subject, "described him in words that he would hear often enough throughout his life-a very competent young man' but 'not scintillating.'" [47] Al played basketball very well; football well (he was co-captain of the team his senior year), hurled the discus well, and was cut from the baseball team when he could not hit the curve. In extracurricular activities, he involved himself in the art and government clubs.

He rose to be leader of the Liberal Party in the senior Government Club.

The Liberal Party debated the Conservative Party on the controversial issues of the day. Gore spoke with a dry, droning delivery. According to classmate John Siscoe: "He [Gore] read his script…he sounded much like he does today."[48] Gore's classmates remember him advocating the recognition of Red China and opposing the dispatch of Marines to the Dominican Republic to prevent another Cuba. This appeasement of Communist dictatorships imitated his father's policy. The Government Club keeps a record of all the legislative debates between the Liberal and Conservative Parties. But for whatever reason, the file record for the 1964-65 Sixth Form, or Senior Class, is missing. As Gore biographer Bob Zelnick dryly observes, "there is no 'controlling legal authority' preventing a former student from purging the record of his high school political views." [49] Like Bill Clinton, Al Gore likes to remove the revealing files of his past to preserve his political viability.

Big Man on Campus Meets His True Love

Because boys punish their presumptuous peers, Al Jr. usually kept his arrogance under wraps. He played by the stern St. Albans rules while piling up good grades and varsity letters. Yet, perceptive classmates of Al Gore observed the robotic character traits now the butt of widespread ridicule. Bill Yates noticed that even as a teenage boy Gore was "not a risk taker." Another one commented, "Al, then as now, was very self-controlled. There was always a tight rubber band wrapped around his waist. He is not comfortable with mirth. He has to work at it." Senator Kefauver's daughter Diane says Gore is "not really close to people. There is distance even between him and close friends. Al took himself very seriously…he was very driven to succeed." [50]

Gore's self-importance won him the nickname "Ozymandias" from some classmates. Ozymandias is the ancient emperor Percy Shelley satirized in the famous poem of the same name. "Look on my Works, ye Mighty, and despair!," Ozymandias cries out at the vanity of his ambitions. Although English was Gore's favorite subject, he pretended not to notice the nickname's point. A classmate explained why Gore was tagged with Shelley's poem: "That suggested the schoolboy's intuition that this was a gigantic figure in our midst. But that there was something wooden, artificial, unreal, monumental about him."

Another classmate who played on the football team with Gore bluntly declares: "He was a stuffed shirt, even then; he was not a kid....He would try to be inspirational, and we would all roll our eyes." The St. Albans Class of 1965 Yearbook editors quoted an Anatole France line under Gore's picture: "People who have no weaknesses are terrible." The editors implied Gore was not truly virtuous, only skilled at camouflaging his sins. They were the first of many observers to perceive this truth.[51]

Part of Gore recognized himself as an uptight prig. Looking for a better half to complement his "wooden" personality, young Al struck gold at the St. Albans Senior Prom in May 1965. He met, danced, and chatted with beautiful, blonde Mary Elizabeth "Tipper" Aitcheson. Tipper, a junior at exclusive St. Agnes School in neighboring Alexandria, had dated several of Al's classmates. She boasted the charm, grace, and fun-loving spirit he keenly lacked. She reassured fragile male egos, played drums in a rock band, and danced up a storm. Tipper could even warm up "Ozymandias" enough to make him laugh. A St. Albans friend of Al and Tipper praises the latter's people skills: "She greets you and fills in conversation when Al goes to the seventy-third stellar galaxy." Al Gore, the wooden stick figure, fell deeply in love. He has carried a torch for Tipper ever since.[52]

Albert Sr. and Pauline approved of Tipper because she shared their hopes for Al's climb to the White House. Tipper eagerly joined the Gore family's pursuit of power. Al had already received early admission into Harvard. Therefore, he urged Tipper to get into a college in the Boston area and follow him there after graduation. Tipper kept her eyes on the prize, and followed Al to Boston. She attended Garland College in 1966.

FOUR

Love Story: Gore's Harvard Years

Marty Peretz: The Poor Man's Allard Lowenstein

In 1970, writer Erich Segal published *Love Story*, a novel about young love at his alma mater, Harvard. *Love Story* proved to be a worldwide best seller and was turned into a famous movie. A quarter of a century later, Vice President Al Gore claimed he and his wife were the models for the *Love Story* couple, Oliver and Jenny Barrett. Segal denied most of Gore's claim. He was "befuddled" and could not understand why Gore made it. Perhaps Segal is unable to comprehend how insecure the only son of a self-made powerful man can be.[53]

Segal did admit to modeling *Love Story*'s Oliver Barrett partly on both actor Tommy Lee Jones and Al Gore, whom he knew while tutoring at Dunster House in 1968. Segal recognized then how Al was "always under pressure to follow in his father's footsteps and that was the conflict, to keep up the family tradition....He was nervous. He was sensitive to being Albert Gore, Jr." But Segal declared Jenny Barrett was not based on Tipper, who he barely knew.[54] Segal was quite right to respond with indignation. Once again, Al Gore, Jr. ridiculously claimed too much credit. But Segal should have paused to wonder why Al and Tipper identified themselves with the tragic young couple. The answer for their self-identification lies in the fact that Oliver and Jenny Barrett were a happy young couple surrounded by Harvard arrogance and emotional turmoil. Al and Tipper Gore serenely glided through the most tumultuous years at Harvard.

Martin Peretz was a 26-year old Harvard instructor in political science who helped create the turmoil and tumult on campus. During the 1965-1966 academic year, when young Al was a freshman, Peretz was probably the most radical member of the Harvard faculty. Even historian John Womack, a registered member of the Communist Party and outspoken supporter of Fidel Castro, did not stir up militance among students to the extent Peretz did. One Harvard undergraduate dubbed him " the school's pet radical." While a Brandeis undergraduate, Peretz befriended Abbie Hoffman, founder of the Yippie radicals. Peretz then went to graduate school at Harvard where he earned his Ph.D. As a young instructor, Peretz irresponsibly whipped students into radically questioning the *status quo*. Then he left them adrift in ideological tumult and turmoil. Jamie Kilbreth, a blueblood member of Gore's Harvard Class of 1969, succumbed to Peretz's powerful influence and became an SDS radical. He was one of those students left adrift. Kilbreth told a reporter in 1999, "I don't think it's unfair to say that Marty radicalized some of his students and then didn't know what to do with them."[55]

Peretz's hero, Allard Lowenstein (1929-1981), did know how to channel the energy of young radical students. Lowenstein inspired undergraduates to become civil rights activists who journeyed down to the Deep South to help black people end segregation and register to vote. Lowenstein also organized the "Dump Johnson" movement that enabled Eugene McCarthy's candidacy to force LBJ to step down in 1968. But Al Lowenstein's character was far more selfless and civilized than Marty Peretz's. Lowenstein cared more for people than for power. He seemed to know and remember everybody. A deranged former student and protégé who he was trying to help murdered Lowenstein in 1981. Lowenstein loathed Communist countries and their American apologists. He could cultivate a close friendship with conservative intellectual William F. Buckley Jr. because they both loathed tyrannies at home and abroad. Peretz rarely befriends a man with different politics than his own. He gets to know people primarily to use them for his projects. Men of old-fashioned honor find themselves irritated by Peretz's feline ways of operating. Unlike Allard Lowenstein, Peretz never denies himself an opportunity to gain and exercise power or seek revenge against his enemies.[56]

Marty Peretz and Al Gore came from contrasting backgrounds. Peretz was a short, squat, Jewish New Yorker with rude manners and radical politics who looked like a "satyr." Gore was a tall, handsome southern Baptist liberal patrician who resembled the man in the Arrow shirt ad. Yet, the two men bonded almost immediately after meeting in 1965. Peretz, who insisted his students address him as "Marty," permitted Al Gore into his elite freshman seminar, "Problems of Post-Industrial Society." Young Al, drilled in deference, continued to call him "Mr. Peretz." Marty decided early on in his seminar that Al Gore was "a historical figure" who could someday be elected President.

Gore decided Peretz, despite his New Left radicalism, was an intellectual dynamo who challenged and stimulated his mind and imagination. Under Peretz's influence, Gore gave up majoring in English, in favor of Government. His grades rose from C's to A's and B's when he switched majors. Albert and Pauline praised Marty for rescuing their son from English Literature. Like Gore's parents, Marty wanted Al to pursue power. But Peretz only wanted to influence Al intellectually, not dominate him emotionally. He acted as a reassuring older brother to Al. Since the fall of 1965, Marty Peretz has reigned as Al Gore's top political and intellectual adviser.

Peretz made Gore a part of his family. Marty was a resident Tutor at Dunster House dormitory, so he had Gore assigned there after his freshman year. Marty's wife Anne, an heiress to the Singer sewing machine fortune, was at first unnerved by Gore calling her "ma'am." Anne, Peretz's patient and forbearing second wife, played a role similar to Tipper's. She acted as a diplomat for her irascible and irritating husband. When Tipper came up to Boston in 1966, Anne mothered and protected her from Marty and Al's Harvard cronies. Many members of the Harvard elite condescended to Tipper as an intellectual lightweight.[57] Anne Peretz also provided the cash when Marty chose to buy and edit *The New Republic*, the most prestigious and influential liberal magazine in America.

As owner and editor-in-chief of *The New Republic* since 1974, Marty Peretz has promoted his various pet causes. Making Al Gore, Jr. President of the United States is probably his top priority. Defending Israel against its many enemies is his second priority. Discrediting Communist regimes is Peretz's third priority. Crusading against traditional sexual mores and restraints, especially those regulating homosexuality and abortion, is Peretz's fourth priority. Peretz allowed his protégé Andrew Sullivan to publish several long articles arguing for same sex marriage. Some wags assert *The New Republic* should be named *The New Sodomist*. Persuading the Democratic Party to follow the Trojan Horse of the Democratic Leadership Council is his fifth priority. Marty Peretz realizes the only way for his cultural values to win the White House is to disguise them in the sheep's clothing of a southern DLC candidate like Bill Clinton or Al Gore.[58]

Peretz forces *The New Republic* staff to abide by his protective concern for Gore. During the 1992 campaign, Marty hung out on Gore's campaign plane "banning publication of all but the

mildest criticism of Al in his magazine." He fired Editor Michael
Kelly in September 1997 for attacking Vice President Gore's
illegal fundraising for Bill Clinton's 1996 re-election.[59] He fired
Senior Editor Jacob Heilbrunn in 1999 for daring to criticize
Gore's handling of Russian foreign policy. Editor Charles Lane
was kicked upstairs to Editor-at-Large in September 1999 for
being too fair to Bill Bradley.[60]

Peretz patrols the magazine constantly to make sure every
employee is on board with his boy Al.[61] Peretz also compels Vice
President Gore to heed his policies. Gore's policy push for
homosexuals and lesbians to serve openly in the U.S. military was
sold to him by *The New Republic*'s editor-in-chief. Peretz also gets
rid of Gore staffers who disagree with his preferences. Richard
Marius, a Harvard historian, authored some fine speeches for
Gore on a free-lance basis. In 1995, Gore hired him as a full-time
speechwriter. But Marius wrote an article on Israel Peretz
disliked. Marty called up Al immediately after Marius was hired.
Gore then notified Marius he had to go.[62]

Peretz influences Gore on war and peace issues. He
persuaded Gore to vote for the Gulf War in January 1991. Peretz
continued to advise Gore on strategy when his protégé became
Vice President. *The New Republic* has constantly urged American
military intervention in the Balkan Wars over the last decade.
Peretz prodded Gore to prevent "genocide" in the Balkans so the
Vice President pushed Clinton hard to intervene.[63]

Although Marty Peretz exerts enormous influence over Gore,
the latter realizes many powerful people regard *The New Republic*
owner as a ridiculous character. They are as repelled by Peretz as
Richard Marius was seeing him at a Harvard book party: "I was
amused when Peretz came in dressed up in a thin gray shirt,
made of silk, I think [,] open to his navel....He swaggered about
the room holding his glass in two hands and looking a bit like an
emperor on progress among his peasants, and if I am not
mistaken, he had recently had a permanent." [64]

Peretz's penchant for sexual liberation repels many members
of the American political establishment. These establishment
characters recognize, as novelist Henry James did,[65] that the
sexual deviant and the political radical are usually found at the
same address. The American power elite distrusts Martin Peretz
for being too zealous about his sexual and political enthusiasms.
Peretz once hoped if Gore became President he would be named
Secretary of State. Now he will settle for being named

Ambassador to either Great Britain or Israel. Whatever Al Gore decides, Martin Peretz will continue to be the leader of Gore's Kitchen Cabinet.

Other Harvard Gurus

Two other Harvard faculty members influenced Al Gore to become a rabid environmentalist. Professor Roger Revelle, who taught earth sciences, alerted Al to the dangers of the greenhouse effect on the environment. Revelle studied the effects of carbon dioxide release on the atmosphere. This lead him to postulate a theory arguing that man's increasing use of fossil fuels (i.e., petroleum and coal) created a "greenhouse effect." This greenhouse effect *could* raise the world's temperatures. As a young Harvard undergraduate, Gore took Revelle's conditional theory and transformed it into the fanatical certainty of "global warming," which he later espoused in *Earth in the Balance*.[66]

Professor Erik Erikson, a psychoanalyst, reinforced Gore's environmentalism by converting him to radical feminism. Erikson distrusted men of action. He thought they were too aggressive and warlike. Erikson published a biography of Martin Luther, *Young Man Luther (1958)*, attributing the great Reformer's actions to inadequate toilet training. If Luther's parents had been more sensitive to his bowels, Erikson argued, that Luther's challenge to the Catholic Church might not have occurred. Erikson propounded his theory of inadequate toilet training to explain many problems experienced by American youth. Poor toilet training helped lead to the widespread "identity crisis" of American adolescents.

Ridiculous as Erikson's crackpot theory is, it once exerted a deep influence on American education. Gore eagerly and fanatically swallowed Erikson's idea of the identity crisis. One overcame the identity crisis by developing through many stages until arriving at the "generativity stage." At this stage, one acquired "the ability to care for many others and to establish and guide the next generation." Women seemed to arrive at this stage sooner than men do. Women were more civilized and caring about the world and its inhabitants than men were. They respected the environment more. Gore's solemn embrace of Erikson's ideas would also later influence *Earth in the Balance*.[67]

Campus Rumbles and the Bust

Marty Peretz infected many students with his radicalism thanks to the Vietnam War draft. The draft put their privileged lives at risk. Apolitical Harvard undergraduates joined the New Left organization Students for a Democratic Society in droves. Harvard's SDS militants demonstrated against the ROTC program, CIA recruiters, and anyone who defended the Vietnam War. The students practiced cultural radicalism as well as political radicalism. They openly smoked marijuana and kept girls in their dorms overnight.

Al Gore joined in smoking dope. His friends in Dunster House dorm remember him passing out several times on the couch after partying too hard with marijuana.[68] But after his freshman year, when he was active in student government, he steered clear of campus politics. Gore's avoidance of politics stood out since Dunster House was a hotbed of SDS politics at Harvard. Al recognized he risked both his and his father's political careers if he did anything reckless. He played lots of pool in the Dunster dorm and went steady with Tipper, who had recently transferred to Boston University from Garland College. Friends remember him enacting his own love story with Tipper. They don't recall him creating any trouble.

In the spring of 1969, just before Al's graduation, Harvard SDS militants stormed and occupied University Hall to protest President Nixon's ending of student draft deferments. The protesters also beat up several faculty members and vandalized the building. Gore's classmates remember many of them being involved in the takeover when the local police came and arrested the SDS occupiers in the famous "Bust." But none of them saw Gore anywhere near the action. Marty Peretz retrospectively claims the student excesses of the "Bust" pushed him away from radicalism and toward the centrist position of the DLC. At the time, Peretz was practicing militancy, not preaching restraint. His pet student Al Gore had already foreseen the dangers of excessive militancy and avoided it. Nothing could be permitted to prevent his pursuit of power. During the turmoil of the 1969 Harvard Commencement, with its many protests and demonstrations against the recent "Bust," Gore behaved as the good boy his parents raised him to be.

FIVE

The Vietnam War Hero

The Agony of Decision

Unlike Bill Clinton, Al Gore chose to bite the bullet and serve in the military during the Vietnam War. But before making this admirable decision, in typical Gore fashion, he explored every option in exhausting detail. He painstakingly weighed the consequences of each option before making his choice. He whined with self-pity about having to make this difficult choice. Young Al sought advice from Tipper, his parents, uncles, Harvard mentors, and peers during his decision process.

While seeking advice, Al expressed his own frank views on the Vietnam War in particular and "American imperialism" in general in a 1969 letter. His written views reflect the influence of Marty Peretz and Erik Erikson as well as his father's appeasement policy toward Communist dictatorships: "We do have inveterate antipathy toward Communism-or paranoia as I like to put it. My own belief is that this form of psychological ailment-in this case a national madness- leads the victim to actually create the thing which is feared the most. It strikes me that this is precisely what the U.S. has been doing. Creating--and if not creating, energetically supporting--fascist, totalitarian regimes in the name of fighting totalitarianism. Greece, South Vietnam, a good deal of Latin America. For me, the best example of all is the U.S. Army."[69]

This inane commentary resembles Bill Clinton's words, written the same year, about "loathing" the American military.[70]

Young Al's analysis of the Cold War combines leftist slurs ("fascist regimes") with amateur psychoanalysis ("psychological ailment," "a national madness"). Like his father, Al Gore did not see the conflict between the United States, the Soviet Union, and their respective allies, as a necessary struggle to the death. He refuses to see the Soviet Union as an "evil empire." Instead, Gore adopts a clinical, condescending tone toward his own country. He diagnoses the desperate efforts of the U.S. to resist Soviet subversion and expansion as mere "paranoia." He accuses the

U.S. of creating and supporting "fascist" and "totalitarian regimes." Gore smears the imperfect allies of America in Greece, South Vietnam, and Latin America. The young Harvard elitist refuses to recognize most foreign governments do not share the customs and practices of American constitutional government. His condemnation of the U.S. Army as fascist is just ridiculous. The Vietnam-era Army bowed tamely to the idiotic political constraints imposed upon it by Presidents Kennedy and Johnson, his father's friends and colleagues. The Army's placid, bureaucratic commanders lacked the passionate wills necessary for fascist conduct. When he ran for President in 1988, Gore repudiated the letter by dismissing it as the ranting of a raw, inexperienced undergraduate. At the time, though, the letter did reflect his true thinking about America's war against Communist regimes. The 21 year-old Harvard undergraduate resented his country for making unfair demands on his privileged life. How dare the paranoid U.S. Government, which paid his father's salary, expect him to serve in its armed forces?

Tipper, Albert, and Pauline claimed they would support whatever choice Al made about serving in the military. Of course, his father preferred Al to serve in the military since it would help in his re-election campaign; and Al's future political viability would be preserved. Pauline mentioned if Al wanted to flee to Canada, she would not oppose him. Pauline's brother, Uncle Whit LaFon, a WW II combat veteran and former state commander of the Tennessee American Legion, urged Al in the opposite direction. Uncle Whit insisted: "there wasn't any question…if they called you up to do it, you did it." When Al expressed religious objections to Vietnam, Uncle Whit retorted," I never knew there was anything in the Baptist religion against war."[71]

Gore's two favorite Harvard mentors, Marty Peretz and Professor Richard Neustadt, both advised him to serve in the military. Peretz hosted Al at his Cambridge home and Cape Cod cottage during the summer of 1969. There he helped Al talk through his options. Although Peretz opposed the war, he thought it was necessary for Al to serve, hopefully in a safe assignment, in order to preserve his "political viability." Almost all Peretz's other protégés dodged the war with medical deferments or conscientious objection. But the leftist guru wanted Al to become President more than he wanted a U.S. withdrawal from Vietnam. Professor Neustadt, a man of the old school who was almost a generation older than Peretz, urged Al to do the hard right in order to earn the privilege of leading his countrymen "25 years from now." Neustadt argued, "if you want any future in politics, you've got to serve."[72]

To preserve his future political viability and help his father's re-election campaign it was necessary he serve. Gore claims he also recognized at the time how underprivileged Smith County, Tennessee boys were being sent over to Vietnam. He says he felt guilt over this fact. This is true to an extent. Many of Gore's intimates remember him expressing grief over Smith County boys he knew who were killed in Vietnam. But if he truly felt guilty over this unfair situation, why did he not volunteer later for a combat unit? It appears his own personal safety and his own future political viability as well as his father's tough campaign were Al Gore's primary motivations. Steve Armistead, his Carthage friend, told him: "Somewhere down the line you'll be in politics yourself, you won't have much choice" but to join.[73] The political careers of both Albert Sr. and Al Jr. demanded the latter join the military. So Al, impelled by the need to preserve the political viability of two careers, decided to join the "best example of all" fascist regimes, the U.S. Army. Like Bill Clinton, Gore spent much time and care preserving his political viability regarding the Vietnam War. Unlike Clinton, Gore chose the honorable course.

Gore's Stateside Army Duty

Al Gore chose to enlist before being drafted. Inside advice from powerful contacts [74] informed him he could obtain pleasant duty if he joined up at the Army recruiting office in Newark, New Jersey. He traveled to Newark in August 1969. Gore took his physical and mental exams, and wound up being classified a military journalist, 71SQ10. This classification guaranteed him little or no combat duty. This plum rating resulted from his voluntary enlistment, fine Harvard record, and the fact he was the son of a U.S. Senator. The Army's high command knew Senator Albert Gore, Sr. was a bitter critic of the Vietnam War. The last thing the beleaguered Army bureaucracy wanted to do was to get the only son of a senior U.S. Senator killed in Vietnam. After eight weeks of basic training at Fort Dix, New Jersey, Gore was sent in late October to Fort Rucker, Alabama to work at the base newspaper.[75]

After reporting for duty at Fort Rucker, Al married Tipper at the National Cathedral, next door to St. Albans School, on May 19, 1970. Almost all members of the wedding party were St. Albans and Harvard friends. Steve Armistead was the only Tennessee friend invited. Everybody else belonged to the northeast corridor establishment. Washington, D.C. and Cambridge, Massachusetts had already won out over Carthage, Tennessee. After a honeymoon, the young newlyweds moved to Fort Rucker. Gore's duty lasted for over 14 months.[76]

Al Gore later criticized the Army for letting Richard Nixon interfere with his Army assignments. He believed Nixon prevented him from being assigned to Vietnam immediately. He thought an immediate assignment to Vietnam would help his father's 1970 political campaign. Despite his own paranoia, the Army was favoring him because of his father. Ft. Rucker was a base close to Tennessee. Al's model service (he won a Soldier of the Month award) and powerful father enabled him to obtain frequent weekend passes. This allowed Al to campaign for his father. Well before the November election, on September 27, 1970, the *Nashville Tennessean* ran a front-page story about how Al Gore, Jr., son of the Senator, was being ordered by the Army to Vietnam in December. This situation assisted his father's election in two ways: 1) Al was going to serve in Vietnam; and 2) Al could campaign in uniform for his father on weekends before the election. He even appeared in a television campaign commercial with his father. Senator Gore, the unscrupulous crony of Armand Hammer, tells his son in the television ad: "Son, always love your country." This gives the lie to Gore, Jr.'s charge President Nixon was interfering with his orders to help defeat his father.[77]

Despite the politically favorable situation created by the Army's orders to Al, Albert Gore, Sr. lost his 1970 election anyway. With only seven months to go in his two-year hitch, Al shipped out for Vietnam a month later than his original orders, in January 1971. He was embittered both by his father's defeat and his own participation in an "immoral war."

Rear Echelon Vietnam Veteran

Gore served only five months in Vietnam, less than half the twelve months average tour for enlisted men. He had a good war. Ordered to the huge Bien Hoa administrative base on January 2,

1971, Gore drew combat pay although he was far from any fighting. Bien Hoa sat only 7 miles from the South Vietnamese capital city of Saigon. His company, the Headquarters of the 20th Engineer Brigade, was a rear-echelon outfit. Gore's superiors back at Fort Rucker recommended him for this cushy duty. Gore's job was to write journalistic copy about the brigade. The front-line troops dubbed the rear area troops who got to live in safe air-conditioned barracks, take hot showers, eat hot food, and take in Saigon night life, the Rear Echelon M----r F-----s, or REMFs.[78]

Except during the 1968 Tet offensive, the Bien Hoa base never suffered from attack by Viet Cong guerrillas or North Vietnamese regulars. The neighboring First Air Cavalry Division, further out on the perimeter, suffered all the mortar attacks. Bien Hoa resembled a prefabricated American city set up in Vietnam, a home away from home. Army engineers had constructed superb highways for the base area, some of them superior to the roads of Smith County, Tennessee. Some of the barracks boasted more comfort and amenities than the dorm rooms at Harvard. Vietnamese servant women cleaned the rooms and shined the shoes of the barrack soldiers every morning. Rock music blared constantly from stereos and jukeboxes. High-grade marijuana and cold beer were available in profuse quantities for bargain prices. So many American troops were continuously stoned even Al Gore was shocked. He cut down on his pot smoking in order to stay alert and preserve his life.[79]

Gore actually aspired to do a little more than just survive. Bored by the routine of the headquarters company, Gore and his journalist buddy Mike O'Hara wangled passes to go visit bases around South Vietnam where 20th Brigade Engineers were building bridges, runways, and barracks. They were curious to see evidence of the war. The closest Gore and O'Hara came to combat was to arrive at firebases hours or even days after a firefight. Military journalists lacked the power and privileges of civilian reporters. The two men ended up filing bland stories, censored by their superiors, about the exploits of the engineers. They saw no actual combat. There are conflicting reports that Gore, the Senator's son, was assigned bodyguards by the Army. Alan Leo, a 20th Brigade photographer with considerable combat experience, was asked by the brigade's commander to protect and keep an eye on the Senator's son. The brass did not want Al Gore, Jr. to become a casualty. So, Leo made sure Gore only went on trips where military security was excellent. Leo said his field trips accompanying Gore were so safe: "I could have worn a tuxedo." [80]

Gore bragged he did guard duty on the perimeter out in the bush to journalist Gail Sheehy in 1988. This claim was just the usual Gore desire to exaggerate his accomplishments. As David Maraniss and Ellen Nakashima of the *Washington Post* conclude: "He (Gore) was a reporter, not an infantryman, and while he was never fully out of harm's way, neither did he face situations where he had to kill or be killed, and he was spared the sight of seeing any buddies die." [81]

After O'Hara left at the end of his tour, Gore grew bored with the Bien Hoa routine. He applied to Vanderbilt University's Divinity School because he wanted to atone for serving in an immoral war. The school accepted him, so on the basis of his good conduct, and he petitioned the Army for early discharge. The Army consented, and Gore flew back to the U.S. on May 22, 1971, 75 days before his two years were up. [82]

SIX

Marking Time:
Reporter, Divinity Student, Law Student

Cub Reporter at the Tennessean

Between 1971 and 1976, Al Gore marked time waiting for a political opportunity to open up for him. For the only time in his life, purposeful Al Gore played the dilettante. He dabbled in three different professions: journalism, the ministry, and the law. He did not complete the training for any of these occupations. He performed with only dogged mediocrity in each of them. Gore did decide, after some doubts, he wanted to enter into public life just as Albert and Pauline planned.

After he arrived home from Vietnam, Gore expressed public bitterness and doubt about entering politics. But privately he was still interested, since his first day back from Vietnam, he called up John Seigenthaler, Editor of the *Nashville Tennessean*. Seigenthaler, now a top executive with *USA Today*, still wields influence over the *Tennessean*. A close friend of both Albert Gores and the Kennedy family, Seigenthaler is the leading public liberal in Tennessee. (His son John Jr. is the NBC correspondent.) Since the early 1960s, Seigenthaler has played the kingmaker role in Tennessee Democratic politics. He helps determine both the elected candidates and the judicial nominees at all levels of the party, whether federal, state, or local. Seigenthaler relentlessly pushes the *New York Times-Washington Post* line on feminism, civil rights, gun control, and Blame America First foreign policy in a traditionalist southern state. The *Tennessean*, is considered the most left-wing southern newspaper.

Immediately after Gore called up Seigenthaler, the latter offered him a reporter's job on the *Tennessean*. Albert Gore, Sr. disagreed with Al Jr.'s decision to become a reporter. The former Senator wanted his son to attend law school, as he and Pauline had, to prepare him for politics. However, Al's decision indicated he understood politics better than his father did. Al perceived how powerful the news media had become in political life. His Harvard senior thesis addressed just that subject. So, he aimed to acquire some experience and skill in journalism before running for office. Gore also planned on making connections in Tennessee politics through working on the *Tennessean*. Seigenthaler, Tennessee's kingmaker, made sure everybody of influence got to meet and know the Gore dynasty's heir apparent. One of Seigenthaler's protégés, a young summer intern named Carter Eskew, befriended Al while both worked at the newspaper. Eskew would later prove himself a valuable hatchet man for both Al Gore and the tobacco industry.

Gore worked doggedly as a reporter at the *Tennessean*. He tolerated the kidding given to a newcomer to the newsroom and tried hard to learn. He was usually assigned to routine local news stories or curiosity pieces. He displayed a flair for research but his prose reflected his robotic personality. As Bob Zelnick, himself an award-winning reporter, observes: "The hundreds of clips from Gore's years on the paper present a mixed picture. Much of the writing is dull. The narrative plods to a wooden cadence with neither pace nor anecdote to invite the reader along. Rarely does Gore enliven the copy with examples to illustrate the point at issue. When he does they are usually buried like wallflowers under a compost heap...Gore feared inspiring emotion in his readers."[83]

The only reporting Gore did that actually affected events involved his investigations of local zoning ordinances. Perhaps Gore found the very dullness of this beat inspiring to his soul. Thanks to some good tips and an authorized wiretap by the local District Attorney, Gore's reporting got two Nashville Council members, Morris Haddox and Jack Clariday, indicted for bribery to change zoning laws. With his usual modesty, Gore bragged during the 1988 Presidential campaign to a *Des Moines Register* reporter how his investigative reporting "got a bunch of people indicted and sent to jail."[84] Journalists who reviewed the actual record challenged Gore on this boast. He backed down and admitted Haddox escaped jail thanks to a hung jury, and Clariday only received a suspended sentence.

Al Gore relentlessly pursued Morris Haddox. He was the young black councilman who took a measly $300 bribe offered in the sting prepared by Gore and the Tennessee Bureau of Investigation. However, Haddox and his attorneys successfully played the race card in two trials. The second trial acquitted Haddox after the first trial ended in a hung jury. Gore testified in both trials against Haddox and was stung when black leaders accused him of racism.[85] Two decades later Gore castigated Kenneth Starr for excessive zeal in pursuing the Whitewater and Lewinsky cases. He also flayed those reporters and Republican politicians who demanded that his illegal fundraising actions for the 1996 campaign be probed by an independent counsel. Does Gore remember how he tracked down Morris Haddox for a $300 bribe?

Considering that Gore once took credit for inspiring *Love Story* and inventing the Internet, this boast about putting people in jail seems mild and modest.

The Dope Smoking Divinity Student

Despite wanting to atone for the sin of serving in Vietnam, Al did not don sackcloth and ashes after returning to Nashville. He and Tipper lived for a few months at the family home in Carthage. They then moved to a house in Belle Meade, Nashville's richest and most exclusive suburb. Belle Meade was all white. Although Gore became a lifelong friend of John Tyson, a black resident of his Dunster House dorm, he felt no compunction about living with Tipper in Belle Meade. The vocal defender of racial quotas who vilifies Republicans as racists resided for four years in a rich, "Whites Only" suburb.

Al Gore practiced habits not usually seen in Belle Meade. He wore his hair long and parted in the middle. He took courses at the Vanderbilt Divinity School advocating radical resistance to government authority and redistribution of wealth. One course, "Theology and the Natural Sciences" advocated zero population growth and a suppression of industrialization. This course, combined with the teaching of Harvard professors Erikson and Revelle, reinforced his rising zeal for radical environmentalism. People and their needs were wrenching the earth out of balance. Control the reproduction and economic activities of people, Gore thought, and we could once again live in harmony with Mother Earth. Probably no resident of Belle Meade resented the rich or felt guiltier about being one of them than Al Gore. Most of all, he smoked marijuana, large quantities of it.[86]

Students of Al Gore's life know he smoked pot regularly, at least until 1972. However, recent revelations by his friend John Warnecke indicate Al smoked both marijuana laced with opium and hashish heavily until the day he declared his candidacy for Congress in February 1976. Warnecke, a fellow reporter on the

Tennessean, supplied Al with his dope. Warnecke reported: "Al Gore and I smoked regularly, as buddies. Marijuana, hash…We smoked more than once, more than a few times, we smoked a lot. We smoked in his car, in his house, we smoked in his parents' house, in my house…we smoked on weekends. We smoked a lot. Al Gore and I were smoking marijuana together right up to the time that he ran for Congress in 1976. Right up through the week he declared for that race in fact." [87]

Warnecke remembered how Gore took pains to conceal his constant pot smoking. Prince Albert feared political enemies were spying upon his recreational drug use. So he insisted Warnecke turn out the lights and close the curtains whenever they smoked marijuana inside his house. While stoned, Al Gore's personality was both expansive and paranoid; Prince Albert boasted about his political future but also worried about the demands it would impose on him. Warnecke went along with his friend's security measures against the detection of their pot smoking but found them amusing. Gore particularly feared his father might find out about his drug use. He also feared losing his political viability in Tennessee. Warnecke resented how Gore avoided him after declaring for Congress in February 1976. Gore thought Warnecke's friendship was now dangerous to his burgeoning political career, so he drifted away from his close friend. Warnecke's testimony contradicts many of Gore's previous statements about his illegal drug use. Warnecke admits he made misleading statements about Gore's drug use to the *New York Times* and *Nashville Tennessean* during November 1987. At that time, he told those newspapers he smoked dope with Gore "a few times. And I told them he didn't like it…I was put under a lot of pressure to lie." [88]

Warnecke testified Gore shouted at him in November 1987 to stonewall any detailed press inquiries into his narcotics use. Prince Albert's advice reminds one irresistibly of Bill Clinton's frequently proffered advice to his many mistresses: "Just deny it." Gore became terrified after Federal Judge Douglas Ginsberg was forced to step down from a nomination to replace Justice Lewis Powell on the Supreme Court. Ginsberg lied about his pot smoking as a young professor. He claimed he had only smoked as a student. But a liberal friend squealed to the press about it during that same month of November 1987. Gore did not want his presidential ambitions derailed for an identical lie. Now the young Senator severed himself from any contact with Warnecke.

Warnecke, who had comforted Tipper during Al's tour in Vietnam, was tossed away. Warnecke discovered the truth of Henry Adams' comment: "A friend in power is a friend lost." [89]

Warnecke has now come forward to talk about his drug use with Gore because: "I was having trouble living with myself being part of this hypocrisy and the lies…The drug laws in this country are ruining the lives of hundreds of thousands of young people, mostly poor young people, people who don't come from privileged backgrounds and wealthy families. It just doesn't make sense that we have a war on drugs."

Warnecke preserved evidence from his drug sessions with Gore. He still holds Prince Albert's personal roach clip. [90]

Warnecke's revelations about Gore's pot smoking are contained in an article by *Newsweek* reporter Bill Turque. Turque's article is excerpted from a new biography of Gore he just published. *Newsweek* editors suppressed the story, perhaps because they wish to help Gore's campaign. Matt Drudge leaked the drug information, and now Warnecke has come forward to confirm it. Warnecke, who plans to vote for Gore in the 2000 Presidential election, says further: "I wish that Al would come clean. I wish that all politicians would come clean…*Newsweek* cut off information that the American people should have had in order to make an informed decision. Knowing that Al Gore used drugs considerably more than he has admitted is important. Let the American people draw their own conclusions about it, let them decide how important it is." [91]

Gore sounds a lot like Bill Clinton when asked about his drug use. Clinton stated during the 1992 campaign: "I did not break the laws of this country." [92]

The Law Student and Man of Property

After drinking in the wisdom offered by Vanderbilt's leftist Divinity School, Gore finally bowed to his father's wishes by enrolling in the university's Law School in August 1974. Vanderbilt, often called "the Harvard of the South," boasted a law school ranking 25th in the country. Its faculty leaned far to the left of most Tennesseans. To attend law school, Gore took a leave of absence from the *Tennessean*. Later he contributed editorials to the newspaper on a part-time basis. But his full-time journalistic career effectively ended. Al Gore studied law to attain power, not to write about it.

The young husband and law student was now also a father. His first child, daughter Karenna, was born in 1973. He was a man of lucrative property as well. Al, his father, and Armand Hammer, worked out a complicated three-way deal for mining and property rights on a parcel of Carthage land recently made available by the death of the owner. Occidental Minerals Corporation, the mining subsidiary of Occidental Petroleum, discovered large deposits of zinc and germanium on the land.

The land was purchased by the Senator, acting as agent for Occidental's mineral subsidiary, as an estate for Al and Tipper. Hammer gave Albert Gore, Sr. $160,000, twice the price of the only other offer, to buy the land. Then he sold it to Gore, Sr., who then sold it to Al Jr. The mining rights then were sold to Armand Hammer, who paid an annual lease to the young couple. Al took out a mortgage on the property for $100,000. The mortgage was quickly paid off in ten years by income averaging $20,000 a year from the mineral leases. In effect, Armand Hammer paid for Al's Tennessee's farm and the mineral lease on it. Albert Sr.'s land purchase was a fiction to enable Hammer to buy Al Jr.'s favor. The idealistic investigative reporter and law student now joined his father in Hammer's back pocket. Al Gore refuses to recognize how he, his father, and Armand Hammer did deals far more corrupt than poor Morris Haddox's $300 bribe.[93]

Now, at age 26, Al owned a house in Belle Meade and a farm with mineral deposits in Carthage. He was a rich man compared to his father at the same age. He probably possessed more total worth than any of his fellow law students. Gore's Carthage farm, like his father's estate, raised tobacco as a cash crop.

Al Gore was not just a family man owning substantial property. He also led a group of Tennessee law students at Vanderbilt Law. They looked up to him as the heir of a liberal political dynasty. Even the Vanderbilt law professors treated him as a pet for the same reason. A fellow student and acquaintance in the Vanderbilt Law Class of 1977 remembers Gore as a mediocre student. Al ranked right in the middle of the class according to this source. He was a gentleman C student who usually received 75% out of 100 for grades. But Vanderbilt law professors like James Blumstein, a leftist emigrant from Brooklyn, fell over themselves to do favors for Al. Blumstein grew angry over the voter resident requirements preventing him from casting a ballot for Albert Gore during the 1970 election, he sued the state of Tennessee and finally won his case at the Supreme Court.

It was obvious to our Gore classmate source that Al aimed to pick up his father's mantle. Tipper and Al joined the law students for their Friday beer bashes. Tipper, as always, was charming and irresistible to any law student who did not defer to Al. In late February 1976, John Seigenthaler phoned up the heir apparent and told him: "Joe Evins (the Democratic Congressman who held Albert Sr.'s old district) is going to announce his retirement tomorrow. The story just came across my desk."

Al Gore was so excited by this notification from the Democrat Kingmaker of Tennessee, he dropped to the floor and did some pushups.[94]

Then, in Bob Zelnick's words: "By the time the weekend was over, he had quit the paper, withdrawn from law school, put his [Belle Meade] house up for sale, trimmed his hair, changed his part to the conventional left side, and outfitted himself in the attire blue suit, red tie, scuffed shoes that would become his political uniform."[95]

Gore also stopped smoking dope and began avoiding John Warnecke. He then traveled with Tipper to the Smith County Court House at Carthage. After throwing up in the men's room, he stood on the courthouse steps and became the first candidate to announce for Evins' former House seat.[96]

James Blumstein, who recently told the *Washington Post* how much he still admired the Gore family, led several of the Vanderbilt law school professors to do a favor for their pet student. These professors offered to waive all the classes he skipped if he wrote research papers for them. Gore accepted this blatant favoritism as his due. Influential people had always eased his progress to power. But because of many distractions, he never got around to taking advantage of this offer of a law degree by correspondence school. For years afterward when he saw Blumstein, Gore would smile and say, "I owe you a paper." [97]

The First Election

Just by being Albert Gore, Sr.'s son, Al Gore, Jr. enjoyed a huge advantage running for the Fourth Congressional District seat. His name, his family's money, and Armand Hammer's money made his victory in the Democratic primary very likely. But Gore dutifully and doggedly denied the voters should elect him on the basis of his father's reputation. Albert appeared at rallies but did not speak at them. Al recognized how many

Tennessee voters still (and accurately) identified his father as a Northeast Corridor liberal. But he did ask for Pauline to make speeches and she cheerfully assented. Often Pauline would say in the presence of her husband and son: "I trained both of them, and I did a better job with my son." In 1999, she was still using this line at the Vice President's political rallies.[98]

Gore's most dangerous primary opponent was Stanley Rogers, Majority Leader of the Tennessee State House. Rogers, with all of his legislative chits, would scare anybody but the heir apparent to the Gore dynasty. Rogers was simply unable to compete with Gore's name, hard work, and financial resources.

Al emulated his father by spending much more cash than his opponent. He overwhelmingly outspent Rogers, putting two-thirds of his own net worth on the line. His campaign expenditures of $188,560 were well above average for a Congressional seat in 1976. Armand Hammer and other friends of his father pitched in with donations. Rogers, a conservative Democrat, tried to paint Gore as a pro-gun control, anti-war liberal like his father. Rogers also hammered away at Albert Gore, Sr.'s connection to Armand Hammer. Gore answered by portraying himself as tough on crime, fiscally responsible, and moderate. He demagogically demanded higher taxes on the rich without mentioning his own wealth. Despite his later posture as a pro-defense hawk, Gore called for less defense spending. In 1976, the defense share of the U.S. GNP was the lowest it had been since 1941. The Soviet Empire was expanding since the U.S. military was so weakened by Democratic Congresses. But Gore pretended the Soviets did not exist. He ignored Rogers' attacks on the Armand Hammer connection. Most of his other campaign themes became drearily familiar after the Democratic Leadership Council patented it to disguise southern liberals in conservative sheep's' clothing.[99]

While pounding away at these issues, Al Gore spoke, as Zelnick puts it, in a "slow, stiff, painfully measured way" to voters. He spoke in "a very sonorous tone" according to Bart Day,[100] much resembling his father's lecturing stump style. Reporter Marjorie Williams captures Gore's oratorical pose: "The athlete's body language suddenly broadcasts a lack of fluency: his arms dangle lifelessly from his shoulders, and he seems to have no joints at all above the waist. The deliberate pauses in the middle of his sentences stretch into yawning silences."[101]

Gore told corny jokes to break the ice. Perhaps the former dope smoking, Harvard elitist thought his father's stuffy speaking style was the best way to impress and reassure the Middle American voters of his district. Al also used several of his father's favorite issues to stir the voters. He resembled Albert Gore, Sr. when he discussed progressive taxation, lower electric rates, and the sacred TVA.

Unlike his father, Al Gore hustled to speak with every voter in sight. He sped over the Fourth District's highways to meet with every possible group. In areas where he trailed in the race, he returned repeatedly to shake hands and talk. Gore's Carthage friend Steve Armistead recalled: "He felt like he had to overcome his father's beating....He overkilled—he'd go back and go back and go back."[102]

He jogged two hundred yards into a field to shake hands with a farmer driving a tractor. David Lyons, a reporter with the Nashville *Banner* newspaper, saw Gore climb a telephone pole to chat with a lineman working up top. As Lyons said: "He [Gore] was just a bulldog, a tenacious campaigner. He just flat was everywhere at every time."[103]

Lyons admitted the news media, including himself, assisted Gore's candidacy: "He really got a free ride in '76."[104] Both the Nashville papers, Seigenthaler's liberal *Tennessean* and the conservative *Banner*, endorsed him. When Gore brushed off questions about marijuana use by the *Tennessean*, the two reporters did not press the point. They certainly did not inquire about the Gore family's relations with Armand Hammer, even when Stanley Rogers explicitly raised the issue. The Tennessee news media openly rooted for Prince Albert. After all, he was one of their own. Gore and his aides, Roy Neel and Ken Jost, all worked for either the *Tennessean* or the *Banner*. The reporters regarded him as a reformer reviving his father's liberal tradition.[105]

Al Gore's hustling, money, and media support paid off. Despite his robotic speaking style, satirized even by his close friends, the Fourth District Democrats gave Al Gore a one third plurality in the crowded primary field. He beat Rogers narrowly, 32% to 29%. This primary victory was Gore's only close election. The heavily outnumbered Republicans of Middle Tennessee did not even field a candidate in the November 1976 general election. Since then, Al Gore's victories came even easier. In neighboring Arkansas, another "southern moderate" won *his* first election with similar themes and a large bankroll. Bill Clinton became Arkansas State Attorney General in Little Rock while Al Gore trooped off to his real home of Washington, D.C. Two powerful wolves had successfully donned their sheep disguises.

SEVEN

A Yankee Liberal in Southern Sheep's Clothing: the House Years

Settling In

Tipper Gore's grandmother, Verda Carlson, sold her Tudor mansion in Arlington, Virginia to her and Al for $208,000 shortly after the election.[106] Al, Tipper, and Karenna now lived in a reasonably priced residence just as Al, Pauline, and Nancy did when they came to Washington 38 years earlier. Proclaiming himself a "raging moderate," Gore deliberately set out to make his incumbency invulnerable. Unlike his father, he chose to never appear too left of his constituents. Gore kept a full constituent service staff in Carthage. He undertook a regular schedule of town meetings throughout the Fourth District during weekends, averaging 150 meetings a year. Gore then pondered how to make a name for himself in the House. There was little money available for social program spending thanks to Great Society entitlements. So Gore cleverly decided to devote himself to arcane technical issues of practical import for people's lives. These technical issues must lend themselves to bi-partisan compromise and agreement. They must also cost little money. Gore recognized his dogged diligence enabled him to master problems of complex detail. So, he campaigned hard to be assigned to technical committees such as those on Interstate and Foreign Commerce, Science and Technology, and Intelligence. Thus was born Al Gore, policy wonk.[107]

The policy wonk surrendered to his constituents' wishes on hot button moral and foreign policy issues. But he only surrendered outwardly. His actual thinking usually mirrored the views of his mentor Marty Peretz. Peretz, now owner and editor-in-chief of *The New Republic*, was becoming increasingly hard line toward the Soviet Union because of its hostility to both Israel and the United States. Simultaneously, Peretz pushed *The New Republic* to the outer envelope of the sexual revolution. The magazine passionately championed unrestricted abortion and homosexual rights. *The New Republic* loved to jeer at southerners, evangelical Christians, old-fashioned Roman Catholics, and anyone else supporting traditional sexual morality. Peretz and his elitist Ivy League staffers conveniently overlooked how the sternest opponents of sexual liberation were also the sternest opponents of the U.S.S.R. As a Congressman, Al Gore mildly disappointed Peretz by often voting against both of Peretz's pet issues.

Assembling the Gore Team

The new Congressman hired staff assistants who became notorious over the next two decades. Peter Knight, an aggressive Cornell and Georgetown Law graduate from Massachusetts, worked as his primary administrative aide. Later he became Gore's Senate Chief of Staff and then an influence peddling lobbyist and fundraiser. Just 25 years old when he began working for Gore, Knight stood out even on Capitol Hill for ardently desiring power and money. He schooled the shy Gore in raising funds from complete strangers.[108] Knight became a prime suspect in several different scandals while chairing the 1996 Clinton-Gore re-election campaign.

Roy Neel, an affable Tennessee "good old boy," specialized in negotiating legislation. He eventually became Vice President Gore's Chief of Staff and then President Clinton's Deputy Chief of Staff. Neel now lobbies for the U.S. Telephone Association.[109] Leon Fuerth, a former Foreign Service Officer from New York, took on the role of Gore's foreign policy tutor. Fuerth, an arrogant Council on Foreign Relations mandarin, loathed President Reagan's bold policies of Strategic Defense and aiding anti-Soviet guerrillas. He still works as Vice President Gore's primary adviser on foreign policy. Gore considers Fuerth the only one of his aides who can match him in intellectual ability.[110] Ken Jost, Gore's Harvard classmate and *Tennessean* colleague served as legislative director. Jost's wife, Eve Zibart, introduced Gore to Roy Neel back in Nashville.[111] Floridian Carol Browner served as an environmental policy aide to Gore. She served so effectively and faithfully that she now serves as head of the Environmental Protection Agency in the Clinton Administration. Knight, Neel, Fuerth, Jost, Browner, and other Gore aides share common characteristics. They have all tried to keep a low profile over the past 8 years. They avoid journalists and publicity and rarely grant interviews. They never criticize or joke about their boss. Only a few Washington insiders know who they are. They work hard and will happily undertake dirty jobs for their boss. If the dirty jobs their boss orders them to do involve questionable conduct, these Gore aides will not flinch. They all give Al Gore unstinting loyalty. He rewards them with ample power and protection. Unlike Bill Clinton, Al Gore always takes care of his subordinates.[112]

The TV Congressman Pursues Bipartisan Issues

Al Gore soon became known as the Class of '76 House Member most eager to appear on TV. Both Republicans and Democrats snickered at his grandstanding. His fellow Class of '76 Member and rival Richard Gephardt nicknamed Gore "Prince Albert" for his constant preening before the cameras. But the driven robot continued to hunt for favorable publicity. Gore ensured he spoke on television March 19, 1979, the first day House proceedings were televised. Although senior Members resented it, appearing on television helped the status of Congressmen within the House. As former Congressman Tom Downey, Gore's closest friend in the House, put it: "If you want to reach your colleagues, the best way is to let them see you on TV or read your name in the paper."[113]

Gore wanted to reach voters, not just colleagues. He used televised House oversight hearings to pursue bi-partisan consumer issues that gained him fame for a low cost. The "raging moderate" picked his spots with great care. Gore always aimed to be crusading on the side of consumer angels against corporate corruption. He took the investigative skills he honed at the *Tennessean* into House oversight hearings. "It's just like being a reporter," he bragged to friends, "only you've got subpoena power."[114]

Gore first used television to reach his audience by a crusade against corrupt infant formulas. He discovered how Syntex Corporation manufactured two brands of formula lacking in chloride. The formulas' lack of chloride contributed to serious illness in infants, sometimes death. The Federal Drug Administration possessed no authority over infant formula due to the then law. Who wanted infant babies to die of inadequate formula? Gore's televised hearings compelled passage of a bill regulating the content of infant formula by the FDA. Gore immodestly took full credit for this very popular legislation. With typical overstatement, he observed how 60% of babies depended on infant formula, "the most significant adjustment in the diet of human beings since the introduction of cooking."[115]

After saving infants from dangerous formula, Gore turned to other riskless and popular consumer issues. He crusaded against carcinogenic children's' pajamas, medical insurance policies bilking the elderly, and corruption in the contact lens industry. He explored the possibilities of biotechnology research and co-authored a pamphlet on the subject.[116] He also designed and passed legislation creating a national policy for organ transplants. The policy linked up donors and recipients and brought the program under Medicare and Medicaid coverage.

Gore, then, looked for another riskless crusade. He found a perfect opponent: the toxic waste dump industry. In late 1978, the whole country discovered Love Canal. Love Canal was a Niagara Falls, NY suburb built over a buried toxic waste dump. The Hooker Chemical Company, a subsidiary of Armand Hammer's Occidental Petroleum, created the toxic waste. It then sold the waste dump land to the City of Niagara Falls. The company warned the city not to allow anyone to live over the site. The Niagara Falls government disregarded the warning and sold building permits for the Love Canal area to developers without informing them of the hazardous waste material in the area. Two hundred frame houses were built in Love Canal. By 1978, many children raised in Love Canal developed horrifying birth defects and some children even died. After neighborhood activists learned of the presence of the toxic waste, they went to the news media to shame government authorities into action.

President Jimmy Carter quickly declared a federal state of emergency in Love Canal in August 1978. He did this to enable its residents to evacuate and move to a safer area. Al Gore likes to claim *he* discovered and publicized the Love Canal scandal. This of course is a lie. Gore did lead the push in October 1978 for House hearings on both Love Canal and a Memphis toxic waste dump in his home state. He was also the acknowledged star of the hearings. Gore showed himself better technically informed on the toxic waste issue than any of his colleagues. He also displayed an extraordinary ability to posture on television. Of course, he refused to mention that his father's friend Armand Hammer chaired the company that created the toxic waste.[117] Gore wanted all the credit for solving the Love Canal problem. He did not want to let the public know his family was close to the ruler of

Hooker Chemical Company. Despite Gore's grandiose claim, his call for the hearings came *two months* after Jimmy Carter declared a state of emergency in Love Canal. Once again, Al Gore took much more credit than he deserved.[118]

Gore also took undeserved credit for writing and enacting the Superfund Bill. The Superfund Bill, Public Law 96-510, is a 1980 Federal statute intended to clean up the most urgent toxic waste sites. Superfund consists of a trust fund administered by the Environmental Protection Agency. Former Congressman Jim Florio of New Jersey originally proposed superfund as a short-term project. Congress was to appropriate $1.6 billion over five years to clean up 400 of the most dangerous toxic waste sites. Gore, with his customary fanaticism, expanded and transformed Florio's modest initial proposal into a never-ending bureaucratic behemoth. The primary problem of Superfund was who should pay for cleaning up toxic waste sites created before any state, local, and federal laws regulating toxic waste were enacted. Were the polluting businesses to be retroactively convicted of violating the law? Gore demagogically insisted only the chemical companies should pay for the cleanup. He refused to consider a compromise whereby the chemical companies and the federal government split the cost 50/50.

Convicting chemical companies of a retroactive crime made for bad law and bad economics. In law, this approach sets a terrible precedent. It tramples over several centuries of established limited liability business law. If a business can be held retroactively liable, few risk-taking entrepreneurs will be motivated to begin new businesses. Therefore, the chemical companies litigated endlessly against their legal responsibility to pay for the cleanup. These lawsuits and EPA countersuits wasted much time and money, perhaps a whole third of Superfund's budget. In economics, the Gore anti-business approach ignores how companies pass along the cost of regulatory compliance to the consumer. Gore's decision to demand chemical polluters pay all the cleanup's cost only meant the consumer-taxpayer would end up footing the bill.

By nationalizing the Superfund cleanup, Gore exacerbated the high costs of the cleanup. He also wasted much money. Gore's refusal to balance costs and benefits of Superfund created an immortal budget monster. The Superfund pork incentives were all rigged in favor of delay. The General Accounting Office concluded in a March 1997 study that the average time of toxic site cleanups increased from 2.3 years in 1986 to 10.5 years in 1997. The GAO study also noted how there was more hazard involved cleaning up a site than in leaving it unremediated. Twenty years after its inception, Gore's Superfund project, once budgeted at 1.6 billion, has now cost 30 billion. The Superfund cost keeps escalating with no end in sight. Gore still boasts about how well he designed the Superfund cleanup.[119]

Gore's oversight of the petroleum industry also revealed his ignorance of business and economics. Despite his friendship with oil baron Armand Hammer, Al Gore did not realize how the petroleum market operated. During the 1979 oil crisis, Energy Secretary James Schlesinger begged Congress to deregulate oil and gas prices to stimulate energy exploration and production. Prince Albert, as his House colleague and rival Richard Gephardt nicknamed him, denounced Schlesinger's suggestion. Gore claimed the oil companies had artificially tightened supply to drive up prices. Deregulation would only make the situation worse: "Sharply higher prices risk simultaneous recession and double digit-inflation. The poor would be devastated; those barely making it now would be pushed beyond their limits. Yet once again, as in 1973-74, the oil companies would thrive, their profits inflated in direct proportion to the crushing economic burden on the country as a whole. In my opinion, our policy should reflect a greater concern for equity and a greater effort to avoid further drastic price increases."[120]

Contrary to Gore's prophecy, petroleum prices dropped drastically after newly elected President Reagan deregulated the petroleum industry in early 1981. Energy costs dropped so quickly they assisted in our country's economic boom. Despite Gore's apocalyptic warnings, there was no recession or double-digit inflation. Rich and poor alike enjoyed cheap prices at the pump. So, Gore now began to complain about how excessive use of fossil fuels released greenhouse gases that caused global warming. Global warming, not the needs of the poor or those barely making it now concerned him. Gore, the privileged rich kid who experienced little contact with poor people, now brushed them aside as he pursued his latest abstract fanaticism. This pursuit later led to writing *Earth in the Balance*.

The Liberal Trojan Horse:
The Democratic Leadership Council

After being trounced by Ronald Reagan's 1980 Republican landslide, some centrist Democrats decided their party needed to change its image. They muttered about also changing the substance of Democratic politics, but recognized too many special interest groups would resist more than cosmetic changes. These Democrats first began informally meeting in 1982, and set up a formal organization called the Democratic Leadership Council, or DLC, in 1985. Most of the elected officials among them were southerners: Senator Sam Nunn of Georgia; Governors James B. Hunt, Jr. of North Carolina, Bill Clinton of Arkansas, and Charles Robb of Virginia; and Congressmen Al Gore of Tennessee and Richard Gephardt of Missouri. The policy intellectuals of the DLC were Cold War intellectuals like Ben Wattenberg, Richard Scammon, and Al From, who refused to join the Republican Party. What the DLC members wanted was for Democratic liberalism to move slowly and stealthily to the middle, so as not to offend centrist voters.

The DLC members, despite their small numbers, enjoyed an influence far out of proportion to their numbers. This influence derived from the yearning of many in the liberal news media that the Democrats nominate a presidential candidate who hid his liberalism under a southern or border-state mask. This ideal candidate would be charming, respectable, and reassuring, unlike Jimmy Carter, and put undercover liberalism back in the Oval Office. This southern candidate would support welfare reform, be tough on crime, and be willing to use force in foreign policy. Of course, the DLC members refused to challenge any of the core values of liberalism: federal deficit spending; high taxes; feminism; gender and racial affirmative action; secular education; gay liberation; and judicial activism. The DLC members emphasized image and packaging, not substance. At heart, they were still big government liberals who refused to trust voters to make their own decisions. They just wanted the national party to not openly alienate centrist swing voters. The favorites for this centrist undercover candidate were all active in the Democratic Leadership Council: Senator Nunn; Governors Hunt, Robb, and Clinton; and Congressmen Gore and Gephardt.

One of the favorites for this DLC stealth role, Governor Jim Hunt of North Carolina, moved early to anoint himself the

"Great White Male southern Hope." He challenged the man most hated by Democratic liberals, Senator Jesse Helms, the leader of the New Right. Despite favorable news media coverage, Hunt lost the bitter and expensive 1984 North Carolina Senate race to Helms. But as events were to demonstrate, all of the other DLC hopes were to remain major Presidential contenders until miscues or bad luck drove them from the field. The Democratic Leadership Council people lacked honesty, but not a sound political strategy. Ten years after their founding, they installed the most gifted as well as the most corrupt of their members, William Jefferson Clinton, in the White House. The DLC even managed to install another member, Al Gore, in the Vice Presidency as Clinton's heir apparent.

The Right-to-Life Congressman

On January 26, 2000, in a New Hampshire debate, Bill Bradley, former U.S. Senator and Democratic Presidential candidate, accused Al Gore of voting for anti-abortion legislation while in Congress. Gore replied the charge was not true. But not surprisingly, Gore lied. Until failing in his run for President in 1988, Congressman and later Senator Gore voted for life and against abortion on 84% of all recorded roll call votes on the issue. Gore did not confine his anti-abortion activity to voting. He spoke against abortion in recorded Congressional speeches and wrote against abortion in letters to many constituents.[121]

In 1977, while a Member of Congress, Gore voted for the Hyde Amendment denying the use of federal funds for abortion except to save the life of the mother. That same year, Gore voted three times against amendments extending funding to abortions caused by rape or incest. In 1978, then Congressman Gore voted to prohibit the use of Department of Defense funds to pay for abortions unless the life of the mother was in danger. In 1980, Gore voted for the Ashbrook Amendment, which prohibited the use of funds in a Treasury, Postal Service, and General Appropriations bill from being used for abortions. In 1983, Gore voted for the Conte Amendment, which prohibited all funds in a Labor-HHS-Education appropriations bill from being used to pay for abortions. In 1984, he voted against the Boxer Amendment to allow federal employee health insurance to pay for abortions in cases other than danger to the life of the mother. To crown all of his pro-life votes, Gore voted for Congressman

Mark Siljander's Amendment defining life as beginning from the moment of conception. Siljander's amendment aimed to extend the Fourteenth Amendment's citizenship protection to unborn children.[122]

Gore did not just vote pro-life as an outward gesture to his constituents. He seems to have inwardly believed abortion was wrong. Al Gore thought abortion was not the "Hard Right" Canon Martin of St. Albans taught him to choose. He definitely thought federal funds should not be used to subsidize abortion. However, Tipper was an ardent pro-abortion feminist. She thought her husband let his background and conservative constituents influence him too much on the issue.[123] Gore said to City Editor Frank Ritter of the Nashville Tennessean well before being elected to Congress: "I know many here will disagree with me but I simply don't believe the government ought to be spending tax dollars on abortions."

He sounded the same theme in a letter to a constituent: "I am a firm supporter of the Hyde Amendment. I will continue to support efforts that are designed to prevent the use of federal funds in a manner which violates the relationship between the government and individual protected by our Constitution." (Al Gore, letter to constituent, 09/10/80).

In 1984, the year of his first Senate race, Gore wrote to another anti-abortion constituent: "As you know, I have strongly opposed federal funding of abortion. In my opinion, it is wrong to spend federal funds for what is arguably the taking of human life. I have been encouraged by recent action in the Congress, particularly in the House, that has indicated greater acceptance of our position with respect to federal funding of abortions. It is my deep personal conviction that abortion is wrong. I hope that some day we will see the current outrageously large number of abortions drop sharply. Let me assure you that I share your belief that innocent human life must be protected and I have an open mind on how to further this goal." (Letter to constituent, Mrs. Marvin Himmelberg, 07/18/84.)

Seven years later, while a U.S. Senator, he explained clearly why he opposed abortion: "During my 11 years in Congress, I have consistently opposed federal funding of abortions. In my opinion, it is wrong to spend federal funds for what is arguably the taking of human life. Let me assure you that I share your belief that innocent human life must be protected, and I am committed in furthering this goal." (Al Gore letter to constituent, 05/26/87).

Despite Gore's later avowals, he *was* a consistent and principled anti-abortion pro-life legislator from 1977-1988. Thanks to his House investigations of biotechnology, Gore certainly knew better than any other Congressman did the scientific evidence indicating when human life began. The fact that Tipper bore him three children between 1977 and 1982, Kristin, Sarah, and Albert III, probably helped him understand how unborn children made their presence felt well before birth.

Al Gore did not jettison the anti-abortion position until after his 1988 Presidential race. That loss convinced him he would never win the Democratic nomination until he joined the pro-abortion feminists. To obtain power, Gore discarded his "deep personal conviction that abortion is wrong." We will explain how Gore performed this flip flop in a later chapter.

The 1984 Senate Race

Al Gore played to television cameras because he wanted to move up from the House to the Senate. Like his father, he aimed for the White House, and wanted to win a Senate seat as an interim step. In December 1983, Republican Senate Majority Leader Howard Baker announced he was retiring as Tennessee's senior Senator. Baker wanted his protégé, Tennessee's popular Governor Lamar Alexander, to succeed him. But Alexander did not want to step down from the Governor's office and the Republicans could not field a strong candidate to defend the seat.

As in the 1976 Congressional seat, Al Gore was handed an easy opportunity to win this Senate seat. John Seigenthaler gave his order to Democrats: the party was to unite behind "Prince Albert." Gore easily raised money with the help of establishment Democrats inside the state and Armand Hammer's help in New York. The Republicans were forced to run State Senator Victor Ashe of Knoxville. Ashe was an inept candidate. He was an acerbic Yale graduate with a condescending attitude toward his fellow Tennessee legislators. Ashe refused to mobilize conservative voters around the moral issues of sexuality, school prayer, and education. Gore, the happy family man with a charming wife and four small children, seemed to be more down-home Tennessee than Ashe. Ashe elicited such resentment from Tennessee conservatives that Ed McAteer, Chairman of the traditionalist Religious Roundtable, ran as a third party protest candidate.

McAteer polled well enough to be included in several Senate election debates. Gore, delighted that his already slight opposition was split, just coasted smoothly to victory. He smiled and joked as much as his robotic personality permitted during tours around Tennessee. Whenever Ashe claimed Gore was an enemy of President Reagan, Gore quickly expressed his eager admiration of the incumbent President. Gore recognized that Reagan was enormously popular in Tennessee. He never dared to openly attack Reagan until the Iran-Contra affair flared up in 1987. Despite the fact Ronald Reagan carried Tennessee with 58.2% of the vote in 1984, Gore polled even better, winning 60.8% of the total to Ashe's 33.9% and McAteer's 5.3%.[124]

Al Gore's 1984 Senate triumph was spoiled by the agonizing death of his beloved sister Nancy by lung cancer. Nancy was a lifelong chain smoker who died before the November election. He would later exploit Nancy's premature death at 46 for public political purposes. But when Nancy died, he grieved along with his parents, Tipper, and Nancy's husband, Frank Hunger. Al Gore was still human enough in 1984 to refuse to politically exploit his grief.[125]

EIGHT

The Big Man Steps Forward: Cold War Wimp

Al Gore spoke on the first day Senate proceedings were televised in 1985. Gore loved speaking because it increased his name recognition for a future presidential run. However, he did not love the tough foreign policy voting choices created by the Cold War during the 1980s. Unlike the crusades against infant formula or toxic waste, the crusade against the U.S.S.R.'s Central American allies ignited bitter political opposition.

Prince Albert Hamlet and the Cold War in Central America

Thanks to the Cold War, Soviet influence spread to Central America after 1979. Using Cuba as a supply and training base, Soviet-sponsored Communists seized power in Nicaragua in 1979. President Jimmy Carter and his leftist foreign policy advisors first bungled Central American policy by not immediately opposing the influence of the Communist faction in Nicaragua. The Communist faction, known as the Sandinistas, imprisoned and exiled the democratic factions who helped them overthrow the Somoza dictatorship. The Somoza family had ruled Nicaragua for four decades before 1979. The Sandinistas then set up a totalitarian government and began importing Soviet advisors and heavy weapons, which included tanks, artillery, armored helicopters, and fighter aircraft. The Sandinistas used Soviet aid to help the Communist faction, known as the FMLN, in neighboring El Salvador. With military aid from the Sandinistas, the FMLN waged bloody guerrilla warfare against the democratically elected government of El Salvador. The Salvadoran military, not known for self-discipline or combat effectiveness, became frustrated and brutal. Massacres of Salvadoran civilians became common on both sides.

Ronald Reagan and his foreign policy advisors asked Congress for military aid to help both the Salvadoran government, and the anti-Sandinista rebels, known as the Contras. President Reagan wanted to help El Salvador to undertake land reform for its peasants. He also aimed to use American military advisers to train and discipline the ill-behaved Salvadoran army. Reagan wanted to help the Contras put pressure on the Sandinistas and ease the suffering of the Salvadoran people. Unfortunately, for President Reagan, the Democrats in Congress, still reeling from the political disaster he had inflicted on them, chose to play dirty politics with this national security issue.

Congressional Democrats, led by Speaker Tip O'Neill, knew the American people were literally gun-shy after the Vietnam tragedy. Polls indicated Americans were timid and undecided about using military force against Soviet-sponsored aggression in Central America. Therefore, O'Neill organized the House Democrats against Reagan's Central American foreign policy. O'Neill discarded patriotism in favor of "Blame America First" rhetorical blackmail tactics. The Speaker did not let politics end at the water's edge. He exploited the Central America crisis. It was the only stick he could use to beat the Reagan Administration with and keep it at bay. The Senate, with its Republican majority and patriotic southern Democrats, refused to play O'Neill's irresponsible and reckless obstruction game with Reagan's Central American policy. O'Neill ignored the Senate's responsible course. He directed his House subordinates to oppose all aid to the Contras and to harass the Reagan Administration's efforts to aid El Salvador.[126]

Gore, like other southern Congressmen with Presidential ambitions, found himself between a rock and a hard place regarding Central America. The rock was Ronald Reagan's overwhelming popularity with southern voters of both parties. The hard place was the continuing dominance of the Democratic Party's nominating machinery by hard left, anti-American fanatics from the Northeast and Pacific Rim regions. Like his father, Al Gore faced the dilemma of doing what his Tennessee constituents wanted or pleasing powerful Democratic leftists in Massachusetts, New York, and California. Instead of doing either Canon Martin's "hard right" or "easy wrong," Gore chose, like his father, to thread his way through the dilemma with a pleasant middle course.

The pleasant middle course involved voting against military aid to the Contras and supporting aid to El Salvador while keeping quiet during the 1979-1990 Central American crisis. Gore appeased the hard Left by voting against the Contras and appeased southern moderates by not denouncing the anti-Communist rebels publicly. When President Reagan asked both Houses of Congress for military aid to the Contras in 1983, 1984, and 1986, Gore voted no all three times. Despite the overwhelming evidence, the Soviets were using their Central American base in Nicaragua to de-stabilize El Salvador, Guatemala, and other neighboring countries, Gore voted against military aid.

Gore voted against helping the Contras even though his mentor Marty Peretz strenuously urged him to back the rebels. While *The New Republic* continued its mindless crusades for unrestricted gay liberation and abortion, it also exposed the murderous terror tactics used by both the Sandinistas and the FMLN. Peretz commissioned articles by Robert Leiken, Mark Falcoff, and Charles Lane. These three men, all leading scholars of Latin America, carefully and meticulously narrated and analyzed the evils done by Communists in Central America. The magazine documented the atrocities done by the Sandinistas and FMLN and the flow of Soviet heavy weapons and advisers to Nicaragua. Even hard-core right-wingers admitted *The New Republic* provided the most thorough and penetrating coverage of the Soviet effort to subvert Central America. The magazine played a crucial role in persuading some southern and Midwest House members to change their minds and back the Contras. The Reagan White House ordered the latest issue of the magazine hand-delivered to its officials to keep abreast of the fluid situation both on Capitol Hill and in Central America. Peretz even put down a revolt by some *New Republic* staff members who regarded him as too pro-Contra.[127]

But Gore still voted like his father, the friend of Armand Hammer and appeaser of the Soviet Union. Try as Marty Peretz might with his former student, Al Gore still chose to do what was expedient for his future Presidential run. Al Gore refused to choose the "hard right" if it meant alienating fellow traveling or pacifist Democratic interests who might prevent his nomination. Gore made a feeble effort to appease Peretz by voting for non-lethal aid to the contras. Non-lethal aid to the contras consisted of food, clothing, shelter, and medical supplies. But as Bob Zelnick, former *ABC News* Pentagon correspondent and Marine officer, wrote, "in terms of higher policy Gore's position was virtually irrelevant. After all, the war in Nicaragua was a battle of bullets, not a food fight."[128]

After news of the Iran-Contra scandal broke in November 1986, Al Gore may have congratulated himself on opposing contra aid. His cowardice and opportunism toward the Cold War in Central America seemed to be reaping rich political dividends. At long last, Ronald Reagan was backpedaling and on the defensive. The Democrats took back the Senate majority in the midterm elections. Revelations that Reagan approved trades of arms to Iran for hostages damaged the President's public opinion standing. Democratic Congressional leaders created a joint House-Senate Committee, modeled on the Senate Watergate Committee, to investigate the Iran-Contra scandal and thus attempted to cripple the Reagan Presidency. The outnumbered and outgunned Contras, fighting heavy Soviet armored helicopters and artillery with small arms, soon would be trampled if military aid ended.

But Oliver North humiliated the Democrats' Iran/Contra Congressional inquisition with a kinetic performance during the late June - early July televised hearings. Millions of Americans finally found out who the Contras were and what Communist enemies they were fighting. The Iran/Contra Committee trembled as thousands of letters and telegrams arrived accusing them of being pro-Communist sympathizers. Al Gore had prudently kept himself off the Iran Contra Committee, probably to please Marty Peretz, so he avoided the much-deserved abuse heaped on the Committee. Oliver North, the designated scapegoat of the Iran-Contra scandal, became revered while the Democratic Congress was reviled.

To his eternal credit, Marty Peretz rallied support for the Contras among Democratic intellectuals and policy wonks. In October 1987, he emceed a gathering of pro-Contra leftists and liberals in Washington, "The Second Thoughts Conference." Disillusioned former supporters of the Sandinistas testified about the abuses and atrocities of Nicaragua's Communists at the conference. Peretz personally lobbied swing Democratic Congressmen to support the Contras. Although Peretz failed to change enough votes for military aid, his heroic efforts shamed Al Gore and other cowardly "moderates" to at least keep the Contras alive with food and medical supplies.[129]

Peretz's close friend and literary editor, Leon Wieseltier, aided the contra cause as well. Wieseltier, a hedonistic egghead notorious for seducing *New Republic* interns and snorting cocaine in vast quantities,[130] bravely defended North's aide Fawn Hall in the press. Hall was the girlfriend of Wieseltier's friend, Contra leader Arturo Cruz Jr. Wieseltier pressed his friends Al and Tipper Gore to support the Contras. Big Bad Leon, as his male detractors nickname him, often took Tipper dancing at glamorous D.C. nightclubs when her husband got stuck in late night Senate sessions.[131]

But the arguments of Peretz and Wieseltier failed to overcome Al Gore's moral cowardice and political calculation. He continued to duck the Contra issue. It endangered him too much with the leftist special interests that decided the Democrats' future presidential nominee. However, two of Gore's friends, House Democrats Stephen Solarz and Les Aspin, did bravely act to help the Contras secure democracy for their country. Those two men pressured the Sandinistas to hold a free and fair election. The Nicaraguan people finally rejected the Sandinistas decisively in the February 1990 public election.

This tremendous victory over Communist tyranny occurred despite, not because of, the actions of Senator Al Gore. Like his father, he refused to wage war against the Soviet Union and its allies. He had voted against funding the anti-Soviet resistance in Angola in 1985. This vote passed with a margin of 29 votes in the Senate.[132] Gore also voted against 1989 Solarz's bill to fund the anti-Communist military resistance in Cambodia. But this bill passed easily in the Senate with a twenty-vote margin.[133]

Too Clever by Half Nuclear Strategist

Al Gore needed some heavyweight foreign policy accomplishments to be rated as a potential President. He had lost his nerve on Central American issues. There were too many dangers involved in that either/or controversy. He needed a life or death issue that was also abstract and difficult to understand, so, he searched for an important national security issue suited to his mastery of arcane policy detail. With adviser Leon Fuerth's help, Gore focused on reforming American nuclear strategy to make it "safer."

Gore grandly claimed he became interested in nuclear strategy while speaking in 1980 to a Girls' State convention in Murfreesboro, Tennessee. He rhetorically asked the young girls in the audience whether they expected to see nuclear war in their lifetimes. A large majority of the girls raised their hands. He then asked them: "How many believe we can change that if we really try?" Only a few hands went up. This epiphany led Al Gore to devote himself to preventing nuclear war.[134]

Regardless of how he got interested in nuclear strategy, once Gore involved himself in the subject he became a fanatic about mastering its details. Under Leon Fuerth's guidance, he studied nuclear warheads, rocket delivery systems, abstruse theoretical war game analyses, and the various arms control treaties America negotiated with the Soviets. After mastering the vocabulary of nuclear strategy, Gore characteristically acted as if he had invented the subject.

Nuclear strategy is based on a balance of terror. By assuming there are two primary nuclear powers, the U.S. and U.S.S.R., nuclear strategy aims to secure a stable balance where neither side thinks it can win an overwhelming superiority over the other. This stable balance is known as deterrence, since both sides seek to deter the other nuclear power from attacking.

President Kennedy and Johnson's Secretary of Defense, Robert McNamara, allowed the huge nuclear strategic superiority enjoyed by the U.S. during the Eisenhower Administration to lapse. McNamara, the leading architect of the Vietnam War disaster, disliked the idea of victory in war. It upset his liberal, logical view of rational humanity. Like his acquaintance, Senator Albert Gore, Sr. McNamara sought to appease the world's most powerful Communist dictatorship. Instead of U.S. nuclear superiority over the Soviet Union, McNamara wanted equality between the two superpowers. He called this equality, "Mutual Assured Destruction," or MAD. McNamara got his wish. The U.S. let its nuclear lead disappear between 1960-1980. As Harold Brown, Carter's Secretary of Defense, noted in the late 1970s about the Soviet nuclear missile program, "We build, they build. We stop building, they build." The disastrous McNamara strategic policy caused the Soviets to become the world's leading nuclear weapons power by 1980.[135]

During the 1980 Presidential election, Ronald Reagan promised to restore American nuclear superiority. Immediately after his inauguration, he did just that. Nuclear research and development was stepped up. Trident nuclear ballistic missile submarines were manufactured in quantity. The Pershing II intermediate missiles, renowned for their superb accuracy, were deployed in Western Europe to counter the intermediate Soviet missiles in Eastern Europe. Reagan also pressed Congress for funds to build and deploy the huge MX Peacekeeper missiles.

The MX, the largest and most powerful of American land-based missiles, wielded a ten-warhead MIRV. MIRV stands for Multiple Independent Re-Entry Vehicle and means the missile throws out ten independent nuclear warheads at once, thus counteracting an enemy missile defense system. Reagan did not just decide to build and deploy new nuclear weapons systems. In a bold policy move, he demanded the U.S. military jettison McNamara's no-win strategy and create an anti-missile, space based, Strategic Defense Initiative making all existing missile systems obsolete.[136]

Al Gore opposed all but one of the changes in nuclear policy instituted by Reagan. The one exception was the Pershing II deployment in Western Europe. Gore proposed his own abstract solution for preventing nuclear war. In a May 5, 1982 article in Marty Peretz's *The New Republic*, Gore explained how American nuclear strategy needed what he called "crisis stability." Crisis stability aimed to make nuclear war less likely by eliminating all MIRV nuclear missiles and replacing them with large, single warhead missiles. This single warhead missile would presumably contribute to stability by making it less desirable for either superpower to deliver a nuclear first strike. Gore's reasoning in *The New Republic* article was complex and confused. Its abstract assumptions resembled Robert McNamara's disastrous systems analysis approach to nuclear war. There were two glaring flaws to Gore's nuclear missile strategy: (1) he refused to acknowledge the existing Soviet overwhelming superiority of MIRVed heavy missiles and that it needed to be counteracted; and (2) he never discussed the technology then available for defense against ballistic missiles. Al Gore never asked how the single-shot Midgetman missile could neutralize Soviet MIRV superiority. He followed his father in foolishly eschewing the possibility of ballistic missile defense. There could be no "crisis stability" if Soviet MIRV superiority was not deterred and defended against.

But Gore's flawed Midgetman strategy won over Les Aspin. Aspin, the House Democrats' heavyweight on defense matters, was a Robert McNamara protégé, so he liked Gore's abstruse analysis. Reagan and his foreign policy advisers found themselves stymied by Congress' resistance to the MX deployment. Many Congressmen refused to deploy the MX in their own districts. In order to win them over, the Reagan team compromised by building Midgetman missiles for centrist Democrats like Gore and Aspin, if they voted for funding and deploying the MX. Gore agreed with one condition: the Reagan Administration must commit itself to a new arms control push. Tom Downey, a New York leftist and Gore's best friend in the House, sneered to Gore that Reagan's advisers "believe that real men don't control weapons, real men build them." Gore replied that any chance for an arms control agreement with the Soviet Union must be pursued. Like his appeasing father, Gore never thought of overthrowing the U.S.S.R., only of co-existing with it. In the spring of 1983, the trade-off votes were consummated. But the Soviets feared the MIRVed MX's much more than they feared the single warhead Midgetman. The latter weapon wasted time and money simply to make an intricate theoretical point. Reagan's SDI offered a much better chance to prevent nuclear war than the puny Midgetman missile. Unlike Gore, the raging moderate who feared bold approaches to the future, Reagan aimed to eventually eliminate nuclear weapons by making them infeasible. At the same time Gore lobbied for his Midgetman deal, Reagan unveiled SDI. Al Gore fiercely resisted SDI just as his father battled the Anti-Ballistic Missile system. He emulated Senator Edward Kennedy's habit of dismissing SDI as "Star Wars." Gore refused to take Reagan's thinking seriously and usually underestimated him. In early 1980, he said to other Democrats, "if only the Republicans would nominate Ronald Reagan (for President), then we'd be all right."[137] Despite the DLC call for fresh thinking, Gore followed stale liberal orthodoxy by opposing SDI as a dangerous, de-stabilizing policy.

He hewed to this de-stabilizing line consistently. In 1985, Gore, newly elected to the U.S. Senate, commented on U.S. nuclear negotiations involving SDI: "'If we embark upon a crash program to develop and deploy such a system, we would be making a mistake.' He added, however, if the Soviet Union is unwilling to negotiate on its heavy offensive missiles, 'The political pressure behind the Star Wars plan will make it difficult to stop.'"[138]

One and a half years later, Gore echoed this same party line on SDI, "There is a group of extremely hard-line conservatives, who see in SDI a means for de-stabilizing the arms race by deploying missile defenses to protect our missile silos. This could challenge the Soviet Union to an accelerated arms race, and, the conservatives hope, pressure the Soviets economically to induce a radical change in their system. But their strategy is not viable. The Soviets have always found the rubles to match our military escalation. We're the ones with Gramm-Rudman (spending limits). To assume they're the ones who would buckle is madness."[139]

Gore's 1987 diagnosis of SDI's effect on the Soviet Union was proved completely wrong in two years. Reagan's SDI strategy was not madness, and was quite viable, as Soviet chief Mikhail Gorbachev ruefully admitted. The Strategic Defense Initiative did accelerate the U.S.--U.S.S.R. arms race and did induce a radical change in the Soviet system. The Soviets could not find the rubles or the technological expertise to match the American military escalation. Those "extremely hard-line conservatives" turned out to be right while the St. Albans-Harvard elitist turned out to be wrong. The USSR ceased to exist. It broke up into several different nations. Reagan's strategy of rendering nuclear weapons obsolete triumphed.

Yet, Senator Gore rigidly refused to abandon the wrongheaded liberal dogmas of nuclear strategy. Leon Fourth, his foreign policy aide, loathed the Reagan approach to nuclear warfare; so, Gore continued to vote to cut funding for SDI. Even after the Soviet rulers testified SDI was the "viable strategy" most responsible for undermining the evil empire, Al Gore supported cuts in SDI research and development. This opposition to missile defense mirrored his father's opposition to the ABM, or Anti-Ballistic Missile Defense of the 1960s and 1970s.

In 1985, his first year in the Senate, Gore offered two different amendments trying to slash the FY 1986 funds budgeted for SDI by Reagan. The two amendments aimed to cut SDI respectively by 36% and 16%. Both amendments failed miserably. But Gore obstinately joined Teddy Kennedy to support another failed amendment trimming the SDI request by a measly 5%. This "symbolic" amendment failed by the same margin as the previous two. All three votes reveal Gore as a partisan liberal Democrat. Like his liberal peers, Gore was eager to barter away the security of his fellow citizens to please the "Blame America First" crowd. Republican Presidents and Senators, not Soviet missiles, were what Al Gore feared.[140]

Despite Gore's posturing as a DLC Democrat, he kept adhering to the liberal anti-SDI position. In 1986, he voted to cut President Reagan's SDI research by 39%. The motion failed by one vote. He then joined Senate Democrats in trying to cut SDI by 33%. Again, this attempt failed by one vote. The Senate Democrats tried to cut SDI because they feared it might work, and thus redound to the Republicans' credit. They ignored the fact that it frightened the Soviet leadership and would protect *all* Americans, Democrats and Republicans.

Unfortunately, for SDI, the voters put the Democrats in charge of the Senate again in November 1986. Gore's hostile attitude to Strategic Defense now had more supporters. In 1988, he voted against an appropriation to set up an accidental launch protection system for SDI. He also voted against an amendment increasing SDI funding by $500 million dollars. Gore voted with the winning side both times.[141]

After Republican George Bush's election as Reagan's successor in 1988, Gore kept trying to slash SDI funds. In 1989, he opposed an amendment increasing SDI funding by $298 million. Luckily, the amendment passed overwhelmingly. Two months later, the Soviets freed Eastern Europe. The Berlin Wall came down. The Cold War ended without a shot being fired. Despite this vindication of the "extremely hard-line conservatives," Gore persisted in his efforts to cut the SDI budget. Gore cast his final vote as a U.S. Senator in 1992 to cut $200 million from the SDI budget. He skipped four crucial votes on SDI campaigning for his DLC running mate, Bill Clinton. Given his past record, he most likely would have voted to cut SDI funding on those four missed votes. Gore voted against missile defense improvements 71% of the time in the 34 crucial SDI Senate votes from 1985-1992. Al Gore, ranked only second to Sam Nunn, his fellow DLC crony, in defense expertise among Senate Democrats. Yet, he decided wrongly on the most vital defense issue of his time.

We documented above how timidly he acted toward Central America, the second most vital national security issue of his Congressional tenure. Thanks to his pride, Presidential ambition, and partisanship, Gore pursued a missile strategy hostile to the very lives of his fellow Americans. He loyally supports Bill Clinton's efforts to retard ballistic missile defense. Rogue nations such as Iraq and North Korea are developing the ability to deploy long-range land-based ballistic missiles armed with nuclear and poison gas warheads. Red China is upgrading its missile systems based on both land and submarines. Thanks to Clinton and Gore's lax attitude toward nuclear espionage and the transfer of militarily useful technology, the Red Chinese Army and Navy now possess all of our nuclear weapons secrets. With just a few more years testing, China's nuclear weapons will reach parity with ours.

NINE

The First Run for the White House: 1988

Is he old and rich enough to run?

Despite thinking and voting wrongly about both Central America and nuclear war weapons, Al Gore gained a reputation as a Democrat wise man on foreign policy. This undeserved reputation, coupled with his "southern moderate" stance on domestic policy, combined to make him a Presidential contender. Gore seemed to typify the "Great White Male Southerner Hope" needed to put liberalism back in the Oval Office. Establishment political and media elites decided his policies and character were "good for the country." These liberal elites decried his pro-life votes on abortion. They forgave his pro-tobacco votes because Tennessee raised so much of the crop. Otherwise, Gore appeared to be an unthreatening, tax and spend stealth liberal who could win back some big southern states in a Presidential election.

But Gore's youth made him a question mark. In the spring of 1987, when the prospective Democratic Presidential candidates had to decide whether to run, Gore was turning 39 years old. On Inauguration Day, 1989, he would be 40 years old. Both of the youngest presidents ever, Theodore Roosevelt, age 42 and John Fitzgerald Kennedy, age 43, were also decorated war heroes, glamorous, charming, and witty characters. Who ever accused the St. Albans Ozymandias of being any of these? The Establishment pundits agreed Gore should wait and pay his dues before running for the Presidency.[142]

Gore's lust for power prevented him from waiting. His arrogant personality also looked at the other contenders and found them wanting in political ability. After his DLC allies Sam Nunn and Bill Clinton took themselves out of contention, Gore saw no one in the pack who could win white southerners' votes. Massachusetts Governor Michael Dukakis was a northeast establishment liberal who had vetoed a mandatory "Pledge of Allegiance" bill. Former Colorado Senator Gary Hart, who later had to withdraw because of a sex scandal, Jesse Jackson enraged white southerners with his racial tirades and friendships with foreign leftist dictators. Congressman Richard Gephardt was enslaved to labor unions and old-fashioned protectionism. These four men constituted the first tier of Democratic Presidential candidates.

Below this first group was a second tier of truly inept contenders. Senator Paul Simon of Illinois was a homely prairie leftist who loathed Ronald Reagan. Senator Joseph Biden of Delaware appeared handsome and charming but gave empty, endless speeches. He withdrew in the fall of 1987 when his plagiarism of English Labor Party leader's Neil Kinnock's speeches was uncovered. Governor Bruce Babbitt was a bumbling candidate who worried about the environment.

After looking over these lightweight opponents, Gore decided to run for the Presidency. But one important problem dogged his prospective campaign: money. He needed around 20 million dollars to make a serious run. A young, junior U.S. Senator, even with Armand Hammer's substantial help, could not raise that kind of money. Thanks to a network of rich Greek-American supporters, Mike Dukakis easily accumulated that sum of money and more. Dick Gephardt could draw on the help of his labor union buddies at the AFL-CIO. Jesse Jackson did not need much money since he was running to blackmail the white Democrat power structure, not win the White House. Al Gore needed a financial angel to get him some seed money fast. He was unable to find one, so he tentatively announced against running in mid-March 1987.

Enter Nathan Landow, Dark Angel

Gore found his campaign angel in Nathan Landow. Landow was a Maryland millionaire real estate developer. During the 1984 campaign, Landow had been Walter Mondale's top fundraiser. His fund raising prowess dated back to 1976, when he played an important role bankrolling Jimmy Carter's 1976 run for the White House. After winning the Presidency, Carter wanted to reward Landow's fundraising efforts with an ambassadorship. He nominated him as Ambassador to the Netherlands. Carter then hastily withdrew the nomination when the liberal *Washington Post* published a carefully detailed expose' on Landow's close friend and business associate, Joe Nesline. Nesline was the gangster "godfather" of bookmaking and other gambling operations in D.C. and its suburbs. Nathan Landow, the angel of Democratic Presidential candidates, associated with mobsters.[143]

The *Washington Post* story revealed the many business partnerships engaged in by Landow and Joe Nesline. It also detailed Nesline's background in organized crime: "Nesline, who lives in the luxurious Promenade high-rise apartment building owned by Landow at 5225 Pooks Hill Road in Bethesda [MD, an affluent D.C. suburb], has been an internationally known gambling figure for forty years. He had long been identified in local police files as the suspected 'godfather' of bookmaking and other gaming action in and around Washington. With an arrest record spanning four decades, Nesline has been charged with bribery and bootlegging as well as gambling. He was convicted of carrying a deadly weapon in the fatal shooting of a man at point-blank range in an after-hours D.C. club in 1951."[144]

But Landow's friend Joe Nesline rose above his small-time hood beginnings to become a big-time gangster. He used Nathan Landow's financial skills to enrich them both. The *Washington Post* story explored the Nesline-Landow partnership's attempts to create casinos: "The proposed Atlantic City hotel-casino project, which never reached fruition because of financial problems, was not the only gambling venture in which Nesline had been involved with Landow. Also found in the raid on Nesline's apartment was a large color photograph of an architectural rendering for another proposed hotel-casino deal on the Caribbean island of St. Maarten's in which Nesline was acting as a middleman..Involved in the St. Maarten's venture were Landow and Edward Cellini, a brother of Dino Cellini, a former associate of organized crime dealer Meyer Lansky. Edward Cellini formerly ran the Paradise Island casino operation in Nassau, the Bahamas for Resorts International, but he was let go."[145]

Landow involved himself with organized crime figures more notorious than Joe Nesline and Edward Cellini. The *Washington Post* story further discusses his business deals with the Gambino Mafia family associate Anthony Plate: "They [officers of the Montgomery County, MD organized crime section] learned from Florida police that Landow had a financial interest in a now defunct operation whose concealed owners allegedly included an identified member of the Carlo Gambino Mafia 'family.'..The business involvement of Landow's that originally attracted the attention of Montgomery County's organized crime unit was an investment of Quaker Masonry Inc., a firm that had offices in

Silver Spring [MD] and in Hollywood, Florida...According to corporate records in Tallahassee, Landow was listed in 1972 as a vice president and director of Quaker masonry...Florida law enforcement authorities reported to other police agencies in October 1973 that Anthony Plate known to them to be an associate of the Gambinos was believed to have a 25% interest in Quaker."[146]

Hanging out with cronies of Meyer Lansky and Carlo Gambino conflicted with Jimmy Carter's 1976 promises to the American people. Carter constantly repeated to Americans he would never lie to them and emphasized his administration would be ethical and upright. Carter's promises resembled Bill Clinton's 1993 claim that his would be the most ethical administration in history. Unlike Clinton, Carter kept a few of his promises about integrity. Carter shelved Landow's nomination to be Ambassador to the Netherlands. However, he did allow D.C. Mayor Marion Barry to reward Landow with some lucrative million-dollar real estate deals in the late 1970s and early 1980s.[147] Carter also permitted Landow to keep helping Democrats raise money for their campaigns.

Soon after Reagan crushed Jimmy Carter in November 1980, Landow visited the latter's Vice President, Walter Mondale. According to Marty Peretz's *New Republic*: "A few days after Jimmy Carter's 1980 defeat, Landow paid a call on Walter Mondale, uninvited, to offer him his full support for 1984. Landow placed his private jet at Mondale's disposal and he personally raised over two million dollars."[148] Landow ranked first among Mondale's fundraisers. But his efforts were unavailing since Mondale lost 49 of the 50 states to Ronald Reagan in November 1984.

After Mondale's fiasco, Landow desperately needed a winner. Raising money for Democratic Presidential candidates was a means to gain power and influence, not an end in itself. When asked by the *Los Angeles Times* in 1987 why he raised so much money for Democratic candidates, Landow replied: "It certainly could relate to policy."[149] This shady real estate developer needed a centrist Democrat candidate capable of winning white southerners' votes to get elected. When Al Gore talked on the phone with Landow in late March 1987, Landow decided this was the "White Male Southern Hope" for Democrats. Landow later declared about Gore, "He has been groomed from childhood to be President."[150] The Maryland real estate fixer made Gore an offer of money he couldn't refuse. Gore decided to think about a run for the White House.

On March 27, 1987, Landow brought Gore together with 17 other members of IMPAC 88. IMPAC 88 was a political action committee created and led by Landow. The PAC's members all had raised money for Mondale in 1984. They were also determined to avoid another disaster. Like their leader and friend Landow, they believed a centrist DLC southern candidate was the way to win in 1988. Landow and his fellow IMPAC 88 cronies pledged $4 million up front to Gore at this meeting; so, Prince Albert decided to run for President. *The Baltimore Sun*, a liberal Democratic newspaper, reported two weeks after Gore's announcement of his candidacy on April 12, 1987, "Mr. Gore said that a group of major Democratic fund raisers led by Maryland developer Nathan Landow 'had played a significant role in getting me to change my mind' about running. At a private March 27th meeting, 17 members of the group pledged to raise $4 million for a Gore campaign and the Senator agreed to reconsider his plans." [151]

Al Gore had come a long way from Canon Charles Martin's "hard right." He was running for President with the financial help of a very shady character. We write about Landow in great detail here because he was later to play large roles in the 1990's scandals of the Clinton-Gore Administration. Landow later worked closely with Peter Knight, the Gore aide who ran the 1996 Clinton-Gore re-election campaign. Knight and Landow engaged in many of the fundraising scandals of 1996. They also worked together in the Indian reservation casino scams covered up by Clinton Interior Secretary Bruce Babbitt.

Landow's ugliest moment occurred in 1998 when he used gangster-style methods to intimidate and spy on Kathleen Willey. Willey was the White House aide who testified about Bill Clinton's attempt to sexually assault her in the Oval Office. Al Gore, the square and family man, allied himself with two shady millionaires, Landow and Armand Hammer, in order to become President and rule over his fellow Americans. [152]

Gore's Southern Strategy: Paving the Way for Clinton's 1992 Run

While Nathan Landow's fundraising made Gore a contender, he still lacked the money to contest every primary and caucus as Dukakis and Gephardt did. So, Gore chose to ignore Iowa and New Hampshire and gambled on sweeping the southern state primaries. Gore planned to emphasize his relatively pro-defense foreign policy views, mastery of technical issues such as high technology and the environment, and youthful vitality. He also intended to attack his rivals' views on crime and trade. If he swept the South as its favorite son, and split the East, Midwest, and West, he thought he could win the nomination. Gore emphasized he was not in the race to settle for the Vice Presidency. In the light of his decision to serve as Bill Clinton's Vice President in 1992, his scornful comments about the Vice Presidency invite derision: "I have no interest in it. I might well turn it down. I probably would. I have no interest in it. Vice President Bush will demonstrate again this year it is a political dead end."[153]

Gore's prediction that Bush would not be elected President in 1988 proved wrong. But the prediction was no more inaccurate than most of Gore's 1988 campaign decisions. Prince Albert's first Presidential campaign demonstrated how disorganized this man was. By waiting too long to announce for President, he found few first-rate campaign managers or organizers available. He ended up hiring campaign aides and speechwriters from the second rank. Gore's kickoff speech, delivered from the Smith County Courthouse in Carthage, bombed. It promised to address everything: political corruption; AIDS; arms control; and Gore's hobbyhorse, the ozone layer. Gore made one promise that looks ridiculous in hindsight after the many scandals of the Clinton-Gore Administration: "Any government official who steals from the American people or who lies to the United States Congress will be fired immediately." [154]

Two keen observers acidly commented on Gore's diffuse announcement speech. Michael Kinsley, one of Marty Peretz's neoliberal protégés, zinged it eloquently: "Gore's style of moderation is to go instead for issues that are 'difficult' in the sense of being obscure or complicated but not contentious. Even Gore's greatest genuine political contribution--his promotion of the 'Midgetman' mobile single-warhead missile--has the flavor of high-minded non-ideological cogitation." Tennessee Governor Ned Ray McWherter, an ally of Gore's who resembles Boss Hogg of *The Dukes of Hazard* television series, looked on the bright side: "You know the guy eating bean sprouts in California probably shook his head in agreement about ozone."[155]

Kinsley's and McWherter's comments were especially damning since they were both well disposed to Prince Albert.

The mistakes made by the campaign were all Gore's, since he micromanaged every decision. Fred Martin, a Mondale organizer in 1984, served as the campaign manager. Martin spoke candidly about his former boss' deficiencies. Gore phoned him 6-8 times each day about everything: "a control freak...He was into every large issue, and every petty detail from Tipper's schedule, to car pools, scheduling, hiring, and thank you notes. He spent an enormous amount of time handling crap."

Gore, Martin testified, is "a control freak...He is totally without discipline. He will put off the task of writing a speech and then pull an all-nighter like a college kid."[156] Martin's picture of Gore as a disorganized control-obsessed person contrasts with the image he presents as a cool, disciplined, decision maker keeping his priorities in order.

Gore was warned in memos by his own staffers to stop stretching the truth. In September 1987, Mike Kopp, the campaign's deputy press secretary, wrote to Prince Albert: "In the past few reporters cared if you stretched the truth...But gone are those days...we are becoming increasingly scrutinized, particularly by the national press."[157]

Kopp's superior, campaign press secretary Arlie Schardt, seconded Kopp's cautionary memo in February 1988. Schardt wrote: "your main pitfall is exaggeration...The main point is to be careful not [to] overstate your role."[158]

Kopp and Schardt warned Gore to discipline himself from exaggerating his accomplishments or claiming too much credit. Gore even lied about the gender of his staffers. In August 1987 he claimed "half of his staff was female and that one of the reasons for 'the mess we are in' on arms control is that women have not been allowed to participate fully in that issue."[159] This claim was quite false.[160] Over a decade before Gore made his false claims about Love Story or the Internet, his staffers were begging him to practice truth and humility. Gore's aides knew the news media would have a field day with Gore's lies and grandiose assertions.

Most of the die-hard liberal press greeted Gore's crusade with little enthusiasm. The same reporters who cheered Clinton four years later found little to admire in Gore. He appeared to be "the school prefect, a self-important goody-goody, who looked as if he'd been born in coat and tie." Bob Zelnick repeats the crack about Gore going among reporters: "How can you tell Al Gore from the Secret Service agents guarding him? He's the stiff one."[161]

The only media celebrity cheering Gore's candidacy in 1988 was Marty Peretz. *The New Republic* ran his editorial gushing for Gore as a man able to set the country on course after Reagan's right-wing follies. America, Peretz proclaimed, "was burdened by debt and driven according to a carefully calibrated calculus of regional conflict, class antagonism, and enmity." Only Al Gore could heal these ills. Gephardt conveyed only "crude populism and unwarranted grievance." Peretz condemned Dukakis for his "rigidity" deriving "from no great passion for ideas, no deep convictions about issues." Dukakis possessed only "an overweening estimate of himself." Dukakis also had not studied with Marty Peretz at Harvard. Peretz's friend Leon Wieseltier echoed this sycophantic worship of Prince Albert: "He [Gore] really does believe that he was born to lead…He believes he is a historical figure."[162]

The historical figure moved left in the fall of 1987 to appeal to hard-core Democratic Presidential primary voters. Gore joined other liberal Senators in the campaign to smear Judge Robert Bork, Ronald Reagan's nominee to the Supreme Court. The pro-abortion feminists, race baiters, criminal rights advocates, and liberal law professors demanded Bork's defeat. Left-wing lobbies in Massachusetts, New York, and D.C. compelled the southern Senate Democrats into doing their bidding. The southern Senators all bowed before Teddy Kennedy as he directed the strategy of the anti-Bork forces. Al Gore acted as a puppet for Senator Kennedy. He pompously and piously condemned Judge Bork for opposing the 1964 Civil Rights Act in a 1964 *New Republic* article. Gore neglected to mention his father had voted against the bill. The press also ignored the fact that Democratic Senate Majority Leader Robert Byrd, a former Grand Wizard of the West Virginia Ku Klux Klan, also voted against the Civil Rights Act of 1964. Bill Clinton, the Boy Governor of Arkansas, and a protégé of segregationist former Senator J. William Fulbright, visited Washington to help vilify Judge Bork. After

Bork's nomination was defeated, all the "moderate," "centrist," southern Democrats who crucified him returned to blaming their party's problems on northeast corridor liberals. It never occurred to the DLC leadership that Democrats lost national elections precisely because they kowtowed to the leftist fanatics who loathed Bork.

After helping to torpedo Bork, Gore returned to the Presidential campaign trail where he often made a fool out of himself during the 1988 Democratic primaries and caucuses. While on the stump, Gore pompously reminded audiences that the Democratic Party could only win the Presidency with the help of southern votes. He modestly claimed he alone of the candidates could gain the "Bubba" vote. Garry Trudeau, the liberal preppie New Englander cartoonist, mocked Gore's explicit southern appeal in *Doonesbury* by portraying "Prince Albert" in a Jack Daniels cap yowling: "Y'all wanna hear my coon dog call?" On another occasion at a southern primary debate Gore strenuously lectured on ozone depletion: "This problem of the greenhouse effect is going to be one of the most severe environmental challenges we have ever faced in the entire history of humankind." Jesse Jackson retorted scornfully: "Senator Gore has just showed you why he should be our national chemist."[163] Jackson's reply hit home. Audiences were quite bored with Gore's sermon on environmentalism so he was forced to drop it as a major issue in the campaign.

Gore's stuffy preaching contrasted greatly with Reverend Jackson's fiery sermons to the same southern audiences

Gore was just too much of a dull D.C. policy wonk to excite his southern base. Southerners seek humor and charm in their politicians. Gore possessed little of those two attributes. He doggedly went out and pandered to southern interest groups. Gore bragged to southern tobacco farmers about how much he understood their crop: "Throughout most of my life, I raised tobacco. I want you to know that with my own hands, all of my life, I put in the plant beds and transferred it. I've hoed it, I've dug in it, I've sprayed it, I've chopped it, I've shredded it, spiked it, put it in the barn, and stripped it and sold it." [164]

Gore shouted repeatedly he supported tobacco subsidies during the short-lived 1988 Presidential campaign. He never mentioned then how his only sister died of lung cancer from smoking tobacco. He happily accepted $16,440 from tobacco political action committees from 1979 until the end of 1990.[165]

Gore did not declare war on tobacco until the Clinton Administration did in the mid-1990s. Only then did he tearfully recount Nancy's painful death from tobacco at the 1996 Democratic convention.[166] But Gore's speeches about tobacco and arcane subjects like high technology and arms control failed to win him many black southern votes. Jackson corralled most of those ballots.

Gore's inability to compete with Jackson explains why Gore did not come close to sweeping the South on Super Tuesday, 1988. Jesse Jackson did better than Gore in both Iowa and New Hampshire. He tied him on Super Tuesday. The southern delegates, who represented a third of all delegates, split their preferences among Gore, Jackson, and Dukakis. Gore won Tennessee, North Carolina, Kentucky, Arkansas, and Oklahoma. Outside the South, he won Nevada. But Jackson won Virginia, South Carolina, Georgia, and Mississippi. Gore finished second in those four states. Dukakis upset predictions by winning the South's biggest prizes, Texas and Florida. Gore finished second in those two states as well. Gore, the wooden campaigner, failed to make much headway among black and Hispanic voters, who gave their ballots to Jackson and the Spanish-speaking Dukakis.[167] Gore disappointed both his own and his supporters' expectations on Super Tuesday. He won only the third largest total of delegates on Super Tuesday. His big southern gamble failed. Both Michael Dukakis and Jesse Jackson had beaten him handily. Gore needed big upsets in Illinois or New York to stay in contention.

Who First Made Willie Horton Famous?

Prince Albert overruled his campaign advisers in favor of his father's desire. He competed in Illinois despite its high media costs and unfavorable demographics. Campaign manager Fred Martin fervently disagreed with the decision of the two Albert Gores. He thought to himself, "The Obedient Son...It was the worst big decision we made during the campaign."[168] The campaign was forced to make loans to compete in Illinois and Michigan simultaneously. The result was disaster. Senator Paul Simon, Illinois' favorite son, edged out Jesse Jackson for victory in the Land of Lincoln. Jackson won a smashing victory in Michigan. Gore, the great centrist hope, barely registered in either contest.

Adding to Gore's humiliation was Armand Hammer's clumsy bullying of Paul Simon. Hammer and his relatives and executives already had poured money into the Gore campaign's coffers. Now the 87-year old tycoon emulated his Soviet secret police friends. He tried to bribe Simon to withdraw from the Illinois primary in favor of Gore. Simon indignantly refused and campaigned that much harder to win the contest. Gore's relationships with both his father and Hammer were costing him.[169]

He journeyed up to Marty Peretz's home state of New York to make a last stand. New York was Dukakis country. Its political culture much resembled Dukakis' home state of Massachusetts. Gore looked around for powerful political allies to help him against both Dukakis and Jackson in New York. The state's governor, Mario Cuomo, refused to back him. But New York City's mayor, abrasive neoliberal Ed Koch, despised both Dukakis and Jackson as leftists. Koch eagerly endorsed the "Great White Southern Moderate Hope."

The endorsement backfired because of both Koch and his friend, David Garth. Koch used his endorsement of Gore to flay Jesse Jackson for his politics of racial grievance and anti-Semitism. Koch killed Gore's black vote by yelling Jews would be "crazy" to vote for Jackson. Garth, Gore's New York media adviser, insisted the candidate oppose Israeli occupied territory negotiations sponsored by President Reagan and Secretary of State Shultz. Prince Albert bowed to Garth's wishes. Gore unwisely injected himself into two avoidable internecine quarrels. He thus cost himself many votes to both Dukakis and Jackson. His noble anti-abortion position elicited bitter opposition from many New York feminists. They openly hissed at his opposition to federal subsidies for abortion. Gore never forgot the bitterness his pro-life stance provoked from the feminists. He probably decided then to completely abandon his anti-abortion position. His New York campaign never recovered from these errors.[170]

Gore was desperate to find an issue enabling him to bounce back in the New York primary. Michael Dukakis, Marathon Man and hard-core liberal, handed him one. Gore's research staff discovered Massachusetts's prisons under Dukakis allowed convicted murderers to take weekend passes, or furloughs, from prison to wander freely. Gore's deputy campaign manager Thurgood Marshall Jr., son of the Supreme Court Justice, received newspaper and magazine stories about the Massachusetts furlough program from opponents of Dukakis in the Bay State.

The *Lawrence Eagle Tribune* newspaper had won a Pulitzer Prize for exposing how two convicted Massachusetts murderers committed additional murderers and rapes while on furlough. *Newsweek* and *Business Week* did pieces on the prison furlough program after the newspaper broke the story. Jack Quinn, the Gore aide in charge of the campaign's debate strategy, was briefed by Thurgood Marshall Jr. about the prison furlough scandal. Quinn then briefed Gore about the prison furloughs so the candidate could use them as ammunition against Dukakis. Gore brought up these prison furlough bombshells during the last New York Democratic primary debate. Gore mentioned the Willie Horton incident without actually naming the convicted murderer who committed a rape-robbery in Maryland while on furlough. Gore then asked Governor Dukakis: "If you were elected President, would you allow a similar program for federal penitentiaries?"[171]

Dukakis replied with a dogmatic arrogance making Gore seem humble, "Al, the difference between you and me is that I have to run a criminal justice system. You never have." Gore insisted Dukakis stop ducking the issue and answer. Dukakis changed the subject and the debate turned to other topics. This exchange would become much debated as Republicans, including we, took note of it.

The *Lawrence Eagle Tribune* and *Reader's Digest* had already unearthed the facts about the Willie Horton case and other abuses of the Massachusetts prison furlough system. Co-Author Floyd Brown, then serving as political director of Americans for Bush, researched these facts about Willie Horton and prison furloughs. We produced a television ad about Willie Horton, based on the published stories regarding the case. On one such furlough, Horton savagely robbed and beat a Maryland married couple. He raped the wife while her husband was tied up.

George Bush's campaign team, led by Lee Atwater, ran their own ads publicizing Dukakis' insane approach to criminal justice.[172] Dukakis' prison furlough policy did more than anything else to win the 1988 election for George Bush. And Al Gore, Democrat darling, handed the issue to Republicans.

Even with the prison furlough issue, Gore flopped in the New York primary. The final score was Dukakis 51%, Jackson 37%, and Prince Albert 10%. Gore recognized reality and "suspended" his campaign. Suspension allowed his delegates to attend the 1988 convention. Publicly Gore disdained the Vice

Presidency. But when Dukakis put him on his short list, Gore indicated eager interest. But Dukakis turned him down for Lloyd Bentsen, a much more experienced Senator who could help him win Texas. Gore watched as the Willie Horton issue he created torpedoed Dukakis in November.

Gore was disappointed in his failure. But the young Senator's showing pleased angel Nate Landow and his IMPAC 88 allies. They promised him support in a future Presidential run. As Landow put it: "We felt good about what we did...We all developed a personal feeling for the quality of the man and his intelligence. He impressed us with his ability, his strength, and his presence. We lost. But nobody was unhappy or disillusioned about their support of him once he got in the race."[173]

When a shady character and his cronies are pleased to do such favors for a man, it indicates they perceive he will do whatever it takes to win the White House. Landow and his friends knew Gore would someday enter the White House and reward them for their support.

Landow was not the only Gore fundraiser who kept faith in the candidate. Maria Hsia decided Gore was going places despite his disappointing 1988 campaign. Hsia was a Taiwanese national who immigrated to California in 1973 as a student. After graduating, she created a business assisting Chinese immigrants to obtain citizenship. Her business thrived; she became rich. Hsia began donating to Democratic candidates in 1982. She met Gore early in 1988 at a California fundraiser for his campaign.

Hsia was so impressed by Gore she invited him and several other U.S. Senators to make a "cultural and educational trip to China" in January 1989. The purpose of the trip seemed murky. In her letters of invitation to Gore and the other Senators, Hsia promised them her friends would help them financially in the future. Hsia's letter to Gore specifically stated: "If you decide to join this trip, I will persuade all of my colleagues in the future to play a leader role in your Presidential race."

Leon Fuerth and Peter Knight foolishly urged Gore to make the trip. Fuerth figured Gore could make some useful political contacts in Red China. Knight, about to become a lobbyist, wanted his boss to obtain lucrative business contacts for his future undertaking. So, Gore traveled with Hsia to meet her clients. Hsia's clients turned out to be front men for the Red Chinese People's Liberation Army. Al Gore and his father both ran errands for Armand Hammer, a top agent for the Soviet

Politburo. Gore now surpassed his father's achievements in serving totalitarian tyranny. Prince Albert now served agents of both the world's biggest Communist dictatorships, the Soviet Union *and* The People's Republic of China.[174]

TEN

Big Changes:
Flip-Flopping on Abortion; the Gulf War Vote

The Fragility of Life: Albert III's Brush with Death

On Opening Day of the baseball season, April 3, 1989, Al Gore took his wife and son to see the Red Sox play the Orioles at Baltimore's Memorial Stadium. Both Al and Tipper became Red Sox fans during their time in Boston. Rooting for the Red Sox was customary among the Harvard-MIT and Boston University college crowd. But it was not customary for native southerners like Al and Tipper Gore. Most native Washingtonians pulled for the Orioles after the Washington Senators moved to Texas in 1972. Unlike most D.C. sports fans, however, Al and Tipper wanted to be part of the New England liberal elite.

The Red Sox/Orioles opener provided an exciting contest that went into extra innings. Alas, for Al and Tipper, their beloved Sox lost. While walking back to their car in the parking lot, young Albert III broke out of his father's grasp. He ran quickly away into the path of a speeding car. The car hit Albert and tossed him into the air thirty feet. The boy rolled another twenty feet along the parking lot until coming to a stop.

Gore ran up to find his son barely alive. He prayed with him and administered CPR with the help of two off-duty Johns Hopkins Hospital nurses. Albert III was then taken by ambulance to nearby Johns Hopkins Hospital. Doctors there diagnosed his condition: an internal concussion; ruptured spleen; crushed ribs; a broken collarbone; second degree burns on his arms and legs; and a bruised lung and kidney. Thanks to the early interventions of the nurses, the renowned Johns Hopkins surgical staff succeeded in stabilizing Albert III's condition. His condition worsened four days later because his spleen began bleeding again. The boy underwent additional surgery on his spleen, which worked to improve his condition. Little Albert began his long recovery from the traumatic ordeal.

Both Al and Tipper took turns sitting by Albert's bedside during his three week hospitalization from April 3-April 23.

Albert's painful ordeal shook his father. Gore experienced such little tragedy and emotional ordeal in his charmed life that he used both these personal experiences in his Vice Presidential nominating speeches in 1992 and 1996. But critics rightly attacked Gore for exploiting the personal ordeals of Albert III and Nancy for political purposes in his nominating speeches.

During Albert's hospitalization, Al Gore decided to dine out with a close friend in Baltimore. He needed a friend to whom he could pour out the secrets of his soul. Gore did not choose to dine out with his Baptist pastor, or Marty Peretz, or a friend from St. Albans days. Instead, Gore chose to do his soul searching with the likes of Nathan Landow. Yes, Landow was a shady front man who hung out with unsavory associates of Meyer Lansky and Carlo Gambino. But Landow proved he cared about Al Gore more than anyone else did outside of his family. Landow had raised the funds necessary for Gore's pursuit of the Presidency. Nathan Landow, not a Baptist minister, knows the secrets of Al Gore's soul.

At Sabatino's, a fine Italian restaurant in Baltimore's Little Italy neighborhood, Gore and Landow met twice to talk during little Albert's hospitalization. As Landow later told an interviewer, Gore discussed the surgical procedures performed on his son with great precision. Gore also told Landow Albert's ordeal convinced him he should spend more time with his family.[175] So, Gore made a strategic decision beneficial to his DLC friend Bill Clinton. Gore would not run for the Presidency in 1992. He would wait until 1996 or 2000 to resume his relentless run for the Oval Office. Until then, the Tennessee Senator would concentrate on being a family man.

The Fragility of Life: Flip-Flopping on Abortion

The family man reminded everyone he had only suspended his Presidential ambition, not abandoned it. Al Gore deliberately set out to get right with the Democratic Party's pro-abortion feminists. Despite encountering the fragility and preciousness of life during Albert III's ordeal in April 1989, Gore cold-bloodedly abandoned his pro-life position. This about-face was made easier by the fact that most of Al and Tipper's friends were pro-abortion liberals.

Al and Tipper Gore socialized mostly with people who supported the right to abortion. Gore's mentor Marty Peretz, for instance, eternally preached the gospel of sexual liberation. Peretz opposed almost all the restraints imposed by civilized Western man on sexuality, including the ancient Hebrew tenets condemning adultery, homosexuality, and abortion. Peretz offered zealous support for Israel as a substitute for traditional Jewish observance of the Torah. Peretz's sidekick, Leon Wieseltier, the product of a strictly Orthodox Jewish family and a talented scholar of Judaism, encouraged Marty in his quest.[176] Wieseltier violated Jewish law by indulging extensively in womanizing and narcotics. Peretz's *The New Republic* campaigned ruthlessly against "repressive" laws restricting homosexuality, abortion, adultery, and pedophilia. Peretz and Wieseltier both regarded the Roman Catholic Church as a repressive opponent of their liberated sexual vision. So, they both recruited Andrew Sullivan, a homosexual English Roman Catholic, to join *The New Republic*. Sullivan became a senior editor of the magazine and the first "respectable" advocate of same sex marriage. All during the 1990s, he pushed same-sex marriage in the pages of *The New Republic*. Sullivan jeered at his own repressive Catholic Church for resisting gay liberation. Sullivan also decried the U.S. military's ban on homosexuals in *The New Republic*.[177] When Bill Clinton undertook to lift the ban on homosexuals in the U.S. military in early 1993, Vice President Gore emerged as the strongest advocate in the Clinton Administration for this unpopular and unprecedented action. *The New Republic*'s Editor-in-Chief and staff, not the voters of Tennessee, persuaded him to take this stance.

Marty Peretz and his cronies wielded great influence with Gore. Still, it took the 1988 loss to motivate him to become a cheerleader for federally subsidized abortion. Tennessee voters approved of his former position. But in order to someday win the New York and California Democratic primaries, and harvest the money of rich feminists, Gore flip-flopped. He converted to the unrestricted abortion position during the four-year period between 1988 and 1992. Two weeks after Bill Clinton selected Gore as his running mate, the Tennessee Senator came completely on board with the hard feminist left's view of abortion. On July 27, 1992, the former pro-lifer became a Senate co-sponsor of the Freedom of Choice Act or FOCA.[178] Gore had refused to back the bill when it was first introduced in January 1990, however, in order to win the Vice Presidency, he became an ardent supporter of FOCA. Gore had the gall to deny on *Meet the Press* that his co-sponsorship of FOCA did not represent a flip flop from a previous pro-life position.[179]

The Freedom of Choice Act represented pro-abortion fanaticism. As its original sponsor Congressman Don Edwards put it: "The [FOCA] is explicit. It provides for *no* exceptions-no exceptions whatsoever. It is a classic one sentence [Federal] statute that says a state may not restrict the right of a woman to terminate a pregnancy-and that is for *any* reason."[180]

The FOCA statute completely federalized the abortion controversy. Before the Supreme Court's 1973 Roe decision, the states had always regulated abortion. In fact, many fervent supporters of abortion rights, such as Yale constitutional lawyer Alexander Bickel, the Legal Editor of *The New Republic*, and Stanford law professor John Hart Ely, decried the Roe decision for usurping the power of states to legislate on the matter. Now FOCA aimed to nullify the Supreme Court's recent 1989 Webster ruling allowing states to impose minor restrictions on abortion. Al Gore, the raging moderate, the centrist Tennessean, announced with his support of FOCA that he was now a San Francisco Democrat, a left-wing activist. FOCA actually represented the doctrinaire godless liberalism the Democratic Leadership Council was founded to combat.

But Al Gore ruthlessly sacrificed all his previous votes and arguments against abortion in order to preserve a future Presidential political viability. To further his cause with the pro-abortion feminists, Gore voted against a federal amendment opposing parental notification for the abortions of minors.[181]

The Fragility of Life: The Gulf War Vote, January 1991

Abortion was not the only life or death issue Senator Al Gore had to confront at the beginning of the 1990s. Seven months after Gore explicitly abandoned his pro-life position, Iraqi dictator Saddam Hussein invaded Kuwait. The Iraqi Army quickly crushed the feeble Kuwaiti army with their armored divisions. The army then occupied Kuwait as a conquered province of Iraq. Oil rich Saudi Arabia, Kuwait's neighbor, gazed fearfully at the Iraqi occupation forces. Saddam Hussein now controlled or threatened a majority of the world's oil reserves. He also threatened a traditional Iraqi enemy, the State of Israel.

The Iraqi invasion of Kuwait came at a difficult time for President George Bush. His Republican allies in the Congress were consigned to minority status in both Houses. Bush had also divided his own party by raising taxes after his famous "read my lips, no new taxes" pledge during the 1988 campaign. Nevertheless, Bush immediately ordered Marine, Navy, and Air Force units to defend beleaguered Saudi Arabia. Then he ordered General Colin Powell, Chairman of the Joint Chiefs of Staff, to assemble heavy mechanized Army units for a possible invasion to free Kuwait. Then Bush and his foreign policy advisers began negotiating with foreign leaders to create an international military alliance against Saddam Hussein and his army.

The Congressional Democrats, led by Gore's DLC ally, Senator Sam Nunn, supported Bush's initial defensive moves. But they played coy about supporting a large-scale military invasion to expel the Iraqi army from Kuwait. The Democrats had failed to win a Presidential election since 1976. They sensed an opportunity to saddle Bush with an embarrassing diplomatic and military defeat, thus ensuring the election of a Democrat President in 1992. Of course, the Democrats' opportunistic policy toward an American defeat was unpatriotic and shameful. Even some Democrats thought so. But this same partisan policy had worked during the Vietnam War to help elect Jimmy Carter in 1976. After all, Johnson's War became Nixon's War in January 1969. During the Nixon Presidency, liberal Democrats like Albert Gore, Sr. washed their hands of responsibility for the Vietnam War and voted against policies that might have created a stalemate for the South Vietnamese. The fall of South Vietnam in April 1975 did not cause these liberal Democrats much anguish.[182]

Despite his patriotic centrist image, Sam Nunn was ready to play the same game with a possible Persian Gulf War. Nunn, like his DLC associates Clinton, Gore, and Robb, lusted for the Presidency. Nunn used his forum as Chairman of the Senate Armed Services Committee to parade a flood of witnesses testifying against a possible Gulf War. Nunn used Republicans like former Defense Secretary James Schlesinger, as well as, many former flag officers to claim that many American casualties would result from an invasion of Kuwait. Nunn advocated patience. The U.S. should be patient and let economic sanctions take effect against Iraq. The military units already in Saudi Arabia were sufficient to deter an invasion.

George Bush decided Saddam Hussein was too dangerous to be left unpunished for his Kuwaiti invasion. The intelligence agencies publicly warned that Iraq was developing nuclear and chemical warfare capabilities in order to intimidate other countries in the Middle East. Bush and his advisers rounded up enough allies to authorize a U.N. Security Council resolution permitting an invasion of Kuwait. With the end of the Cold War, the U.N. was now friendly to U.S. interests. The United Nations Security Council complied on November 29, 1990 with a resolution authorizing a U.S. led Allied invasion to expel the Iraqi invaders "by any means necessary," i.e., war, if they did not pull out by January 15, 1991. Bush informed the Congress he would build up the Allied forces in Saudi Arabia to 400,000 men. If Saddam Hussein did not withdraw by January 15, then the Allies would drive them out by force.

Nunn, Senate Majority Leader George Mitchell, and the other Senate Democrats balked at Bush's policy. They chose to give peace and the sanctions a chance to change the mind of the bloodthirsty Iraqi dictator. With the January 15 deadline approaching, the Iraqi forces had not moved a millimeter out of Kuwait. On January 8, Bush asked Congress for a resolution authorizing the use of force against Iraq. For the next three days, Congressmen and Senators debated the resolution. In the House, Bush won his vote easily. Les Aspin, the Democratic Chairman of the House Armed Services Committee, along with Stephen Solarz, swayed many Democrats to join the Republicans in authorizing war. Aspin and Solarz, unlike Sam Nunn, chose patriotism over political expediency. Neither man was seeking the Presidency. Both men also recognized how dangerous Saddam was to America's friends in the Middle East and the world's oil supply. Both Aspin and Solarz believed U.S. forces could do the job with fairly low casualties. Enough Democrat hawks joined with Republicans to keep the vote from being close.

The Senate was a different story. Swollen liberal egos and Presidential ambitions combined to make the Senate vote close. Sam Nunn twisted arms to follow his peace and sanctions policy. Republican minority Bob Dole pressured his Republicans and southern Democrats to support the President. There were only 44 Republican Senators. Two of them, Mark Hatfield and Charles Grassley, were defecting, Dole needed to peel off eight Democratic Senators to carry the Gulf War resolution.

Al Gore, who had just been re-elected in Tennessee with 68% of the vote, was not worried about losing his Senate seat. However, his Presidential ambitions were quite another matter.

Voting the wrong way could ruin his next shot at the White House. This vote was the biggest of his career. It did not involve safe subjects like infant formula, toxic waste, or pollution of the environment. Prince Albert agonized about how the vote affected his next run for the White House. George Mitchell and Sam Nunn assumed he would go along with the party line against an immediate invasion. However, Gore experienced great pressure from his mentor Marty Peretz to support Bush's war resolution. [183]

Despite being a social liberal, Peretz did think clearly about American foreign policy ever since his shift from the left during the early 1970s. As he did during the Central American crisis, which was resolved less than a year before the Gulf War vote, Marty Peretz pressed *The New Republic* to publish superb articles about the Gulf Crisis. Peretz's Israeli sympathies compelled him to be even more hostile to Saddam Hussein than he was to the Sandinistas. The magazine ran pieces by the best analysts of the Middle East. It also published superb writing by a young journalist accompanying Allied forces in the Gulf, Michael Kelly. *The New Republic* coverage pointed to an inescapable conclusion: Iraqi forces must be crushed sooner rather than later. Marty relentlessly hammered this conclusion home to his prize student, Al Gore. [184]

Gore did not let his mentor Marty Peretz down. Gore decided, in the biggest vote of his public career, to support Bush's proposed invasion. It was hard opposing his DLC crony Sam Nunn. Nunn spent considerable time persuading Gore to follow his lead, but Peretz's view prevailed. Prince Albert decided Saddam Hussein demanded swift punishment by American military power. Gore characteristically demanded a high price for his vote. In Bob Dole's and Minority Whip Alan Simpson's recollection, Gore demanded plenty of time for a long speech to be delivered on TV. According to the *New York Times* in 1992, "Senator Bob Dole charged... that Senator Al Gore, the Democratic Vice Presidential nominee, tried last year to trade his vote on the Iraq war resolution for a prime-time speaking slot during floor debate. Mr. Dole said Mr. Gore asked him: 'How much if I vote with you? How much will you give me tomorrow morning?' Then he went to [Democratic Senate Majority Leader George] Mitchell to see how much time he would get if he voted against the resolution."[185] Dole, desperate for votes to pass the war resolution, surrendered to Gore's petty demand. The Republican Senate leader "penciled in" Gore "for twenty minutes of prime speaking time."[186] Marla Romash, Gore's press secretary, tacitly admitted Dole's charge was accurate by timidly saying, "It's standard procedure for people who are undecided to the last moment to ask both sides whether any floor time might be available."[187] Even when the vote concerned a life and death issue like going to war, Gore worried most about presenting himself favorably on television. Al Gore joined nine other Senate Democrats, all DLC stalwarts, to vote with 42 Republicans for the Gulf War. The final vote was 52-47.

Sam Nunn and George Mitchell both resented Gore for leaving the Democratic reservation and joining the Republicans. Nunn thought Gore deliberately snubbed and second-guessed his superior understanding of military affairs. He was noticeably cool to Gore for several weeks after the Gulf War vote. Mitchell was even more hostile. Several other Senate Democrats emulated Mitchell's shunning of Gore. The obedient son did not want to alienate any future political supporters. So, Prince Albert made sure to take gratuitous shots at President Bush and Republican Senators to prove his partisan loyalty.

Gore warned Republicans not to gloat as the Gulf War proceeded speedily and successfully. He ran interference for the Democrats who voted against the Gulf War resolution. To quote *The Almanac of American Politics, 1992* : "[A]fter the war, Gore quickly stepped forward to attack Republicans who were attacking Democrats who voted against the resolution- a deft partisan move that helped Gore with his fellow Democrats and at the same time spotlighted his own vote[e.]"[188]

Gore's skillful tacking managed to increase his future Presidential stature while preserving his partisan reliability.

The first euphoric days of the Gulf War ended with the February 28 cease-fire. Within weeks both the Kurdish and Shi'ite minorities within Iraq rebelled against Saddam Hussein. President Bush was caught in a dilemma. He did not want Iraq to dissolve into three separate states but he also wanted Saddam removed. Turkey, a close U.S. ally, was troubled with its own Kurdish minority. The Turks were terrified their Kurds would unite with Iraq's Kurds and form their own nation. Almost every Middle East country feared the fundamentalist Shi'ite Muslims. The Kurds and Shi'ites represented a problem with no solution. While U.N. forces observed the cease-fire and watched, the Iraqi ruler suppressed both rebellions with armed helicopters and his Republican Guard divisions. After both massacres by the Iraqi forces, the remaining Kurds and Shiites fled to respective safe zones marked out by U.N. forces. While the U.N. invasion phase of the war occurred, even pro-war Democrats like Gore were compelled to defer to George Bush's leadership. The massacre of the Kurds and Shiites offered partisan Democrats an opening to blast Bush.

Gore acted as the designated hit man against the Republicans. His credentials to second-guess Bush were burnished by his pro-Gulf War vote. Gore initially asked in January 1991 that U.S. forces limit themselves to expelling the Iraqis from Kuwait.

"We are not seeking the surrender of Iraq. That has been made clear. No one in a position of responsibility is talking about the conquest of Iraq. It is doubtful that the conquest of Iraq is anything that this Nation would ever want to seek. Even if it were adopting that as a stated goal, it would be a terrible mistake, for reasons we can all certainly see clearly. Any effort to expand our objectives so as to include the military conquest of Iraq would certainly blow apart the core of international consensus upon which all else depends...Above all, it seems to me that the United States needs an outcome minimizing the amount of exposure we must subsequently accept in the Middle East." [189]

This January 1991 speech stresses the limited and confined aims of the Gulf War. Less than three months later, in April, Gore "forgot" what he said in January and accused George Bush of committing an atrocity worthy of Joseph Stalin: "Gore, a possible presidential candidate...faulted President Bush for not defending the Kurdish population in northern Iraq from the forces of Iraq's president, Saddam Hussein. 'It defies our sense of moral justice,' [Gore] said. 'It erodes our sense of compassion.' [Gore] compared the decision not to defend the Kurds to the Russian army's decision to stand outside Warsaw near the end of World War II, 'postponing liberation deliberately to give the Nazis just enough time to finish butchering the Polish resistance.'" According to Gore, George Bush was just as cold-blooded and cruel as Comrade Stalin. [190]

Gore followed up this outrageous analogy with a fresh accusation in July. Once again Gore conveniently ignored his past comments from January: "He [Gore] accused Bush of consciously deciding in the final days of the war that it would be in U.S. interests to let Saddam stay in power. 'I think that was a very serious mistake,' Gore said." [191] A week later Gore echoed the charge: "It was clear what he [Saddam] was up to and then immediately following the military action, the war, he [Bush] made an historic mistake in allowing Saddam to violate the U.N. cease-fire terms and begin massacring the Kurds in the north and the Shi'ites in the south on the mistaken assumption that it was in our geopolitical interests to allow the government he [Saddam] represented to reconsolidate its power and he [Bush] expressed the hope that the military would overthrow him."[192] Al Gore tried to rewrite the history of his own strategy toward the Gulf War. But the quotation from his January speech indicates he was more, not less, timid about Saddam Hussein than George Bush. Al Gore lied about his past strategic views of the war in order to smear Bush for petty partisan advantage. Gore managed to tar his finest moment in public life, the Senate vote on the Gulf War. He eroded this brave vote for the same reason he abandoned his noble anti-abortion position: to win the Presidency by kowtowing to the leftist groups who control the Democratic Party.

ELEVEN

Eco-Freak: Gore's Fanatical Environmental Crusade

The Southern Baptist Becomes a New Age Neo-Pagan

Al Gore claims his son's near-death ordeal inspired his crusade to "save" the environment. It forced him to "look inside myself and confront some difficult and painful questions about what I am really seeking in my own life, and why." The environmental crisis reflects his own disquiet, "an inner crisis that is, for lack of a better word, spiritual." Gore recognizes hypocrisy in his own life: using air conditioning while driving to give a speech on how chlorofluorocarbons undermine the ozone layer, "my own tendency to put a finger to the political winds and proceed cautiously."[193] However, thanks to the conversion caused by Albert III's crisis, Gore will not dodge his duty to the environment any longer. Al Gore will now eschew "the failures of candor, evasions of responsibility and timidity of vision that characterizes too many of us in government." He realizes his mundane political concerns mean nothing next to the fate of our Mother Earth.

Gore's pious cant, as usual, conceals a true portrait of his life. His previous environmental hypocrisy consisted of more than turning on his car's air conditioner. He personally benefited from industrial exploitation of the earth's resources. His Tennessee farm was strip-mined for zinc by three different companies, one of them Armand Hammer's mining subsidiary. Zinc mining demands the use of toxic chemicals like acetone, cyanide, and heavy metals.[194] Gore also grew tobacco on his property and worked as a real estate developer building houses while in law school. Building houses does not conduce to preserving the environment. Like his father, he vocally supported the Tennessee Valley Authority. The TVA was certainly guilty of exploiting the environment and it also produced nuclear waste from its atomic reactors. In his youth, Al Gore swam and water-skied in a Carthage lake created by a TVA dam project. Before converting from mild conservationism to radical environmentalism in 1989,

Al Gore enjoyed exploiting the earth's resources for profit and pleasure.

For whatever reason, Gore turned away from enjoying the earth. He abandoned a balanced, cost-benefit approach to using natural resources. During his House and early Senate career, he fervently crusaded against toxic waste, as we discussed in Chapter Seven. Gore also denounced open dumping, and strip mining. His denunciations of these two practices reeked of hypocrisy, since both occurred on his Tennessee property.[195] Prince Albert had bored listeners about the "greenhouse effect" depleting the ozone layer ever since his Harvard days. This "greenhouse effect" caused "global warming," a dangerous rise in the earth's temperature. Both friends and enemies endured his environmental admonitions patiently. Worrying about the environment was a standard liberal litany ever since the 1960s. Al Gore's speeches about ecology before the late 1980s displayed a reasoned, if tendentious, approach to man's relation to nature. Gore still appeared to revere God more than planet Earth.

But now the Southern Baptist stopped looking heavenward. Instead, he began to fanatically worship "Mother Earth" like a New Age zealot. Environmentalism became his ersatz religion. In 1990, he sponsored the Congressional legislation creating Earth Day. Gore's bill now offered a solemn Federal blessing to this neo-pagan ceremony. Gore took the Senate floor to sound "warning after warning on global warming, arguing that the costs of not taking action now could be enormous; he backed a five-year phase-out of CFC's [chlorofluorocarbons] from all sources to protect the depleting ozone layer." He indicted the Bush Administration for being indifferent to his pet cause of CFC's. Gore managed to get "a CFC ban through the Senate and, with the help of Sam Nunn, got some of his plans incorporated in Nunn's defense-environmental package."[196] Al Gore now regarded the ozone layer as a vital component of national security. In his mind, CFC's now constituted a greater danger than nuclear missiles.

Earth in the Balance

To warn us of the environmental dangers engulfing us, Al Gore wrote and published a long book, *Earth in the Balance* (1992). One wag immediately dubbed it, *Mein Planet*. Its fervent, fanatical, tone somewhat resembled Adolf Hitler's *Mein*

Kampf. Gore also frequently used metaphors from Nazi Germany to ram home his extreme propositions about our environmental crisis. While certainly not purveying the evil vision of Hitler's work, *Earth in the Balance* does reveal its author as a coercive utopian. Al Gore is dedicated to imposing his ecological values on our society. The book cries out for balance, humor, and an understanding of differing views. Its author cannot countenance a complex approach to nature. Man's relation to nature is reduced to a simple-minded conspiracy model of man's exploitation of nature. People's priorities must take second place to Gore's environmental creed: "We must make the rescue of the environment the central organizing principle for civilization."[197]

People are the problem, Gore explicitly declares. There are too many of them. They exhaust the world's limited resources. Gore falls for the overpopulation propaganda purveyed since the 1920s but already discredited by demographers P.T. Bauer, Julian Simon, and Nicholas Eberstadt in the 1970s and 1980s.[198] These three scholars proved our planet is currently capable of feeding and housing *eight* times our current population. Gore conveniently ignores these demographers' existence. Instead, he recycles the lies and myths of Paul Ehrlich's *The Population Bomb* (1968). Ehrlich's book is a hysterical polemic promoted by Sierra Club fanatics over the last three decades. It directly inspired the founding of the organization Zero Population Growth. Ehrlich's hold over Gore emerges in this clumsy passage: "And when an overpopulated nation overgrazes its pasture land, causing a collapse in its ability to provide food the following year, it is if the force of its collision with nature has pushed it abruptly backward in a crushing blow, like a dashboard striking the forehead of a child."[199]

When Gore wrote this nonsense, China, India, and Indonesia, all poor, "overpopulated" nations, had been easily feeding their people for a decade. Gore also neglects to blame himself and Tipper for overpopulating the earth by breeding four children, two more than necessary for parental duplication. This oversight is in keeping with Gore's usual hypocritical practice toward nature. Ignoring the contrary evidence, Gore obstinately insists we are overpopulating.

This overpopulating leads us to crisis. Gore irritates the reader with characteristic mixed metaphors warning of the coming ecological crisis: "What lies ahead is a race against time.

Sooner or later the steepness of the slope and our momentum down its curve will take us beyond the point of no return."[200]

This passage mixes a race, a mountain climb, and an overseas aviation flight to confusing effect. Sensing the reader is not convinced by these mixed metaphors, Gore pulls out all the stops. He likens our earth's plight to the atrocities of Nazi Germany against the Jews: "Our political awareness often seems shaped like this grid [space deformed by a black hole]...In a similar way the Holocaust shapes every idea we have about human nature."

And, "Yet today the evidence of an ecological Kristallnacht [the night of glass-breaking atrocities against German Jews] is as clear as the sound of glass shattering in Berlin."[201]

Gore asserts we humans are doing to nature what Hitler and the Nazis did to the Jews. He does not use Stalin or Mao to scare us into awareness of our earth's crisis. Perhaps, like his father, Gore regards cruel Communist dictators as purveyors of progress. His refusal to discuss Communist dictatorships is notable since Western visitors to recently liberated Iron Curtain countries and Red China all commented on the environmental degradation inflicted by Communist regimes. Despite his heated rhetoric about the Nazis, Gore fails to spell out how man's exploitation of nature resembles Hitler's gas chambers and concentration camps. We must accept this outrageous claim on his mere assurance.

Gore then combines the Holocaust metaphor of our ecological crisis with a world civil war analogy: "We now face the prospect of a global civil war between those who refuse to consider the consequences of civilization's ruthless advance, and those who refuse to be silent partners in the destruction." [202]

Gore obstinately ignores how a genuine global civil war, the Cold War, has only recently ended. Unlike Gore's fantasy of an environmental civil war, the Cold War truly did cause millions of people to die. Perhaps discussing the Cold War demands giving credit to Ronald Reagan, a man Gore despises as a man of inferior intellect. Or he could denounce Saddam Hussein's setting on fire of the oil fields and offshore derricks in Kuwait. Saddam's oil atrocities created a major ecological crisis in the Gulf region the year before Gore published his book. But Gore prefers discussing his fantasy wars rather than analyzing real wars. He is convinced our ecology suffers from the highest form of crisis: global war.

Many expert reviewers of *Earth in the Balance* refused to believe Gore's thesis of an ecology crisis equivalent to a global war. Gregg Easterbrook, a renowned scientific writer for *Newsweek*, flatly rebutted Gore's contention: "There is no scientific consensus that a crisis exists."[203] Easterbrook was a former *New Republic* editor and friend of Gore boosters Marty Peretz and Leon Wieseltier. An avowed liberal and defender of the environment, he could not be accused of political bias against Prince Albert. He followed up his *Newsweek* review with a careful essay, "Green Cassandras," in the *New Republic* criticizing Gore's apocalyptic thesis of global warming harming the earth. Easterbrook chided Gore for his unbalanced and tendentious thesis: "Gore's environmental oratory is out of control... Gore, and environmentalists generally, find it especially painful to acknowledge that there has been significant progress on most fronts in the United States in recent decades."[204]

If a reader refuses to accept on faith Gore's claim that a crisis exists, then the book is just a long exercise in "junk science." Junk science refers to scientific claims that are unable to be verified or just dressed up political propaganda. *Earth in the Balance* partakes of both attributes. The main scientific claim of the book concerns the "global warming" created by greenhouse gases undermining the ozone layer. Gore breathlessly announces: "that global warming is real and the time to act is now." Later he writes: "we are in the process of altering global temperatures by up to three or four times that amount and causing changes in climate patterns that are likely to have enormous impact on global civilization."[205]

Contrary to Gore's contention, there is little evidence to confirm the existence of global warming. His own teacher, Professor Roger Revelle of Harvard, the man who alerted Gore to the danger caused by greenhouse gases, testified to this effect. In 1991, the year before *Earth in the Balance* was published, Revelle reversed his previous belief and said: "The scientific base for greenhouse warning is too uncertain to justify drastic action at this time. There is little risk in delaying policy response."[206]

Two eminent scholars of climatology, S. Fred Singer of the University of Virginia, and Chauncey Starr of the Electric Power Institute, co-authored an article with Revelle published by the Cosmos Club, site of Al's youthful bus stop. Their April 1991 *Cosmos* article warned against taking the global warming thesis as proven.[207]

Gregg Easterbrook, in his *New Republic* analysis of global warming, used the article by Revelle, Singer, and Starr, to demolish Gore's dire warning that drastic action was immediately necessary. George Will and Richard Lesher drew on the article for similar purposes in their columns in the summer of 1992.

Instead of bowing his head and accepting legitimate criticism from his late teacher, Democrat Vice Presidential candidate Gore reacted in trademark fashion. He decided Singer and Starr were Republican operatives attacking him for political reasons. Gore refused to pause and remember the article was written a year before *Earth in the Balance* appeared and the 1992 Democratic convention occurred. Revelle had died late in 1991, so he was unable to personally refute his former pupil's paranoia. Gore bullied Revelle's Harvard research assistant,[208] Justin Lancaster, into denying the article represented Revelle's true views. Gore also put his Senate aide, Anthony Socci, to work undermining the scientific credibility of S. Fred Singer and Chauncey Starr. Both Lancaster and Socci wrote several letters to the editor of various publications libeling Singer and Starr for falsifying Revelle's thinking in the *Cosmos* article. Such ruthless tactics later became painfully familiar during the Clinton-Gore Administration.

Singer fought back by filing a five-count libel lawsuit against Lancaster, Gore's hatchet man, on April 16, 1993. On April 29, 1994, Lancaster surrendered. He and his lawyers settled by retracting the statements libeling Singer for falsifying Roger Revelle's thinking on global warming.[209] Nobody was able to make Al Gore apologize for creating the libels in the first place. Much like Bill Clinton, Gore lets others suffer for his mistakes and leaves a path of personal destruction in his wake.

Gore ignored Revelle's change of mind on global warming while writing *Earth in the Balance*. He only became concerned about Revelle's argument when it seemed to threaten his political power. Gore's intellectual rigidity persisted when he chose a cure for his arrogant diagnosis of global warming. A dire global illness demanded an immediate, expensive, and painful prescription. Gore decided that a "Global Marshall Plan" was in order: "Improbable or not, something like the Marshall Plan—a global Marshall Plan, if you will—is now urgently needed...The new plan will require the wealthy nations to allocate money for transferring environmentally helpful technologies to the Third World and to help impoverished nations achieve a stable population and a new pattern of sustainable economic progress.

To work, however, any such effort will also require wealthy nations to make a transition themselves that will be in some ways more wrenching than that of the Third World, simply because powerful established patterns will be disrupted."

Since the Marshall Plan cost the U.S. 2% of its Gross National Product, or GNP, between 1948-1951, Gore proposes the same GNP percentage be devoted to saving the environment in the Third World. Gore never bothers to ask whether the U.S. taxpayer wants to spend this amount on foreign environmental aid. However, he recognizes it is a tough sell. In his narrated cassette version of *Earth in the Balance*, Gore omits the pages, 298-305, where the Global Marshall plan is discussed. He lied about making the global aid proposal when debating Vice President Quayle in October 1992. Reading the pages mentioned easily discovers the lie. Gore lied about the $100 billion Global Marshall Plan in order to maintain the fiction he and Bill Clinton were budget conscious New Democrats.[210]

Al Gore's solution to our "environmental crisis" does not stop with a global Marshall Plan. This feminist "beta male," as his adviser Naomi Wolf describes him, seeks to convert all aggressive alpha males to his persuasion. We mentioned in Chapter 4 how Professor Erik Erikson's condemnation of masculine aggression influenced Gore. In *Earth in the Balance*, he reveals his debt to Erikson by debunking his own sex: "Western Civilization has emphasized a distinctly male way of relating to the world... Ultimately, part of the solution for the environmental crisis may well lie in our ability to achieve a better balance between the sexes, leavening the dominant male perspective with a healthier respect for female ways of experiencing the world."[211]

Gore does not explain what "leavening the dominant male perspective" means in concrete policy. Perhaps it is mere rhetoric, like his earlier lie that half of his staff was female.

Outlawing automobiles may be a means of "leavening the dominant male perspective." Following his Harvard teacher Erik Erikson here, Al Gore sees men as too aggressive, warlike, and exploitative. Men must learn to practice the feminine traits of peacefulness, patience, and nurture. The world's most famous beta male abhors that notorious symbol of masculine aggression, the internal combustion engine. Men become so excited about their powerful, gleaming, gas-guzzling, environmentally destructive cars. In Gore's New Age neo-pagan theology, fossil fuels replace the role of Satan. The internal combustion engine replaces human pride, the means of Satan's seduction. Discarding the internal combustion engine will allow us to conquer our pride and rescue the environment from satanic fossil fuels. The global warming threat will then be ended.

Gore proposes we begin to quickly abolish automobiles from the earth. First, the federal government must enforce "new laws to mandate the improvements in automobile fleet mileage, but much more is needed." Next, "it ought to be possible to establish a coordinated global program to accomplish the strategic goal of completely eliminating the internal combustion engine over, say, a twenty-five year period." Anybody resisting this draconian federal solution to our "environmental crisis" must submit to Chairman Al's Little Red Book: "We now know that their [automobiles'] cumulative impact on the global environment is posing a mortal threat to the security of every nation more deadly than that of any military enemy we are ever likely to again confront."[212]

Yes, cars are more dangerous to us than the missiles of Red China, North Korea, or Iraq.

Eliminating automobiles in twenty-five years dwarfs any of the utopian schemes pursued by Lenin, Stalin, Hitler, or Mao. Al Gore thinks bigger than any of those twentieth century coercive utopians. Gore plans on using federal law, not the *Gulag Archipelago*, concentration camps, gas chambers, or the *laogai* to rid the world of cars. He confidently expects the American people to surrender to this utopian vision. Bill Clinton, understandably enough, asked his running mate to bury this idea during the 1992 and 1996 campaigns. When your campaign slogan is "Putting People First," you don't want to scare off the voters depending on the 138,450 jobs in auto assembly plants, much less the ones working in related industries.[213]

Gore is dead serious about abolishing the automobile if he gets the chance. When queried by reporters about this proposal, he stands by it and everything else in the book: "I'm glad it's [*Earth in the Balance*] out there, and I'm glad I wrote it, and I'm behind every word 100 percent."[214]

He has repeated this comment several times up to the 2000 campaign. Only one other man rates *Earth in the Balance* as highly as its author. When FBI agents broke into the shack of Ted Kaczynski, the Unabomber, in 1996, they found he owned a copy of *Earth in the Balance*. The FBI agents noticed the Unabomber had heavily underlined and carefully annotated his copy of Gore's book. It amused the agents that Kaczynski found his fellow Harvard graduate to be such an inspiration.[215]

Gore's Environmental Hypocrisy

Gore condemned mining in *Earth in the Balance*. He wrote: "Just as men tear husks from elephants' heads in such quantity as to threaten their extinction, we are ripping matter from its place in the earth in such volume as to upset the balance between daylight and darkness."

Gore refused to mention how he earned royalties of $215,000 from the zinc mine on his property from 1978-1991, for an average of $25,000 a year.[216]

Gore assailed road building and bulldozers for cutting man off from his natural relation to the environment: "Precisely because we feel no connection to the physical world, we trivialize the consequences of our actions. We are, in effect, bulldozing the Garden of Eden."

But four years earlier, during the 1988 campaign, he praised his father for helping institute the interstate highway system: "I remember my father's work on the interstate highway program. I remember the thrill of going out to see the bulldozers turn the first ground. I was proud of him."[217]

Gore praises and damns bulldozers. He gives us no criteria to explain why his attitude toward these earthmovers changed so much in four short years.

Gore's hypocrisy appeared again when a clean water issue in his home state arose. He wrote lyrically about clean water in *Earth in the Balance*: "The rains bring us trees and flowers; the droughts bring taping cracks in the world. The lakes and rivers sustain us; they flow through the veins of the earth and into our own. But we must take care to let them flow back out as pure as they came, not poison and waste them without thought for the future."[218]

Yet, four years previously, during the 1988 campaign, he flip-flopped on a 1984 campaign promise to clean up the once pristine Pigeon River flowing through western North Carolina and east Tennessee.

The Pigeon River flows through the Smoky Mountains, one of America's most scenic and unspoiled areas. Most of the land around the Pigeon comprises a National Park and National Forest. The Champion Paper Company of North Carolina polluted the Pigeon during the 1980s and 1990s by pumping dioxin-producing discharge into the river. The Environmental Protection Agency tried to crack down on Champion's polluting of the Pigeon in early 1987. The agency demanded Champion stop its dioxin discharge. However, two North Carolina Democratic politicians, Congressman James Clarke and Senator Terry Sanford, got to Gore. They offered him endorsements for their states' 1988 Democratic Presidential primary in return for calling off the EPA from Champion. Gore concurred by personally persuading Tennessee environmental officials to put off their demand that Champion stop dumping pollutants into the Pigeon River. Champion then offered Gore a $1000 PAC contribution for his 1990 campaign. One Tennessean who crusaded to clean up the Pigeon River blasted Gore's sellout: "He is right out front on rain forests and other issues outside the United States when it won't cost him any votes, but I don't consider him an environmentalist at all."[219]

Gore resembles the Champion Paper Company in his personal practice toward the land. He flays both water pollution and open dumping in *Earth in the Balance*. Yet, Gore's own Carthage farm contributes to both these problems. There is an illegal open dump on the farm. The dump consists of pesticide containers, aerosol cans which damage the ozone layer, old tires, used filters filled with waste oil, and unrecycled cans and bottles. Gore's neighbors observed this open dump for many years since 1980. One of them says: "I'm appalled at what I've seen." Gore's property borders on the scenic Caney Fork River. His neighbors worry the pesticide and other toxins from the containers in Gore's dump may leak into the river. Gore is too busy pointing out the sins of other polluters' to clean up his own.[220]

Al Gore continued this attitude toward waste disposal as a Congressman and Senator. When pork barrel projects benefiting his district or state were imperiled by environmental considerations, he lobbied the Interior Department and EPA to exempt the projects from federal regulations. Gore intervened in this fashion for the Tennessee Valley Authority's Upper Duck River project, the Columbia Dam and Reservoir, and the Tellico Dam project.[221] He is also careful to never attack the corporations who do the polluting. Gore criticized the disastrous chemical accident in Bhopal, India, but not Union Carbide, the company responsible for 2,500 lost lives. Al Gore happily accepts contributions from corporations and unions involved in polluting. His PAC money comes from: Pennzoil PAC; the Petroleum Marketers' Association of America; Texas Gas Transmission Corporation PAC; the Oil, Chemical, & Atomic Workers Intl. Union Committee; the Gas Employees PAC; 3M PAC; and the various sugar lobbies such as the Hawaiian Sugar Planter's Association and the American Sugar Cane League. The Democratic Leadership Council, which Gore helped found, accepts donations from Dow Chemical and the American Petroleum Institute.[222] How can Gore be taken seriously as a crusader for pristine environment when he takes checks from the businesses most guilty of pollution?

Like his friend and boss Bill Clinton, Al Gore combines the worst attributes of socialism and capitalism, bureaucracy and bribes. Their DLC "centrist" liberalism prefers influence peddling to free market competition. Clinton and Gore like to sell government favors to big business for a price. They certainly enjoyed doing favors to the world's leading polluter country, the People's Republic of China. The Clinton-Gore team happily allowed technology useful to the manufacture of nuclear weapons to be exported to the PRC. Nothing pollutes like atomic waste. But Gore never condemns the Red Chinese for ruining the environment with their atomic testing. When Gore condemns corporate polluters, he is only partly serious. He only punishes those polluters who refuse to reward him with cash and political favors. When environmental preservation and political power come into conflict, Gore will always choose power.

TWELVE

Huck and Tom: Why Clinton Picked Gore as his Running Mate—The 92 Campaign

Gore Postpones—Clinton Goes For It

Al Gore told Nathan Landow in April 1989 he would not run in 1992 because of Albert III's ordeal. In August 1991, he made his vow official. But there were other reasons. Gore finished dead last in a Presidential poll among Democrats with 8%. Thanks to the successful waging of the Gulf War, George Bush seemed unbeatable in 1992. Al Gore rarely challenged the odds in politics. His Gulf War vote was the shining exception. Two of the DLC Senate stars, Sam Nunn and Chuck Robb of Virginia ruined their chances. Nunn bungled on the Gulf War and Robb embroiled himself in embarrassing sex and political scandals. The Cold War still continued as long as Gorbachev and the Communist Party held power in the Soviet Union.

However, simultaneous with Gore's announcing of his non-candidacy, the Cold War ended. The Red Army and KGB hard-line oligarchy tried to overthrow Gorbachev's glasnost government and restore their predominance. The coup failed, and the Russian people began embracing democracy and dissolving Communist totalitarian institutions. The Cold War, which had conditioned American politics since 1946, no longer existed. President George Bush had already damaged the Republican Party and his election chances by increasing taxes. The Republican coalition, already shaky after Bush's mistakes, unraveled further with the Cold War's end. The major reasons for voting Republican no longer existed.

The 1992 Democrat Presidential nomination now became desirable. As Gore friend and aide Robert Squier put it, the failed Soviet hard-line coup joined with Gore's pull out to change political circumstances: "Two things happened today: Gorbachev and Clinton were both liberated."[223] Squier was right. Bill Clinton, who had refused to run in 1988 for the same "family reasons" Gore now used, was the Democrat best situated to take advantage of these changed circumstances.

Clinton was not the only centrist Democrat intending a 1992 run. Nebraska Senator Bob Kerrey was also a contender. Both Clinton and Kerrey enjoyed taking risks. Clinton's risk-taking involved dealing with criminals and performing adultery with several hundred women.[224] Bob Kerrey took his big risk by serving as a Navy SEAL commando during the Vietnam War. He earned the Congressional Medal of Honor but lost a leg in combat. Kerrey loathed Clinton for being a liar and draft dodger. Clinton envied the respect Kerrey always received. But the Nebraska war hero could not compete with the Arkansas liar's phenomenal political sixth sense. Kerrey was also damaged by his vote against the Gulf War. After lying his way out of several well-known scandals, Clinton finished second in New Hampshire to Massachusetts liberal Paul Tsongas. He then brilliantly executed the Super Tuesday southern strategy Gore tried to pull off during the 1988 campaign. "Slick Willie" swept the southern primaries, then won New York. If the Democrats could exploit H. Ross Perot's Reform Party candidacy against the Republicans, then they could win in November. Clinton boasted the intuitive skills Gore conspicuously lacked. He was the finest Democratic political animal since Franklin Roosevelt.

Hungry for the Presidency, the fractious Democrats united quickly behind Clinton. Ron Brown, the slick Chairman of the Democratic National Committee, skillfully and ruthlessly protected Clinton from the few journalists pressing inquiries into "Slick Willie's" dark past. Brown, no choirboy himself, knew about Clinton's lies, sexcapades, and criminal associates. In a pre-emptive strike against damaging news stories, the DNC Chairman sent a letter threatening television and radio station managers with federal reprisals if they ran ads about Clinton by our group, the Presidential Victory Committee.[225] Ron Brown played this hardball because he knew Clinton could not win if the truth emerged about the real Slick Willie.

Clinton was a DLC poster boy: an obvious white southerner talking tough about foreign policy, crime, and welfare while constantly taxing and spending to expand government.

Clinton's Decision to Pick Prince Albert

Clinton, the complete political animal, coldly studied the flaws of his Presidential candidacy. Even his supporters thought he sorely lacked necessary attributes: a reputation for integrity;

experience in foreign policy; the image of a good family man; experience working with Congress; and a pro-environment record. Slick Willie needed a Vice Presidential candidate who possessed all those attributes. His Vice Presidential nominee must also be unfailingly loyal and skilled at raising campaign cash. The candidate had to be a darling of the most powerful liberal factions: the pro-abortion feminists; the gay liberationists; the plaintiff trial lawyers; the public employee and teachers' unions; the affirmative action lobby; the telecommunications industry; and the news and entertainment media. In May, Clinton put Warren Christopher in charge of a committee to pick his veep. Christopher was the California lawyer notorious for being Jimmy Carter's emissary to release the Iranian hostages. He was to investigate, sound out, and decide which of the prospective nominees best fit Slick Willie's needs. Florida Senator Bob Graham was considered the front-runner.

While Clinton and Christopher were pondering the Vice Presidential choice in June, Gore attended the United Nations Conference on Environment and Development. The UNCED met in Rio de Janeiro, Brazil to consider two of Al Gore's pet issues: "global warming" and biodiversity. UNCED wanted to impose regulations upon and extort money from the U.S. for supposedly being most responsible for creating these two "problems." Ronald Reagan enjoyed thumbing his nose at such U.N. efforts to embarrass and blackmail America. But Bush foolishly consented to send a delegation to this U.N. boondoggle, thus legitimizing its proceedings. He handed Al Gore, who represented the Senate Democrats, a stick to beat up the Bush Administration's environmental record.

Gore, the son of a longtime UN official, knew how to exploit the Rio Conference for the Democrats. He beat up Bush's environmental policy in daily press briefings. Gore used the non-existent "global warming" and "biodiversity" crises to show up Bush as an uncaring and cowardly President. Gore frightened some voters into thinking that Bush, who gave the EPA a higher budget and more leeway than any previous President, did not care about Mother Earth. Gore stooped low, as he always does, in his attacks. He analogized the Bush Administration's policy toward the environment as "a Greek tragedy."[226] Gore's daily attacks blistered the Bush officials at the conference. Even the President himself appeared foolish as he personally addressed the conference to tell it the U.S. would not abide by its resolutions.

Clinton and Warren Christopher both noticed how effectively Gore smeared George Bush at the Rio Conference.

The two men also took account of how Gore's foreign policy record camouflaged Clinton's weaknesses better than Bob Graham's or any others did. While Graham, unlike Sam Nunn, did vote for the Gulf War, he lacked Gore's detailed grasp of defense issues. Bob Graham could not defend the Democratic case against SDI with Gore's skill. Gore had served in Vietnam. This helped blunt the dangerous draft dodger charge against Clinton. It also showed up Dan Quayle, who serviced in the Indiana National Guard. Al Gore also did not believe partisan politics stopped at the water's edge. Gore publicly blasted Bush's Iraq policy. Gore also voted to authorize funds for the ridiculous "October Surprise" investigation. This snipe hunt aimed to find proof that the 1980 Reagan campaign conspired with the Ayatollah Khomeini to prevent the Iranian hostages' release before the 1980 election. Only fanatically partisan Democrats took the effort seriously.[227] Ironically, given later events, Gore also freely attacked Bush for appeasing China after the Tiananmen Square massacre in 1989.

On technical domestic policy, Gore beat out all the Vice Presidential contenders. None of them shared Gore's detailed grasp of health care, telecommunications, and environmental policy. James Carville, Clinton's campaign adviser, had made affordable heath care a powerful issue. Gore's Capitol Hill experience would help in designing and passing health care legislation. Telecommunications and computers were becoming extremely important to the economy. Gore's understanding of their future development was a big asset to a Presidential candidate. The Tennessee Senator also enjoyed excellent relations with the corporation executives in both those industries. This would help in tapping them for campaign donations.[228] As Governor of Arkansas, Clinton had allowed polluters free rein if they contributed to his campaign funds. But he recognized the environmentalist "greens" were now an important part of the liberal coalition. Gore shored him up with those voters.

Prince Albert also enjoyed excellent rankings from the labor unions. Old-fashioned manufacturing or service unions no longer comprised a large part of the national vote. But public employees' and teachers' unions picked up the slack from the decline of smoke stack industries. Contrary to his DLC image, Gore, like Clinton, is a big spender and thus a big taxer. Like his father,

Gore never met a tax he did not like. He voted for raises in personal income taxes, corporate taxes, estate taxes, and capital gains taxes. In *Earth in the Balance*, Gore even proposed two innovative taxes on carbon dioxide and a virgin materials fee. During two years, 1989 and 1990, the National Taxpayers Union dubbed him the Senate's biggest spender.[229] His career House-Senate ranking by the liberal Americans for Democratic Action (ADA) put him at 71% for his career. A centrist would rank around 50%. This ranking looks centrist only when compared with Ted Kennedy and Barney Frank's ranking. The 71% ADA ranking indicates Gore is eager to raise taxes to fund programs benefiting liberal special interest groups.[230]

Gore also helped him with social issues. Social issues are actually a liberal code word for moral issues. Like Gore, his fellow Southern Baptist, Clinton once opposed abortion. In order to win feminist support and to please Hillary, Clinton abandoned his pro-life position. Clinton's flip-flop made him sympathetic to Gore's flip-flop. Both Clinton and Gore realized you crossed the feminists at your own peril. Feminists are the most powerful interest group in American society. They proved it by preventing Bill Clinton's removal from office by the U.S. Senate for perjury and obstruction of justice in 1999. Clinton also liked Gore for his ties to the gay liberation movement. The crusaders for homosexual rights enjoyed disproportionate influence due to their zeal and generosity to sympathetic politicians. Thanks to his long friendship with Marty Peretz, Gore was close to the leaders of the gay liberation movement. Gore pushed harder for letting gays serve in the U.S. military than Clinton.[231] Peretz's *The New Republic*, the leading American liberal magazine and the incubator of many DLC policies, would be championing the Clinton--Gore Administration, if Al Gore were Vice President. Clinton surely factored this into his calculations.

Clinton even telephoned Peretz to ask about Gore as a possible Vice Presidential nominee. The fact that Clinton called Gore's mentor indicates how much he leaned toward choosing the Tennessean. Peretz told Clinton he preferred seeing Gore at the top of the ticket but that his former student would make an outstanding vice president. To aid Gore's case, he praised his personal qualities to Clinton: "This is a man who will never knife you in the back. This is not a gossiper. This is someone whose own views about personal honor would guarantee that you would not have someone who was cooking up trouble against you."[232]

Peretz was awed by these characteristics because he so conspicuously lacked them himself. With his propensity for scandals, Clinton knew he needed such loyalty.

Gore offered Clinton more than loyalty and credibility with the feminists and foreign policy figures. He also shared the Arkansan's desire to preserve affirmative action quotas to satisfy feminists, as well as, organized black and Hispanic grievance groups.[233] Both men preferred letting Federal judges legislate from the bench about abortion, gay rights, and gender-racial quotas, thus sparing elected politicians from feeling the heat. They both used litmus tests on prospective judges before elevating them to the bench. Clinton and Gore both opposed Judge Robert Bork's nomination to the Supreme Court in 1987. Gore, despite his moderate image, was one of the few southern Senators to vote against Judge Clarence Thomas' nomination to the Supreme Court in 1991.[234]

Besides agreeing with him on policy questions, Clinton felt personally comfortable with Gore. He most appreciated five qualities of Al Gore. First, Al enjoyed a faithful and happy marriage with Tipper. Clinton, given his own flawed relationship with Hillary, was awed by the Gore couple's serenity. He also knew Al and Tipper's happy marriage was politically helpful to him. Second, as a policy wonk himself, he admired Gore's capacity for hard work and mastery of detail. Clinton enjoyed and benefited from talking shop with Al Gore. If he became President, Clinton wanted to hand off some important issues to his Vice President to allow extra time for extracurricular activities. Third, Clinton valued Gore's unstinting loyalty and fierce partisanship. Clinton sometimes laughed at Gore's grim belief that Democrats were always doing God's work. But he knew Prince Albert's ruthless partisanship would be indispensable during the tough battles ahead. Fourth, Gore was a Southern Baptist like himself. Unlike Michael Dukakis, a northeast corridor elitist, Clinton figured he and Gore could put an easy, reassuring, smiling, southern drawl face on liberalism. They could both charm southern centrist swing voters into returning to the Democratic Party of feminists, abortionists, gay liberationists, Jesse Jackson, mandated quotas, ACLU lawyers, and nuclear freezers. Events proved Clinton's prediction accurate. Fifth, Clinton valued Gore's political discipline. "Al the Robot" always stayed on message. He refused to be distracted by mundane human concerns. Although it gave him a deserved reputation as a bore and zealot, Gore pounded away relentlessly on whatever duty or subject concerned him. Clinton himself was easily distracted from the subject at hand. Slick Willie knew he needed Al Gore's discipline to keep him on track.

A close adviser of Gore wanted him to keep away from Slick Willie. Pauline Gore warned her son back in the mid-1980s: "Bill Clinton is not a nice person. Don't associate too closely with him." [235]

The 1992 Campaign—July to November

Bill Clinton notified Gore he was his Vice Presidential pick on July 8, 1992. Gore, who described the Vice Presidency back in 1987 as "a political dead end" (See Chapter 9), accepted Clinton's offer. His father had only aspired to the Democratic Vice Presidential nomination (See Chapter 2), but the son actually achieved it. Gore flew to Little Rock, met with the Democratic nominee, and then was briefed by the campaign aides. The Vice Presidential nominee needed few lessons. James Carville, Clinton's spin-doctor with the media, raved about the same message discipline Clinton noticed: "He was, in my opinion, the best: somebody disciplined on the message, as good a national candidate as I've ever seen out of either party. It's extremely rare for a Democrat, but he had unbelievable message discipline." [236]

Clinton and Gore traveled to the Democratic Convention in New York City by tour bus from Little Rock. This clever gimmick helped the two men to mesh their campaign styles on the stump. It also showcased Clinton's two great qualities as a campaigner: his energy and empathy. The bus tour helped them later win the battleground states of Illinois, Ohio, and Pennsylvania. On July 15, Clinton was nominated in New York. That same day, Ross Perot withdrew his candidacy. Instead of helping George Bush, the move assisted Clinton. From that day forward, the Clinton-Gore ticket never trailed in the opinion polls. Al Gore accepted his nomination with a speech exploiting the personal ordeal of Albert III's accident. This speech also attacked all the alleged sins of Bush and the Republicans. [237]

After the convention, Clinton used Gore for various hatchet man tasks. Gore accompanied Clinton on some of the bus tours. Clinton noticed how the Washington press corps, especially the women reporters, favored Gore more than they did him. This represented a reversal from 1988, when the reporters constantly mocked and jeered at "Al the Robot" and the "Wooden Indian." Clinton encouraged Gore to run interference for him with the Fourth Estate. Prince Albert continues to perform this thankless task for his boss to this day. He then prepared for his October 13 debate with Dan Quayle and Admiral James Stockdale. Perot had re-entered the race with his Reform Party candidacy and named Stockdale as his Vice Presidential choice. Stockdale was not a very good debater, but Quayle called attention to Clinton's lies and to Gore's proposed Global Marshall Plan in *Earth in the Balance*. Gore denied Clinton's lies and created one of his own about the Global Marshall Plan. Gore timidly refused to defend Clinton against Quayle's accusation that the Arkansan was a notorious liar. Perhaps Gore recognized defending Clinton's reputation for integrity was impossible. Ironically, the former pro-lifer spent much of the debate mocking Quayle's anti-abortion stance. While Quayle probably won the debate, Gore allowed him to score few points.[238]

Gore usually stuck to the campaign slogans of: "It's the economy, stupid!" or the even more vacuous "Putting People First!" However, he was hauled out as a hatchet man against Bush's foreign policy in many smear speeches. Gore repeated rumors that the Bush Administration did dirty deals with Iraq involving the crooked Bank of Credit and Commerce International and a Commodity Credit Corporation grain exchange. Gore also accused the Bush Administration of exporting high technology supercomputers and satellites to Iraq. These items would enable Iraq to develop nuclear weapons. Gore's charges about Iraqi policy were later proven untrue. However, they worked to keep Bush on the defensive. Bush did not help himself by running one of the worst Presidential campaigns ever. Gore also ripped into Bush for coddling the Communist Chinese regime by exporting sensitive satellite technology to it. Both Clinton and Gore bashed Bush for putting *realpolitik* and trade above human rights. They promised to revoke China's Most Favored Nation status if human rights violations continued. Given later developments, this criticism proved bitterly comical.[239]

Despite the Clinton-Gore campaign's lies, it easily won the Presidency on Election Day, November 2, 1992. Its 43% share of the vote was enough to beat the Bush-Quayle team's 37%, and Perot-Stockdale's 19%. Al Gore was now just a heartbeat away from the White House.

THIRTEEN

The Loyal Soldier:
The Most Powerful Vice President Ever

Bill Clinton kept his promise to hand over the portfolios for several important matters to his Vice President. He gave Al Gore responsibility for (A) White House relations with the Congress, (B) foreign relations with Russia, the Ukraine, Egypt, and South Africa, all countries vital to U.S. strategic interests, (C) nuclear arms control and SDI issues, (D) environmental issues, (E) the reinventing government and consolidation program, (F) telecommunications and computer policy, and (G) raising money for the 1996 Clinton-Gore re-election campaign.

Before assuming these responsibilities, Marty Peretz threw a lavish, pre-Inauguration party in Washington, D.C. for Al and Tipper Gore on January 19, 1993.

Don't Ask, Don't Tell

Al Gore immediately demonstrated his clout in the Clinton White House. He asked the new President to announce an executive order overturning the ban on homosexuals and lesbians in the U.S. military. He made this request during the transition period between the election and inauguration. The "raging moderate," thanks to the influence of Marty Peretz, took a militantly pro-gay position on this issue. *The New Republic* had campaigned for over a decade to overturn the military ban on homosexuality. The magazine claimed the ban represented a civil rights discrimination. It saw this radical "reform" as simply righting a persisting injustice. Issuing an executive order approving of homosexuality and lesbianism in the military ranks meant overthrowing the Uniform Code of Military Justice, or UCMJ, the statues created by Congress to govern the American military. Although Bill Clinton broached this explosive change of policy with his southern charm, it still provoked a firestorm of reaction. Sam Nunn, Clinton and Gore's DLC pal and Senate Armed Services Committee Chairman, expressed his fierce opposition. Since Nunn had proved wrong about the Gulf War,

Gore paid him little heed. Nunn's stand cost him the opportunity to be Secretary of Defense. The top defense job went instead to Gore's pliable Gulf War ally, House Armed Services Chairman, Les Aspin.

Clinton and Gore could handle Sam Nunn's resistance to gays and lesbians serving openly in the American military. General Colin Powell, Chairman of the Joint Chiefs of Staff and America's most powerful black man, was another matter entirely. Powell was enraged by this Clinton-Gore "reform." The Army General quickly used his prestige to put the Commander-in-Chief and the Vice President on the defensive with a pre-emptive strike. Powell openly announced: "Open homosexuality would have a very negative effect on military morale and discipline."[240] Behind the scenes, Powell twisted arms and whipped up respectable opinion. Other members of the Joint Chiefs openly expressed their disagreement with President Clinton. Democrat, as well, as Republican Members of the Congress protested allowing avowed homosexuals and lesbians to serve in the U.S. military. Opinion polls showed heavy majorities of the American people opposed "reforming" the American military to allow open gays and lesbians to serve. After encountering this bitter resistance to the proposed change in military regulations, Bill Clinton began to back off.

However, his implacable Vice President had only begun to fight. Al Gore obstinately persisted in the effort to overturn the military's ban on homosexuals and lesbians. He appeared on the *Today* show on April 16, 1993 and pulled no punches: "Well, first of all, I'm not for the ban. I think it's an issue of discrimination, and I think that the standard ought to be of behavior, not status. And I feel very strongly about that."[241]

Gore revealed his true fanatical self in this *Today* interview. He refused to consider any opinion or conviction other than his own view on gays in the military.

In private, Gore kept pushing to overturn the ban. But Bill Clinton betrayed his Vice President's grim crusade for gay liberation. Clinton thought the violent reaction to overturning the ban endangered his re-election. So he compromised on the matter by ordering Defense Department official Jamie Gorelick to craft the now famous "don't ask, don't tell" policy with Congressional leaders and the Joint Chiefs. The military would not ask recruits if they were homosexual or lesbian, and the recruits, if they were of that persuasion, would not admit it. This legalistic cop-out replaced the unambiguous UCMJ policy of banning same sex inclinations or behavior. Gore seethed at this Clintonesque compromise but kept quiet. And the compromise's author, Jamie Gorelick, was rewarded with the third-ranking post at Justice.

Did Gore remember his own earlier comments on homosexuality during the 1970s and 1980s? While making his first House run in 1976, candidate Gore: "says he is opposed to removing legislation regarding the 'abnormal' practice of homosexuality, but says it is 'senseless' to try and enforce such laws.[242]

Eight years later, while making his first Senate run, the same candidate sounded the same theme: "I don't pretend to have an understanding of homosexuality that sustains a discussion of its roots....but I do not believe it is simply an acceptable alternative that society should affirm."[243]

In 1987, Al Gore commented again on homosexuality while making his first run for the Presidency. He opposed providing specific legal protection for sexual preference: "I also do not think we need a bill to protect the specific category—that is, sexual preference."[244]

Five years after opposing specific legal protection for sexual preference, Gore flip-flopped. He was now insisting on legal protection for same sex preference in the American military, a branch of society demanding absolute obedience in order to function. Apparently, Gore opposed homosexuality in his early years only to appease his conservative constituents in Tennessee. He told Tennessee voters what they wanted to hear only in order to get elected.

The Largest Tax Raise in History

Gores demonstrated anew he was a tax and spend liberal in 1993. Clinton and his economic advisers proposed a budget with huge tax increases. Senator Daniel Patrick Moynihan, the Democratic Chairman of the Senate Finance Committee, criticized Clinton's plan as "the largest tax increase in the history of public finance in the United States or anywhere else in the world." [245] Clinton agonized over the political effect his 1993 tax hikes would exert on the 1994 elections. His foreboding on that score turned out to be accurate. The Republicans seized control of both Houses of Congress for the first time in four decades in

1994. But Al Gore bluntly urged him "Get with the G-------n program!" [246]

Gore sulked because his pet tax on energy consumption, based on British Thermal Units, or BTU's, had passed the House in 1993 but was killed in the Senate by Democrats from oil and coal producing states. Clinton's Secretary of the Treasury, Lloyd Bentsen, a close friend of the oil industry, encouraged these Senators to reject Gore's BTU tax. If the BTU tax had passed, as Bentsen wisely recognized, it probably would have triggered a recession. Gore neglected to prepare the legislative ground for this unpopular energy tax. He just arrogantly assumed it would sail through with the rest of Clinton's 1993 tax increases because he authored it. The BTU tax's defeat left him crushed and cautious.[247] *Earth in the Balance*'s author decided to regulate oil drilling to control the supply for fossil fuels on the supply end since his BTU tax would not be passed to control it on the demand end.

Gore worked hard to push through Clinton's batch of tax increases. When the Senate tied 50-50 on the Clinton tax increase bill, Vice President Gore presided over the Senate to cast the deciding vote. Gore, like Clinton and his economic advisers, justified the tax increases as necessary to balance the federal budget. But Al Gore had always voted in the House and Senate against balanced budget amendments aiming to prevent Congressional deficit spending.[248] Only once in his career did he vote for a balanced budget amendment. The one bill he supported tried to assign all responsibility for federal spending to the President, a solution that was clearly unconstitutional.[249] Gore revealed his genuine view of balanced budgets while running for President in December 1987: "Americans have many cares and many concerns, only one of which is balancing the federal budget. We cannot let any one of those vital concerns keep us from doing the things we must do to protect the nation's security, to hone our competitive edge, or to meet immediate and inescapable needs."[250]

By constantly surrendering to "immediate and inescapable needs," Federal politicians like Al Gore created a four trillion-dollar national debt. The new Vice President, unlike President Ronald Reagan, believed expanding government was the best way to solve human ills. Al Gore has spent almost his entire adult life either holding or running for Federal office. A permanent Federal office holder will rarely, if ever, vote to keep spending within means.

Corruption: From Russia With Love

When the Ukraine split from the Soviet Empire after 1991, an explosive problem emerged. Many Soviet nuclear missiles were still stationed within the former satellite country's borders, and the Russian government wanted the missiles returned to them. The Ukrainians preferred keeping the missiles to deter Russia from trying to re-conquer them. Gore played a key role in persuading the Ukrainian President, Leonid Kravchuck, to return the nuclear missiles back to Russia.[251] Whether Gore's intervention with Kravchuck will help keep peace between the Ukraine and Russia remains to be seen.

But Al Gore did inflict lasting damage on American policy toward Russia. He and Deputy Secretary of State Strobe Talbott, a Clinton crony since they were both Rhodes Scholars, both backed the wrong horse in Russian Prime Minister Victor Chernomyrdin. Chernomyrdin was a corrupt, incompetent ruler. Yet Gore and Talbott wrongly saw him as the man indispensable to reforming Russia. Chernomyrdin, they thought, would undertake Russia's much needed conversion to free market economics. They believed in the Russian Prime Minister though he was known to praise Joseph Stalin's memory.[252]

Gore and Talbott spent much time persuading Chernomyrdin to privatize the Russian economy and expand trade with the U.S. The two men also lavished American tax dollars to help Chernomyrdin enact reforms. They pressed the International Monetary Fund (IMF), to pour billions of dollars in foreign aid to Russia. Chernomyrdin supervised the flow of this cash. He also oversaw the technological assistance offered by the American government. Chernomyrdin assured Gore and Talbott he agreed with their aims. He promised them both Russia was becoming a liberal democracy of limited government and a vibrant private sector. Gore and Talbott naively believed Chernomyrdin's promises. They both boasted of their close personal relationships with the Russian Prime Minister. The "Chernomyrdin Channel," as they referred to it, guaranteed close and beneficial relations between the two former enemy superpowers. The U.S. and Russia would march happily together toward the future in a "strategic partnership."[253] This phrase, "strategic partnership," was hauled out again by the Clinton Administration to characterize the American relationship with the People's Republic of China. A strategic partnership with Russia, in Gore and Talbott's thinking, meant trust, cooperation, and affection would replace the former Cold War attitudes of rivalry and mutual suspicion.

Gore and Talbott's utopian vision proved mistaken. Russia today combines the worst features of both communism and capitalism. Political and economic corruption flourishes. The Russian Mafia, comprising many former KGB officials, operates many protection rackets and murders anyone who criticizes them or refuses to make payoffs. Their organized crime network extends around the world. The Russian Mafia's tentacles reach even into the U.S. They control many narcotics rings, nude dancing clubs, and even National Hockey Association players.[254] Thanks to Victor Chernomyrdin looking the other way, many billions of dollars in foreign aid was siphoned off by the Russian Mafia into numbered Swiss bank accounts. The IMF funds pumped in to prop up Russia's currency did not reach its intended recipients.

The CIA gathered extensive evidence for several years on Chernomyrdin's personal corruption and his relations to organized crime. After compiling "conclusive evidence of the personal corruption" of Chernomyrdin, the Agency wrote up a secret report in 1995 and sent it to the White House. A *New York Times* story in November 1998 reported Gore's reaction to the CIA's report: "Instead, when the secret CIA report on Mr. Chernomyrdin arrived in the office of Vice President Gore, it was rejected and sent back to the CIA with a barnyard epithet scrawled across its cover...At CIA headquarters in Langley, Va., the message seemed clear: The Vice President did not want to hear allegations that Mr. Chernomyrdin was corrupt and was not interested in further intelligence reports on the matter...As a result, CIA analysts say they are now censoring themselves. When, for instance, the agency found that it cost a German business executive $1 million just to get a meeting with Mr. Chernomyrdin to discuss deals in Russia, it decided not to circulate the report outside the CIA officials said."[255]

Prince Albert refused to believe anything derogatory about his crony Victor Chernomyrdin. After all, Chernomyrdin resembled Gore's late patron, Armand Hammer. Al Gore's reaction to the CIA report resembled a Chinese emperor executing a messenger bringing bad news. As *The Moscow Times* commented on the same story: "The message was—and is—that President Bill Clinton, Gore, and other high-ranking U.S. officials are not interested in any information that would question their decision to deal with Chernomyrdin and other Russian leaders on a close, personal basis." [256]

Three long years after Gore received the CIA's dossier on Chernomyrdin, President Boris Yeltsin asked the Duma, the Russian Parliament, to reappoint Chernomyrdin as his Prime Minister. By that time, thanks to many of Chernomyrdin's policies, the Russian stock market had collapsed and the economy was in tatters. Most of the Duma reacted to the bad news by reverting to their anti-market Marxist leaders. They decisively rejected Chernomyrdin. Yeltsin was forced to fire him in March 1998. Gore's uncritical embrace of Chernomyrdin backfired. The Vice President was unable to prevent the Russians from shipping arms to America's enemies. "Russia...continues to export weaponry abroad no matter what the Gore-Chernomyrdin Commission decides on paper," [257] Jacob Heilbrunn of *The New Republic* observed. The Russian people were more hostile to the U.S. than they were in 1993. They saw the American government favor a corrupt Prime Minister allied with the Russian Mafia. As David Remnick, a Russia expert, put it: "Chernomyrdin represents a longed-for predictability abroad, but to Russians he represents the worst of Yeltsin's government: corruption, privilege, and an almost delusional disregard for the public." [258]

Al Gore's bad judgment reinforced the worst elements in Russian public life. Incredibly enough, Gore continues to socialize with Chernomyrdin and to consult him for advice on Russian affairs. Gore gushed last year about his corrupt Russian crony in an unintentionally comic manner: "There's just no doubt that we have the ability to talk with one another in total candor and in total confidence that neither is trying to pull the wool over the other's eyes." [259]

On the 2000 campaign trail Gore constantly calls attention to his superior understanding of foreign policy.

The Uranium Deals with Russia

Gore cut Chernomyrdin into another lucrative deal. This deal involved weapons-grade uranium necessary for producing nuclear weapons. Russia and its former satellites possessed the world's largest arsenal of nuclear weapons and nuclear grade material. Clinton sent Gore to Russia to negotiate an agreement to manage its nuclear weapons and nuclear material. The two politicians worked out a $12 billion twenty-year agreement. The deal pledged the U.S. Enrichment Corporation (USEC), a federal agency, to buy highly-enriched, weapons-grade uranium from Russia, then convert it to lower grade uranium suitable for reactors in American power plants. This deal supplied the cash-poor Russian government with dollars to pay its nuclear scientists. Paying the Russian scientists kept them happy so they did not offer their expertise to unfriendly governments such as Iran, Iraq, or North Korea. The weapons grade nuclear material would thus be under the control of the United States.[260]

This uranium deal worked well until 1996. That year Congress privatized the USEC. Thomas Neff, the MIT weapons expert who designed the uranium deal, protested against the privatization of the USEC. The action would result in less cash for the Russian uranium. Some Russian officials might be tempted to sell the uranium for more cash to the rogue regimes of Iran, Iraq, and North Korea. Vice President Gore could have stopped privatization of USEC if he had lobbied against it. Considering Gore's fanatical enthusiasm for the public sector, it seemed puzzling he had eagerly signed off on privatizing the USEC as part of his "reinventing government" project.

After USEC was sold for $1.9 billion, it went public and sold its shares to investors. Gore's willingness to privatize it became clear. Wall Street investment bankers and large law and lobbying firms friendly to the Clinton Administration cashed in big for $75 million in underwriting, legal, and lobbying fees. J.P. Morgan & Company, one of the investment bankers involved, hired Gore's former domestic policy adviser, Greg Simon, for $10,000 a month to help it select the newly privatized company's directors.[261] But USEC's going private affected its original mission of keeping weapons-grade uranium under control. The price of uranium plummeted as USEC was glutted with supply of the substance. The Russian authorities, protested at the drop in price. They threatened to send their weapons-grade uranium to unfriendly countries.

So, the Clinton White House added a $325 million sweetener to the Russian government to compensate for the drop in price. These supplemental bribes will have to be paid until 2015. Thomas Neff estimates the total cost for buying the uranium back from Russia will cost $2.1 billion, or $200 million more than USEC sold for. So much for "reinventing government" and making it less costly. Gore accomplished his real mission; he secured future campaign cash and good will from rich banking, law, and lobbying firms. However, Gore continues to uphold the Clinton Administration's observance of the now irrelevant ABM Treaty of 1972.[262]

The Environment Czar

Gore's former aide, Carol Browner, serves as the nominal chief of the Environment Protection Agency. Bruce Babbitt serves as the nominal Secretary of the Interior. Dan Glickman serves as the nominal Secretary of Agriculture. But the real power over EPA's, Interior's, and Agriculture's land management is exercised by Al Gore. The U.S. Forest Service, a bureau of the Agriculture Department, recently developed a proposal to ban the building of roads through 60 million acres of the country's national forests. The House Resources Committee traced the Forest Service's proposal back to an illegal collaboration between the White House, the Department of Agriculture, and environmental activist groups. The Resources Committee reported on February 21, 2000 that the environmental groups provided "draft language, legal memoranda, and survey research data to the administration officials." The chief Administration official named in organizing the proposal was White House Chief of Staff John Podesta.[263] Podesta's boss Bill Clinton delegated all environmental matters to Vice President Gore. So, the illegally created proposal is probably Al Gore's brainchild.

The national forest proposal is not the first or even the most important of Clinton White House executive orders concerning the environment. The executive orders creating vast national monuments out of Western states and restricting offshore drilling along the Florida and California coasts also result from Gore initiatives. Gore deserves much responsibility for reducing the number of oil drilling rigs in the U.S. from 530 to less than 135. The Vice President knows he cannot impose his radical environmental agenda through congressional legislation. There are just too many evil Republican reactionaries in the Congress seeking to pollute our air and water. So, he resorts to Presidential executive orders or illegal collaborations such as the one discussed in the paragraph above.[264]

The Kyoto Negotiations

Al Gore did not settle for regulating only American energy production. He also tried to regulate the entire world's use of fossil fuels. Environmental activists in Europe and North America managed to stage a global summit on global warming in Kyoto, Japan during early December 1997. 160 countries sent delegations to this conference on a problem many reputable scientists do not consider serious. Developing countries such as the People's Republic of China and India resented environmental standards being imposed upon them. As usually happens at most world conferences, little agreement could be reached on a way to enforce standards on countries that wanted to disregard them.

Few sensible people took the Kyoto conference and its decisions seriously. The United States Senate wisely decided not to accept any agreement negotiated at Kyoto that: (1) refused to hold developing countries to the same emissions standards as industrialized countries, or (2) imposed serious economic hardship on American society. The Senate vote was 95-0. The Senate signaled by this vote its unanimous refusal to abide by the kind of treaty likely to be negotiated at Kyoto.

Gore has done much to fan the flames of "global warming" hysteria and wanted to save face for his efforts. Gore flew out to Kyoto determined to make the U.S. a signatory to whatever global warming treaty the Kyoto conference devised. Gore authorized the American delegation at Kyoto to display "increased negotiating flexibility." [265] So Gore led the U.S. to sign a treaty which the Senate had already unanimously warned it would not ratify. The utopian treaty pledged the U.S. to cut its greenhouse gas production by one third between 2008 and 2012, thus putting two million people out of work and ending economic expansion in order to solve a problem few quality scientists thought existed. Senate Republicans drooled over the prospect of voting the Kyoto treaty down before the 2000 elections. Clinton and Gore refused to submit the treaty to the Senate for that reason. Gore pretended not to notice that his Kyoto effort was a delusion. He had saved face, and that was what mattered to him.

Reinventing Government

Clinton gave Gore the task of reorganizing the federal bureaucracy to make it leaner and more efficient. The President hoped to mollify the Perot voters with this reorganization and his deficit reduction tax plan so they returned to the Democrat fold in 1996. Gore knew the President did not expect him to produce more than cosmetic changes that presented a good image for the new Administration. Both men spent almost all their adult lives on public payrolls. Neither of them can intellectually conceive of any activity that does not require government supervision. Besides, Clinton and Gore both recognized how most Federal civilian bureaucrats or contract employees voted Democratic. It would be folly to alienate such a key Democratic constituency. So, Gore set out to make some cosmetic changes in the Federal work force.

President Clinton called his new reorganization effort The National Performance Review. He announced it on March 3, 1993 with Gore at his side. Under Gore's guidance, the Review intended to create a government that "works better, costs less, and gets results Americans care about." The wonder is that more people did not laugh out loud when Clinton uttered these words.

Gore solemnly followed up on his boss' empty promise. On September 7, 1993, the Vice President pompously proclaimed the National Partnership for Reinventing Government (NPRG). Gore asserted the goal of the NPRG was to eliminate 252,000 jobs from the Federal budget. These jobs comprised 12% of the civilian, non-postal work force. If these positions were removed, the taxpayers were supposed to be saved $108 billion. "I think we face a unique environment where the need to get changes [sic] across the board," he said at a dry press conference. Appearing on NBC's *Today* show the next morning, Gore appeared more animated about the reinventing government charade: "We're downsizing the federal government by 12 percent, cutting the bureaucracy dramatically."

Of course, Gore's reinventing government effort was a sham. His 1999 NPRG web site declares: "Government was reduced by 351,000 positions. Reductions occurred in 13 of 14 departments. (Justice increased crime fighting.)"[266]

About three fourths of the Federal employees laid off during the Clinton-Gore Administration worked in foreign policy departments and agencies. After cutting Defense Department jobs, Clinton and Gore ordered them to perform more duties and tasks than they were equipped to do. Morale plummeted and re-enlistment rates sank.[267] But Clinton and Gore turned a deaf ear to military complaints. Both men disdained the armed services and regarded their personnel as obedient lackeys who should keep quiet. Cutting the armed forces' budgets while increasing their missions did not seem to bother Clinton and Gore. The military downsizing that made the "reinventing government" mission seem successful. With the end of the Cold War, the employees at the Defense Department and the U.S. Information Agency were headed for elimination even if George Bush had been re-elected.[268] Reagan's Cold War victory caused the Defense and U.S.I.A. cuts not a tough-minded "reinventing" government choices by Clinton and Gore.

Bill Clinton's bragged that the federal civilian work force "is the smallest it's been since John Kennedy." Columnist Robert Samuelson punctured Clinton's claim: "True. But the drop reflects the end of the Cold War-and not the 'reinventing government program.' The non-defense work force (almost 1.2 million) is nearly 40 percent higher than in 1963, when Kennedy died. It's also higher than any year before 1988, except for three years (1978-80) in the Carter presidency."[269]

The few civilian Federal cuts made by Gore's "reinventing government" mission involved lower level employees. The higher pay grade employees have actually increased both in numbers and pay. As the *Washington Post* observes: "But the one part of the reinventing effort that has touched virtually every agency—the downsizing—has not turned out as Gore planned. Although hundreds of thousands of jobs have been cut, there has been no dramatic increase in the government's management layers. In fact, it appears the bureaucracy is becoming top heavy."[270]

The *Arkansas Democrat Gazette* wrote: "The typical government employee is in a significantly higher pay grade and has received more merit raises than was normal before the White House began in 1993 to "reinvent" the government by eliminating 300,00 jobs."[271]

Gore used smoke and mirrors budgeting to lure back some Perot voters in 1996. Gore also lavished more favors on high-level Democratic federal civilian employees to keep them loyal for both Clinton's 1996 race and his own run in 2000. So Prince Albert did accomplish his mission of assisting the Democrats' election prospects. In that sense, he was right to boast that NPR "has become the largest and by far the most successful government reform effort in U.S. history[.]" [272]

Bag Man for the High Tech-Telecom Industry

Al Gore is a technocrat. Technocrats believe in using new technologies to force change upon society. Computers and telecommunications offered an effective method of using information to control the direction of the future. The complexity and novelty of both these industries appealed to Gore's love of the abstract. Gore took the trouble to master the intricacies of computer systems so he could talk to the people who designed and operated them. Gore's desire to please the high tech business executives was less than altruistic. He wisely prophesied how rich and powerful these high tech gurus would become in the future cybernetic world. If his high tech wonks hit the jackpot, they would remember how Gore listened closely to them when most people dismissed them.

Gore's gamble on high tech turned out to be right. With his usual modesty, arrogant Al claimed "During my service in the United States Congress, I took the initiative in creating the Internet." [273] Even for Al Gore this constitutes a monstrous exaggeration. The founder of the Internet was actually the U.S. Army. In 1969, the Army set up a worldwide computer network, the ARPANET, for its supply-logistics system. *The Almanac of American Politics, 2000* puts Gore's contribution to the Internet fairly: "if he exaggerated when he claimed to be responsible for 'creating' the Internet, he did much to promote it." [274] Gore's role was to promote, not create, a worldwide Internet modeled on previous networks like the ARPANET. Al Gore could not settle for just calling himself a promoter. He had to describe himself as an inventor comparable to Thomas Edison, Alexander Graham Bell, or Guglielmo Marconi.

Although Gore is no technical genius, high tech executives appreciated his hard work for them. As they say in their high tech lingo, Gore "gets it" about their thriving new industries. [275] The high tech executives share Gore's New Age approach to shaping the future. Silicon Valley, the high tech industry sprawl near San Jose, California, became Gore Country. The Vice President tapped these executives for campaign cash during Clinton's 1992 run. The high tech fat cats now enjoy a close relationship with both Gore and his boss.

Gore's Vice Presidential staff calls these Democrat Silicon Valley donors the "Gore tech" group. They comprise 15 of California's leading computer and telecom executives. Since 1997 the "Gore tech" group flies to Washington for regular monthly meetings with the Vice President. This group meets with Gore to discuss their needs and preferences regarding Federal regulation and taxing. The executives include: Marc Andreessen, the Chief Technology Officer of America Online, Inc.; Scott Cook, Chairman of Intuit, Inc.; Charles Geschke, President of Adobe Sytems, Inc.; Chris Larsen, President of E*loan, an online loan service company; Sanford Robertson, founder of Robertson Stephens & Company, an investment bank based in Silicon-Valley and a founder of E* Offering, an online trading company; and L. John Doerr, partner in Kleiner, Perkins Caulfield and Byers, a venture capital firm in Silicon Valley.[276] All these high tech power brokers made the maximum contribution of $5000 to Gore's Leadership 1998 PAC war chest for his 2000 Presidential run. Since 1992, Sanford Robertson has donated the enormous sum of $503,100 to the Democratic Party and its individual candidates. Over the same period, the "Gore tech" group gave $1,397,373 to Democrats, a majority of it to the D.N.C.

The group got full value for their cash contributions. Thanks to their lobbying and donations, every American who makes a telephone call since January 1, 1998 must pay a 3% flat tax. Al Gore and his St. Albans School friend, Reed Hundt, then Chairman of the Federal Communications Commission, or FCC, deserve blame for this tax. They devised it as a method to fulfill Gore's demand that every school in the U.S. be accessible to the Internet. This "E-rate" tax raises $2.3 billion a year. Its revenue, after administrative costs eat up much of it, will be passed on to the schools by way of a Federal bureaucracy. Thanks to the regulating power of the FCC, Hundt was able to impose the 3% tax without a Congressional vote. He did it by bureaucratic fiat.[277]

Although it is a wonderful tool for schoolchildren to learn with, neither Gore nor Hundt asked the American people or local school boards whether Internet access was necessary. The two prep school buddies just arrogantly assumed their tax was in the public's best interest. They both also knew the tax served the interests of Gore's Silicon Valley donors. The "Gore tech" group now possessed a lucrative market for its services in the schools.

While the "Gore tech" gang exulted over its good fortune, long-distance carriers and the regional Bell operating companies protested their misfortune. They complained so effectively that Hundt and the FCC allowed them to pass on more than 80% of the tax's cost to the long distance carriers. It is no coincidence two of them, Bell South and Bell Atlantic, rank second and thirteenth among Al Gore's career patrons.[278] The Vice President was not beholden by campaign cash to the long distance carriers, such as AT&T, MCI, and Sprint. So he and Reed Hundt ignored their pleas.

The long distance carriers bitterly resented having to bear almost all the burden of an undemocratically imposed tax. So they retaliated against the FCC by carefully itemizing the E-rate tax cost, and who imposed it, on all their bills. Enraged long distance customers raised a clamor to the FCC. Vice President Gore hammered the long distance carriers and their customers' tit for tat. He ordered the FCC, packed with his political cronies, to forbid the carriers to itemize the charge on their bills. Like a Soviet commissar, Gore figured there would be no fuss over the tax if it were hidden.[279]

This "hidden" tax hits the average telephone customer for $30 a year. Before the money eventually goes to the schools, it takes an intermediate stop at the Schools and Libraries Corporation. The Schools and Libraries Corporation is one of the three non-profit operations created to run the "E-rate" program. Gore crony and White House lobbyist Ira Fishman ran the SLC, which began in November 1997, from its founding until September 1998. Fishman proved too incompetent and he resigned. However, he drew a $200,000 annual salary and $50,000 "performance bonus" for his failed effort. Fishman also managed to spend $ 4.4 million with no benefit to anyone. The General Accounting Office even charged the SLC was illegal.[280] FCC Commissioner Harold Furchtgott-Roth, a conservative Republican who was not a Gore crony, slammed the costs of the SLC and the other two non-profit operations as "exorbitant and unjustified."[281]

Furchtgott-Roth's criticism was accurate. However, in one of the many wasteful Federal-big business scams characterizing the Clinton-Gore Presidency, E-rate went forward. As Charles Lewis, the renowned watchdog of influence peddling puts it: "Now that the 'E-rate' program is up and running, some of Gore's top patrons have climbed aboard the gravy train. Bell South and Bell

Atlantic each made millions of dollars providing telephone lines to schools. So did software companies like The Learning Company, a division of Mattel Inc., which makes educational software and Cyber Patrol, a program that blocks students from accessing pornographic sites from school. The Learning Company, Gore's No. 7 career patron, offers a discount on its Cyber Patrol program to schools participating in the E-rate program. And, of course, connecting all those classrooms—some two million of them—to the Internet won't accomplish much without the computers, monitors, hardware, and software needed to surf the Web. Hundreds of high-tech companies—from chip makers like Intel Corporation to software companies like Netscape and Microsoft Corporation—stand to profit handsomely from E-rate."[282]

The E-rate program profits Gore's high tech patrons. They make a killing on it. However, it will do little or nothing to solve the verbal and mathematical illiteracy of American children. If a child cannot read or write, hooking up to the Internet will not benefit him.

Al Gore will always shill for the unions and bureaucracies who vote for Democrats. After all, he, Tipper, and his four children were all rich enough to attend exclusive private schools like St. Albans, Sidwell Friends, St. Agnes, or the National Cathedral School. The "E-rate" program, like most Clinton-Gore "reforms," is not designed to benefit the general public. It is aimed at rewarding fundraising patrons such as the "Gore tech" group. The program also seeks to reward Gore cronies like former FCC Chairman Reed Hundt. In 1999, according to *The Washington Post*, Hundt raked in $2 million.[283] In practice, the Clinton-Gore Administration aims at "Putting Powerful People First."

Exploiting Nancy's Death from Lung Cancer

As we learned in Chapter 9, Al Gore liked to brag about his relationship with tobacco. Even after his sister Nancy died of lung cancer in 1984 caused by smoking, Gore continued to accept PAC money from tobacco lobbies and to grow tobacco on his farm. From 1979-1990, he accepted $16,440 from tobacco PAC's.

As the Clinton Administration decided to wage war against the tobacco companies, Gore flip-flopped on the tobacco issue. He got with the program and began to excoriate every facet of the tobacco industry. Gore hit a new low by deliberately exploiting Nancy's death in his Vice Presidential nomination acceptance speech at the 1996 Democratic Convention in Chicago. He vowed, "until I draw my last breath, I will pour my heart and soul into the cause of protecting our children from the dangers of smoking."[284] Al Gore did not mention how he enriched himself from the smoking habit during the first half of his life.

Quickie Citizenship for Immigrants

The Clinton-Gore team was elected with only 43% of the vote in 1992. In order to ensure their re-election in 1996, they needed more votes than they received in 1992. What better way to accomplish this, than to literally create new voters? Vice President Gore set himself in April 1995 to naturalizing immigrant voters who could be counted on to vote for the Democrats in 1996. He established "Citizenship USA," designed to accelerate the naturalizing process for immigrants by eliminating legal logjams.[285]

As the *Los Angeles Times* revealed, the real reason Al Gore enacted "Citizenship USA" was articulated by one of his aides: "[A] top aide to the vice president proposed ways to 'lower the standards for citizenship' and acknowledged that the program could be viewed as 'a pro-Democratic voter mill.'"[286]

Gore was eager to conquer the Republicans with an accelerated citizenship process in 1996. The Vice President added 1.3 million voters to the rolls with "Citizenship USA" but in his haste he naturalized many who were criminals.

In a blistering editorial, *The Wall Street Journal* wrote: "INS [Immigration and Naturalization Service] officials presided over shocking lapses in 'Citizenship USA,' a crash program to clear immigration bottlenecks that resulted in 180,000 people becoming citizens without proper background checks before the 1996 election. It was later found that at least 5,000 of these new citizens had been arrested for felonies."[287]

Vice President Gore does not worry about whether he helped felons to gain citizenship and the vote. He only worries if they betray his hard work and vote Republican.

Cutting Corners with Big Labor

The 1996 Clinton-Gore campaign needed to mobilize labor unions to win re-election. It was easy to win the endorsements of the AFL-CIO and the United Food and Commercial Workers, or UFCW. John Sweeney, President of the AFL-CIO was a leftist Democrat who hated Republicans and free markets. Douglas Dority, President of the UFCW, thought much like Sweeney. Clinton-Gore 1996 did not need to do much to win these old unions backing, especially when Republicans controlled both Houses of Congress.

Securing the backing of the teachers unions demanded loyalty to the status quo. Because Clinton and Gore both opposed school vouchers, teacher testing, pupil testing, and any other measure aimed at making public schools accountable for their performance, they easily won the endorsement of the two large teachers' unions: the mighty National Education Association, or NEA; and the smaller American Federation of Teachers, or AFT.

Of course, neither Clinton nor Gore believed public schools effectively educated children. They indicated their real attitude to public schools by enrolling Chelsea Clinton and the four Gore children in expensive, exclusive private schools such as Sidwell Friends, the National Cathedral School, and Al Gore's own alma mater, St. Albans. Clinton and Gore were not concerned if their fellow Americans' children were not learning how to read, write, or calculate. They were only concerned with winning the NEA's and AFT's endorsements.

Vice President Gore's Reinventing Government sham earned him and Clinton the gratitude of Gerald McEntee, President of the American Federation of State, County and Municipal Employees, or AFSCME. McEntee recognized Clinton and Gore did not want to reduce government or hold its employees accountable. McEntee decided to help the Clinton-Gore campaign by obtaining the endorsement of the largest and most notorious labor union, the International Brotherhood of the Teamsters.

Teamsters' President Ron Carey had a problem. Like the Clinton-Gore team, he faced a tough re-election in 1996. His opponent, James Hoffa, was the son of the most famous and important President of the Teamsters, Jimmy Hoffa. To beat

Hoffa, Carey needed lots of cash contributions. McEntee, McEntee's subordinate Andy Stern of the AFSCME International Division, and Rich Trumka, the Secretary-Treasurer of the AFL-CIO, cooked up a complex scheme to assist Ron Carey's re-election. These three union officials worked with Clinton's top fundraiser, Terry McAuliffe, the Finance Chairman of Clinton-Gore '96, to illegally embezzle money from the Teamsters' treasury, launder it by donating it to Democratic political organizations, then order the latter to donate it to Ron Carey's re-election campaign. The Democratic organizations acted as straw donors for the laundered Teamsters funds. McAuliffe worked directly with Carey's subordinate, William Hamilton, the Teamsters' Governmental Affairs Director, to accomplish the scam. McAuliffe has played complex games with union pension funds before, often for his personal financial benefit.[288] McAuliffe is most famous for lending Bill and Hillary Clinton the money to buy a house in Chappaqua, New York, for Hillary's 2000 Senate run. He also played a leading role in the infamous White House Coffees of the Clinton-Gore 1996 campaign. The Teamsters money laundering scam helped elect both Clinton and Carey in 1996.

However, Hoffa cried foul at the crooked Teamsters' election. The Justice Department investigated, discovered Hoffa's complaint had merit, negated the results of the union election, and indicted William Hamilton. Hamilton was convicted of defrauding the United States, embezzlement, wire fraud, lying to the FEC, and perjury. Evidence obtained in Hamilton's trial also placed direct responsibility for the Teamsters fundraising scam on McEntee, Stern, McAuliffe, and McAuliffe's two subordinates at the DNC, Laura Hartigan and Richard Sullivan. All five of these officials play leading roles in the Gore 2000 campaign. McEntee and Stern ordered their unions to endorse Gore before the primaries, and McAuliffe, Hartigan, and Sullivan are all working to raise money for Gore's campaign.[289] Al Gore's campaign will be quite embarrassed if any of these five figures are indicted for their parts in the Teamsters election swindle.

The Solicitor-in-Chief: Clinton-Gore Looks East

Thanks to its own foolishness, the Clinton-Gore Administration provoked a bitter backlash in the 1994 Congressional elections. The Republicans seized control of the

House for the first time in forty years, and grabbed back the Senate they lost in 1986. Bill Clinton and Al Gore's grand schemes for further socialism were now stymied. It was at this time that Clinton turned to Dick Morris, the Republican political consultant for help. Morris used his "triangulation" tactic to gain time for Clinton and help him win re-election in 1996. "Triangulation" is the tactic of falsely accusing the Republicans of "threatening" Social Security and Medicare in the 1996 Presidential election. This tactic demanded a huge sum of money up front for television advertising. This money was "soft money," i.e., money used for political issue advocacy. Soft money can be raised in unlimited amounts and is relatively unregulated. Hard money is campaign money directed to a specific candidate and is carefully regulated. Clinton and Gore set out to bombard the electorate with television commercials accusing the Republicans of ruining Social Security and Medicare. They ended up spent $40 million on these television ads that ran constantly during 1996.[290]

To obtain all this cash, Bill Clinton asked his Vice President for help. Gore had established connections with Maria Hsia and her clients back in 1988, as we mentioned in Chapter 9. Clinton also knew Gore possessed many more fundraising contacts than the President himself did. Not coincidentally, Bill Clinton already knew James Riady and John Huang of the Lippo Group, two associates of Hsia. Gore organized the fundraising operations by Hsia, Riady, and Huang to get cash from Communist Chinese officials and front businesses to ensure the Clinton-Gore Administration's 1996 re-election. Gore got Clinton to make lobbyist Peter Knight, Gore's former aide, campaign manager of the 1996 Clinton-Gore campaign. Knight acted as the ringleader of the elaborate conspiracy to evade the federal election laws.[291]

Knight worked with Hsia, Riady, and Huang to organize the infamous White House coffees and Lincoln Bedroom visits. At these affairs, Communist Chinese nationals, usually not knowing a word of English, got to meet Clinton and Gore in exchange for donating cash to the campaign or the Democratic National Committee. Of course, since almost all of these donors were *not* U.S. citizens, the cash contributions were illegal under American election laws. Hsia, Riady, Huang, and Democratic fund raising officials tried to launder the hundreds of thousands of dollars in illegal foreign money by putting the cash donations in the names of American citizens serving as "straw donors," then reimbursing the straw donors from their personal accounts. At the notorious Buddhist temple fundraiser in Hacienda Heights, California, the Buddhist nuns wrote out checks in their own names to the DNC. Then Hsia, Huang, and other American citizens involved in the scam reimbursed the nuns and monks for their pains.

Al Gore, Mr. Clean according to his carefully crafted image, did not worry himself about breaking the law. Gore participated in the 1996 campaign fund raising scandal in order to get re-elected and retain power. As Bob Woodward, the *Washington Post* expert on political scandals, writes: "Gore played the central role in soliciting millions of dollars in campaign money for the Democratic Party during the 1996 election.... Gore became known at the DNC[Democratic National Committee] as the administration's 'solicitor-in-chief'"[292]

Al Gore outperformed his father when it came to selling out America's interests to a foreign totalitarian dictatorship. The Red Chinese were incredulous at the White House access they enjoyed from the Clinton-Gore Administration.

Dire consequences flowed from the Clinton-Gore decision to rent out the White House to the agents of foreign Asian governments. The People's Republic of China began bullying Taiwan in a way not seen since the 1950s. When Red China threatened Taiwan and the small islands of Quemoy and Matsu in the late 50s, President Eisenhower threatened them with nuclear attack. The PRC calmed its actions and rhetoric immediately then. Now the PRC refused to take Clinton's bluffs seriously. Its rulers maintained steady pressure on Taiwan to submit to its rule. Red China also continued its aggressive espionage efforts in the U.S. to learn American nuclear and high technology secrets.

The Clinton-Gore team responded to Chinese aggressiveness with more appeasement. In March 1997, Gore visited Beijing to reassure the Communist Chinese Politburo. He asked the Chinese rulers to buy more American products. Then the Vice President raised his champagne glass in a toast to Communist China's Prime Minister, Li Peng. Li Peng had ordered the massacre of the student demonstrators thronging Tiananmen Square in 1989. Just days later, an opponent of Gore addressed the Chinese dictators in franker terms: "In March 1997 [Republican Speaker Newt] Gingrich traveled to China and articulated bluntly to its leaders basic American policies which

Vice President Al Gore just days before had been at pains to slough over[.]"[293]

Gore forgot his own words uttered in 1991 against George Bush's conciliation of the PRC: "[Bush] placed so much importance on that principle [geopolitics] that he sent close associates to have a very pleasant exchange of views and even raise their glasses in toast to those who were responsible for Tiananmen Square, very soon after the tragedy occurred."[294]

Once again, "Putting People First" meant putting only powerful people first.

Senator Bob Kerrey, D-Nebraska, Clinton's most bitter critic in the Democratic Party, was revolted by the Clinton-Gore courting of Red China. Kerrey, a Vietnam War Medal of Honor winner and amputee, did not bother to hide his indignation at the admittance of Communist Chinese agents into the White House: "We invited agents of foreign governments into coffees at the White House, at a time when critical national-security decisions were being made, and being made about China. It was embarrassing, and it made me sick."[295]

FOURTEEN

The Solicitor in Chief : Gore's Defense of Clinton Administration Scandals

We do not want to overwhelm our readers with the multiple scandals of the Clinton-Gore Administration. So we will confine ourselves to analyzing the major scandals in which Al Gore played a leading role. We will also study how Al Gore tried to defend indefensible acts committed by himself and his boss, Bill Clinton.

No Controlling Legal Authority

Bill Clinton and Al Gore broke almost all existing federal fundraising laws to win the 1996 Presidential election over Bob Dole, 49% to 41%. Peter Knight, Gore's trusted friend and aide since 1977, oversaw these fundraising abuses as Chairman of the 1996 Clinton-Gore campaign. The two main abuses involved: illegally accepting funds from foreign nationals, most of whom were agents, or even high officials, of the People's Republic of China; and Vice President Al Gore's lying to the FBI about his illegal Dialing for Dollars program of calling for donations from the White House, which is federal property.

Al Gore's breaking of campaign finance laws appeared to be even more serious and widespread than Clinton's. Unlike his boss, he possesses little knack for covert operations. Gore's chicanery occurs out in the open. Gore's most notorious foray was the Buddhist His Lai Temple incident in Hacienda Heights, California. Hacienda Heights is located in Orange County, just south of Los Angeles, where Maria Hsia and John Huang's based their illegal operations. The Vice President appeared there April 29, 1996 at what he lamely called "a community outreach event." This community event involved shaking down Buddhist nuns and monks, who had taken a lifelong vow of poverty, for thousands of dollars. The superior of the nuns and monks, Venerable Master Hsing Yun, the founder of the Fo Kuan Shan order, had met and dined with Gore in Taiwan in 1989. Hsing

Yun wrote a 1996 article about their meeting. In it, the Venerable Master recounted how he said to Gore in 1989: "You can become president of the U.S. He was excited upon hearing that and said 'I will visit you when I become president.'"[296] Gore visited Hsing Yun as Vice President for the purpose of shaking down the temple for money.

This visit was needed so Maria Hsia and John Huang could launder the dirty money handed to them by their Asian contacts.

Comically surrounded by saffron-clad Asian Buddhist nuns, standing in front of an immense pagoda, Gore lent his august Vice Presidential presence to an illegal laundering scam by agents of China's Communist government.

A video camera recorded a grinning Gore, wearing a flower lei, walking reverently with Hsing Yun, the Buddhist monk Master, and Maria Hsia. He gravely presented his lei to the Buddhist shrine. Then Gore posed for photos with Hsia's donors and Democrat VIP's before sitting down to lunch with the 150 attendees. One of the donors included Ted Sioeng, a Chinese émigré to Belize, who enjoys close business relations with Red China's rulers. Huang and Hsia had hurriedly solicited most of these donors to appear just the day before. Peter Knight's subordinate, Maely Tom of the DNC, joined with Huang and Hsia to help round up the donors. The only community these three money launders were reaching out to was fat cats available on short notice. Don Fowler, Chairman of the DNC, showed up to shower his official blessings on the temple event.[297]

Gore lied by claiming he did not know fundraising occurred at the temple event. The National Security Council staff found out about the event and warned him not to attend it. As a *Washington Post* story stated: "Vice President Gore's office was told by an NSC staff official to proceed with 'great, great caution' in deciding whether to attend what Gore's office explicitly described as a 'fund-raising lunch' at a Buddhist temple in Los Angeles last year....The White House dispatched Vice President Gore to the 1996 event after deciding the concerns were unfounded."[298]

Gore himself admitted on March 11, 2000 to *The New York Times* that "I made a mistake going to that temple."[299] After four years of denial, he finally admitted the truth after Maria Hsia was convicted for lying about the event. The only concern at the White House was paying the bill for all those television ads vilifying the Republicans. National security concerns ranked well down the list.

John Huang knew he was engaging in illegal activity. Huang, co-conspirator with Hsia and James Riady at laundering the illegal Asian money, testified at Hsia's Federal trial in early 2000 that she handed him an envelope containing $100,000 on April 30, 1996. This was the day after Gore's visit to the temple. Huang further testified that most of the money in the envelope was reimbursed by the temple. Reimbursement, in effect, means the illegal money was laundered. Religious institutions are forbidden by law to engage in such financial transactions. If they do, they lose their tax-exempt status. The hapless Buddhist monks and nuns were used as "straw donors" for the laundering. Prosecutors at the Hsia trial displayed evidence indicating Hsia helped arrange $65,000 in illegal reimbursements to Clinton-Gore campaign donors by using temple funds. Checks were exhibited showing how Hsia used temple funds on three occasions between 1993-1996 "to reimburse her own political donations."[300] The DNC itself tacitly admitted the money was illegal by later returning most of this dirty money to its donors.

Maria Hsia could not take back her actions, though. For lying to the Federal Election Commission about the true source of funds for the Buddhist temple event and two other Clinton-Gore fundraisers in Los Angeles and Washington, D.C., Maria Hsia was found guilty on five felony counts by a Federal D.C. jury on March 2, 2000.[301] Al Gore, in private, said he has "long enjoyed the wonderful friendship" of Maria Hsia.[302] Will Janet Reno continue to ignore Al Gore's responsibility for handing Maria Hsia a leading role in the 1996 Clinton-Gore campaign? On March 10, 2000, the *Los Angeles Times* ran a story about a memo by Charles LaBella, the Justice Department official in charge of investigating the fundraising scandals. The memo, which Reno suppressed, urged her to appoint an independent counsel to investigate Gore's role in the fundraising scandal.[303]

Al Gore also performed other illegal acts without Maria Hsia's help. Bob Woodward's sleuthing revealed Gore made fundraising phone calls from the White House for the 1996 campaign. Peter Knight, Gore's long-time hatchet man, prepared the "call sheets" listing the personal attributes and financial targets for each fat cat called by the DNC's "solicitor-in-chief." [304] Gore also lied about calling for hard money donations, even though a memo by his Deputy Chief of Staff, David Strauss, indicated some of Gore's calls were to solicit hard money campaign donations. "Count me in on the calls" was what Gore said to Strauss. Gore's flimsy excuse was that he did not hear the hard money calls discussed by Strauss since he needed to frequently visit the restroom from drinking too much iced tea. He also told the FBI agents he "did not recall" the events in question.[305] Soliciting campaign funds from Federal property violates both the 1883 Pendleton Act and the 1939 Hatch Act. Al Gore clearly broke Federal law. After Woodward broke this front page story in the *Washington Post* on March 2, 1997, Prince Albert faced a serious problem for the first time in his cautious and calculated political career.

Instead of patiently stonewalling against the truth, like his boss Bill Clinton, Gore panicked. He huddled with his counsel Charles Burson in a damage control conference. Burson was not a specialist in campaign finance laws. He did not adequately prepare his unstrung client. The next day, Gore called a press conference to spin his actions. Mike McCurry, White House Communications Director, a master of protecting Clinton from media inquiries about the Administration's many scandals, recognized Gore was not ready to deal with his own scandal. McCurry urged Gore to stall until a Clintonesque defense for his Dialing for Dollars scheme could be mounted. Gore, ever arrogant, ignored McCurry and went ahead with his press conference.

The press conference was a disaster for Gore but a feast for comedians. The Vice President exhibited all his worst qualities. He was haughty, foolish, and frightened. Instead of owning up manfully to his mistakes, he compounded them by denying them and engaging in special pleading: "My counsel—and Charles Burson (sp) is my counsel here—my counsel advised me that there is no controlling legal authority or case that says there was any violation of law whatsoever in the manner in which I asked people to contribute to our re-election campaign."[306]

Burson advised Gore to mention the phrase "no controlling legal authority" once in his spin session. Instead, Gore repeated the ridiculous phrase *seven* times. "No controlling legal authority" provided rich fodder for comedians. The phrase indelibly etched an image of bungling, self-righteous, criminality on Al Gore.

Gore lied several times in the press conference. He claimed he only made "a few" phone call solicitations from his White House office. The "few" calls actually numbered 56.[307] Gore

asserted the Hatch Act forbidding Federal employees not to
engage in politics while on federal property did not apply to him.
It does. He further claimed, "All of the charges related to the
telephone calls were made to the Democratic National
Committee." This was a lie since the White House itself later
admitted 20 of the long-distance phone solicitations were not
charged to any political credit card.[308] Kenneth Lyons, President
of the National Association of Government Employees, called on
Gore to resign for violating Federal Employee Ethics. Gore
ignored Lyons' request. Al Gore, the man in charge of reinventing
the federal government, decided to reinvent federal job ethics for
himself.

Despite abundant evidence documenting Gore's violation of
Federal employee and fundraising laws, he escaped prosecution
by the Justice Department. Janet Reno, the most corrupt
Attorney General in American history, chose to turn a blind eye
to scandals by high-ranking Clinton Administration officials.
Reno settled for pursuing small fry scapegoats taking the fall for
their bosses. She refused to hold high officials accountable for
their misdeeds. She also allowed Bill and Hillary Clinton to
determine who her key deputies were, even when they were twice
convicted felons like Webster Hubbell. Janet Reno's Justice
Department operated under the White House's close control.

Reno had already ignored Travelgate and the FBI files scandal
involving former Gore aide Craig Livingstone. Nixon aide
Charles Colson went to federal prison for examining one FBI file
without authorization. Craig Livingstone and his White House
superiors received 900 FBI files on Reagan and Bush
Administration officials and Members of Congress without a
glove being laid upon them. Clinton, Gore, and their cronies
clung to the files in order to stymie any aggressive investigations
into Clinton Administration misdeeds. Reno refused to probe
who gave Livingstone unauthorized access to such sensitive and
potentially scandalous material. She accepted the Clinton White
House's proffered explanation that the incident was a
"bureaucratic snafu."

Reno allowed Clinton, Gore, and their cronies to obfuscate
the Whitewater investigation by Independent Counsels Robert
Fiske and Kenneth Starr. Reno said nothing when Clinton's
hatchet man James Carville conducted an unprecedented public
smear campaign against Kenneth Starr's character.[309] Reno
pretended Starr was not her subordinate or responsibility. With

such a record, it was no surprise Janet Reno resisted naming an independent counsel to investigate Vice President Gore's fundraising machinations. She continued to ignore the fund raising scandal even after FBI Director Louis Freeh and Justice Department official Charles La Bella both wrote reports recommending the need for an independent counsel to probe the Clinton-Gore fundraising abuses.

The Scandals of Nathan Landow and Peter Knight

Nate Landow, at Al Gore's request, helped raise $600,000 for Bill Clinton's 1992 and 1996 elections. He was disappointed his patron had to settle for the Vice Presidency. Landow tried to establish an intimate relationship with Bill Clinton. But he was unable to become one of Clinton's many Friends of Bill, or FOB's. It seems the President disliked him. Perhaps Clinton had more than enough shady friends already. But Gore gave his favorite mobster angel a chance to earn the President's good will in 1994.

A close Clinton crony was in trouble. Independent Counsel Kenneth Starr indicted Clinton's Arkansas associate, former Deputy Attorney General at the Justice Department Webb Hubbell, for overbilling legal clients. Hubbell faced both a possible prison sentence and huge legal bills. Starr possessed enough evidence to convict Hubbell. Clinton worried that Hubbell might cooperate with Starr's investigation and finger him, Hillary, and their aides. So the Clintons ordered hush money to be paid to Hubbell. The notorious Riady family, among others, handed nearly $800,000 in hush money over to Hubbell for small or non-existent services. Landow tried help consisted in trying, in journalist Al Hunt's words, "to arrange a favorable real estate deal involving a Washington office building for the former top Justice Department official."[310] When Hunt discovered the deal in 1997, he asked Gore's office if they knew of Landow's deal. Gore's spokesman lied to Hunt: "Late yesterday, the vice president's office said Mr. Gore did not know of Mr. Landow's offer to help Mr. Hubbell."[311]

Landow also lied about the deal in a letter to *The Wall Street Journal* after Hunt's column appeared. He claimed the story "that I tried to arrange a real estate deal for Webster Hubbell is totally false and without foundation."[312] Hunt stuck to his reporting, declaring: "I know he [Landow] lied then."[313]

Landow's lying was only beginning. He and Peter Knight undertook to make more easy money from their friendship with the Vice President. The two men joined together to work a scam involving Indian reservation lands. The Cheyenne-Arapaho Indian Tribe had struggled for years to recover a petroleum-rich parcel of Oklahoma land seized from it in 1869 by the Federal government. The parcel of land boasted oil and gas reserves worth hundreds of millions of dollars. The tribe contributed $107,000 to the 1996 Clinton-Gore campaign to spur the Administration into aiding its case. But the huge sums donated by the Communist Chinese made the generous Cheyenne-Arapaho contribution seem piddling. It earned the tribe's representatives a Clinton White House luncheon, but no action.[314]

Richard Grellner, the Tribe's attorney, contacted Nathan Landow to get things moving. Landow told Grellner to pay his buddy Peter Knight a $100,000 retainer and $10,000 monthly fee to present the tribe's case to the White House. Landow also demanded a 10% cut of anything the land earned, including possible revenues from oil and natural gas. Grellner and the Tribe blanched at the Landow-Knight team's attempt to make an offer they couldn't refuse. The Tribe was already strapped for cash and could not afford Landow's price. Out in Oklahoma they had no experience dealing with shakedown artists. They were shocked enough by this incident to report it to the Senate Governmental Affairs Committee.

The Committee investigated the Cheyenne-Arapaho tribe's story about Landow-Knight's offer during 1997 and early 1998. Landow stonewalled the investigation with his usual shady methods. He urged Michael Copperthite, a Democratic fundraiser and partner with him in the Cheyenne-Arapaho scam, to lie to FBI agents investigating the tribal land deal. Landow said to Copperthite: "You're going to be contacted by Justice Department people probably and/or law enforcement people and I want to go over with you what the truth is, so that you can tell the truth."[315]

Copperthite then recounted how Landow concocted a perjurious cover story: "So then he [Landau] does this whole story that doesn't even match up to anything that happened and then says, 'Now that's the truth isn't it? You're going to tell the truth.'…He was lying to me."

Landow's advice resembles Bill Clinton's similar admonition to Monica Lewinsky about her upcoming testimony in the Paula Jones suit: "Just deny it." [316]

Landow offered Copperthite a bribe to keep quiet. The Maryland dark-angel promised his partner a job in Al Gore's 2000 Presidential campaign. As Copperthite reported: "[Mr. Landow] said, 'We're all going to be part of the big happy Gore family some day and this will all pass over.'… He was clearly telling me to keep my mouth shut, play along and I would be taken care of—or un-taken care of." [317]

Copperthite refused to follow Landow's perjurious advice or to accept his future bribe. He cooperated fully with FBI agents and the House and Senate Investigative Committees.

The Committees reported that Landow's Cheyenne-Arapaho land deal was indeed crooked. According to the investigation, "a collection of Democratic fund-raisers and operatives …fleeced" and then "abandoned" the Cheyenne-Arapaho Tribe. [318] The Democratic National Committee embarrassed by Landow's scam toward the Indians, offered to return the tribe's $107,000 donation.

Despite the Senate Governmental Committee's damning revelations, Nathan Landow stuck to his perjurious story. *Frontline*, a PBS program, interviewed the Marylander about his role in the Indian land scam. He gave an unrepentant account blaming the Cheyenne-Arapaho tribe for its own troubles: "They want the land given back to them on a platter….They brought in innocent people like me. They're a bunch of goddamned uneducated Indians." [319]

Al Gore's close friend is not only a bully, perjurer, and whiner, but also a bigot who despises Native Americans.

Landow played the thug again soon after the Indian land deal imploded. He stooped to conquer and terrify Kathleen Willey. Willey is the former White House aide who testified Bill Clinton sexually groped her in the Oval Office. Landow, just as he had with Michael Copperthite, tried to bully Willey into concealing the truth about Clinton's sexual assault of her. Willey's testimony would strengthen Paula Jones's civil lawsuit against Clinton for sexually coming on to her in Arkansas. Landow knew Willey was vulnerable and financially bankrupt after her husband's suicide over money problems. He saw an opportunity "to ingratiate himself with Gore and [Peter] Knight," [320] as *The Weekly Standard* put it, by preventing Willey from testifying.

Landow leaned harder on Kathleen Willey than he had on Michael Copperthite. Two months after she was subpoenaed to testify in the Jones lawsuit, Landow acted. His real estate firm chartered a private jet on October 6, 1997 to fly Willey from her Richmond, Virginia home to Landow's estate on Maryland's Eastern Shore. During Willey's two-day stay at his estate, Landow constantly pressured her to deny Clinton's misbehavior. "Don't say anything," he advised Willey. If Willey said "nothing happened" during her encounter with Clinton, then she could not be contradicted.[321] Willey informed the grand jury Landow offered her a small gift to cooperate: a chartered flight to New York City so she could go Christmas shopping. Landow's actions clearly constituted witness tampering.

When questioned later about the October meeting, Landow admitted talking to Willey about her "mental anguish" but asserted that any evidence of witness tampering was "absolutely untrue."[322] But Landow did not believe his own claim. When summoned to testify on possible witness tampering before Kenneth Starr's grand jury, Landow refused. As *The Washington Post* reported: "Landow refused to testify before Starr's grand jury last summer [1998] citing his Fifth Amendment right against self-incrimination. He has denied any wrongdoing and said he invoked the right on the advice of lawyers when prosecutors refused to give him immunity in exchange for his testimony about his dealings with Willey."[323]

Landow tried to squelch Kathleen Willey's damaging testimony with less savory methods than witness tampering. The dark angel's lawyer, Saul Schwartzbach, hired Jarrett Stern, a private investigator, to spy on Willey's movements. Stern felt uneasy about the assignment. As *The Washington Post* reported: "Stern's lawyer, Edouard Bouquet of Bethesda, told the network [ABC News] his client felt uneasy about what he was asked to do and called Willey, using an alias, to warn her someone was out to do her harm."[324] Landow, as usual, denied he was interested in leaning on anybody. He had "no knowledge" that Schwartzbach hired Stern to investigate Willey.[325]

Nobody believed Landow's denial. It appears Landow bullied Willey in order to please Al Gore and Peter Knight, not to help Bill Clinton. A Washington financier familiar with Landow testifies: "It would not be atypical for Nate to insert himself into [the Willey affair] or for him to tell Willey things as if he were acting at the behest of the White House, when in fact he had no such authority."[326]

Landow recognizes how Gore and Knight, two privileged yuppies who led sheltered lives, would be impressed with his tough guy tactics against hostile witnesses if it worked.

Although Peter Knight cannot match his friend Nate Landow in tactics, he can match him in greed. Besides breaking campaign finance laws and trying to exploit the Cheyenne-Arapaho Tribe, Knight engaged in a profitable scam with the Molten Metals Technology Company. Molten Metal, of Waltham, Massachusetts, was a company devoted to reprocessing dangerous nuclear waste materials into safe, "non-radioactive solid materials."[327] Many established corporate giants like General Electric, Getty Oil, and Allied-General Nuclear Services tried and failed to make a profit reprocessing nuclear waste materials into solids. There was little reason to think a tiny concern such as Molten Metal would experience better luck at waste reprocessing.

However, on April 18, 1995, Vice President Al Gore put his arm around William Haney, President of Molten Metal, at one of the company's factories in Fall River, Massachusetts, and asserted: "Molten Metal is a success story, a shining example of American ingenuity, hard work, and business know-how."[328] What motivated Gore to gush over a small, obscure company operating in a high-risk industry?

The answer was Peter Knight and Molten's Vice President for Governmental Affairs, Victor Gatto. Knight knew Haney from the 1988 Gore campaign, when Haney acted as a field coordinator.[329] Gatto was a Harvard classmate and crony of Gore's. William Haney put Knight on retainer for "$7,000 a month plus lucrative stock options. Haney even gave a gift of 640 shares of the company's stock, worth some $10,000 at the time, to Knight's thirteen-year old son."[330] Haney also donated $82,000 to the 1996 Clinton-Gore campaign and the DNC. Thanking Haney for Molten's campaign contributions, Knight wrote back: "Your participation in this program will give you a special place of significance with the Vice President and put you first in line."[331]

Peter Knight moved Molten to the front of the line. The Department of Energy awarded Molten $6 million in nuclear waste contracts during the spring and summer of 1995. In November 1995, the Department's nuclear experts concluded Molten's technology did not work to reprocess the nuclear waste.

The experts recommended the Department stop issuing contracts to Molten. The Energy Department's Undersecretary, Thomas Grumbly, a close friend of Knight's and a former Gore aide, overrode the experts' recommendation. The Energy Department awarded another $27 million worth of government contracts to Molten Metal.[332]

Despite this government largesse, Molten folded. It seems its executives did not know what they were doing. In October 1996, the company's stock price sank when management announced they overestimated the revenue from Energy Department contracts. The stock price plunged from a high of $40 per share to less than a nickel per share. Molten filed for bankruptcy in December 1997.

Spurred by angry investors initiating a shareholders' suit, the House Commerce Committee investigated the business affairs between Knight, Grumbly, Gore, and Molten Metal in November 1997. Although the Committee found plenty of sleaze, Reno's Justice Department, as usual, found nothing worthy of prosecution. The Justice Department investigated Knight and then closed the case. Gore was relieved for his friend and aide: "Peter Knight is one of the most honorable, honest men I have ever known in my life" he told *The New York Times*.[333] Next to Armand Hammer, Maria Hsia, and Bill Clinton, Peter Knight does appear honorable and honest.

Al Gore truly believes Peter Knight, influence peddler and bookend to Nate Landow, is destined for higher things. William Haney clued us in a letter to Knight's future in a Gore Administration: "Our objective is to keep you [Knight] and other[s] of the more talented people with us right up until you are Secretary of State."[334]

Imagine, we could have a Secretary of State who sells out our national interests to Chinese Communists and cheats struggling Native Americans.

Defending Clinton During the Early Days of the Lewinsky Scandal

In January 1998, Bill Clinton finally reaped bitter fruit from the Paula Jones sexual harassment lawsuit. Matt Drudge, the Internet reporter, broke a story suppressed by *Newsweek* about a junior White House staffer, Monica Lewinsky, who carried on an affair with the President. Clinton, like mobster angel Nathan

Landow, committed witness tampering with Lewinsky, who was subpoenaed as a witness for Paula Jones' lawsuit. Monica's friend, Linda Tripp, turned in Lewinsky to Kenneth Starr's investigation. We cannot detail here Clinton's cover-up, perjury, and obstruction of justice during this scandal. Instead, we will study the defenses Gore offered of his boss and friend's impeachable conduct.

Al Gore behaved like a loyal servant during Bill Clinton's crisis. He was certainly tempted by the prospect of succeeding his boss if impeachment occurred. But he tempered this by remembering the fate of Gerald Ford 24 years earlier. If Gore arrived in the Oval Office the easy way, like Ford, he would probably become the victim of his predecessor's crimes. So Gore urged all his cronies to stand pat for Clinton during the crisis if they wanted to win in 2000.

Gore tried to tailor his rhetoric to suit the developing circumstances of the crisis. On January 22, 1998, he professed to believe in Clinton's lie that he had no affair with Monica Lewinsky: "The President denied the charges and I believe it...He has said he will cooperate fully with the Independent Counsel. And you will see that is exactly what he does....Beyond that, he is not only the President of the country, he is my friend."[335]

Gore repeated this message of humble trust in the President through the winter, spring, and summer of 1998. Gore also pretended not to notice Nathan Landow's bullying of Kathleen Willey during the same time period. As *The Sacramento Bee* reported in April 1998: "His response to all subsequent questions about the Lewinsky case has been to reiterate his faith in the president's denials."[336] Gore kept a low profile and avoided press questioning. While Clinton delayed, denied and avoided press conferences, Gore kept silent. On July 30, Gore praised Clinton at a joint appearance to end speculation the Vice President was distancing himself from his boss: "Each and every day, President Bill Clinton makes an enormous difference for our families and for our communities because he understands the promises and he cares deeply about your future. I'm intensely proud to serve with him."[337]

But Gore couldn't be found when Clinton testified before Starr's grand jury in mid-August. Al took Tipper and the kids to Hawaii for a two week vacation. In typical fashion, Gore aides lamely insisted the Vice President planned the vacation before the date for Clinton's grand jury testimony was determined.[338] Gore watched Clinton's defiant televised "apology" in Hawaii. After the telecast, Al called Bill. He told the President "that Tipper and I have him and his family in our hearts and in our prayers." Then Gore released a short statement to the press: "I am proud of him—not only because he is a friend—but because he is a person who had the courage to acknowledge mistakes. I am honored to work with this great President on his agenda for the nation and I believe it is time to put this matter behind us—once and for all—and move forward with the business of the United States of America."[339]

Gore ignored the grave evidence indicating Clinton committed perjury, witness tampering, and obstruction of justice. Instead, he urged the country to accept the President's half-apology and "put this matter behind us—once and for all." Never did Gore admit Bill Clinton put the country through seven months of needless agony and strife.

The Starr Report, the 98 Elections, and the Impeachment

Independent Counsel Kenneth Starr crosschecked Clinton's grand jury testimony against Monica Lewinsky's testimony. The evidence indicated Bill Clinton committed perjury, obstruction of justice, and witness tampering while stonewalling Starr's investigation of the Lewinsky affair. Starr's staff wrote a report regarding impeachable offenses Clinton committed. Then Starr sent the report and all his evidence to the House Judiciary Committee for consideration of impeachment proceedings on September 11, 1998.

Al Gore responded in character to Starr's report. Instead of realizing Bill Clinton had provoked a constitutional crisis by breaking the law and not admitting it, Gore reduced the situation to a partisan contest. No matter how criminal or foolish Clinton's actions, he was a Democrat first. He condemned Clinton's personal conduct but denied it was impeachable. He also reinforced Clinton's determination not to compromise with the Congressional Republicans and meet them halfway. Clinton and Gore decided together to just brazenly dare the Congressional Republicans to defy the public opinion polls and impeach Clinton.[340]

On September 12th, the day after Starr's report appeared, Al Gore publicly cast himself as a constitutional expert. He dismissed the evidence of impeachable offenses: "I do not believe this report serves as the basis for overturning the judgment of the American people in 1992 and again in 1996 that Bill Clinton should be their president."[341] He did not bother to analyze Starr's report and explain why its evidence did not justify impeachment. In Gore's mind, partisanship and holding onto power justified his stance.

After Clinton's grand jury testimony aired on television September 21, Al Gore began hitting the Republican Congress even harder. The next day, the Vice President slammed the two chambers for preferring "investigation over legislation....The Republican Party seems to want partisanship, not progress....Instead of rolling up their sleeves and doing their job, they give us personal attacks on the president....my friend, our president and leader Bill Clinton has been good for the United States of America....[He has been] at the heart of America's new strategy for success."[342] Gore's blind partisanship enabled him to blithely overlook the various major scandals of the Clinton-Gore Administration: Whitewater; Travelgate; Filegate; Secretary of Agriculture Mike Espy's corruption; HUD Secretary Henry Cisneros' lies to the FBI; the late Commerce Secretary Ron Brown's influence peddling; as well as the biggest of them all, the campaign finance conspiracy to raise illegal foreign money. Gore, like his boss, refused to recognize how the Administration had provoked the Republican Congress beyond endurance. He and Clinton both assumed the Republicans would lose their nerve as they had before during the last three years. Gore flippantly dismissed Clinton's damning videotaped testimony: "My overall impression was that it was much ado about not much new."[343]

Instead of counseling compromise and caution to Clinton, Gore pressed him to activate the Democratic core of feminists, minorities, and public employee unions. Gore thought it especially important to frighten minority voters into showing up at the polls. Clinton agreed with the man he calls: "the greatest Vice President in history." The President encouraged Gore to flay the Republicans in Congress. Campaigning for Gray Davis in California, Gore shouted: "We say health care, they say investigation. We say environment, they say investigation. We say education, they say investigation."[344] The same man who, for purely partisan purposes, voted for the "October Surprise" snipe hunt now denied Republicans a chance to investigate major scandals involving matters of grave importance.

Gore pumped up the volume of his campaign against Congressional Republicans. On September 29, he lashed out: "The only thing they can agree on is personally attacking the President....It's astonishing, at a time when the business community is saying, 'You've got to stabilize these markets overseas,' they won't do it.... What have they been spending their time on? Investigating the president....I believe the Congress of the United States ought to get on with the business of the people."[345]. Two days later at a fundraiser, the Vice President blasted the same target: "All they can agree on, among themselves, is their hatred of President Clinton."[346]

While publicly excoriating Congressional Republicans, Gore privately joined Clinton in an "extensive last-minute lobbying effort to urge wavering House Democrats to vote against the Republican plan for an open-ended impeachment inquiry."[347] The lobbying failed. Over thirty House Democrats, mostly Southerners responding to their constituents' wishes, joined with the Republicans in authorizing an open-ended inquiry. But Gore still underestimated the seriousness of the House Republicans. On October 14, he discounted the probability of impeachment. Bill Clinton "will be reprimanded by Congress," he predicted. "They'll come up with some scenario for closure which is way short of impeachment."[348]

Two days later, Gore echoed his fulsome praise of William Jefferson Clinton: "There is one person who's at the center of all the progress in our country. And that is our President, Bill Clinton."[349] When the Vice President mentioned progress, he could only have meant material progress, for Clinton represented regression in moral terms. Al Gore wrote a long book, *Earth in the Balance*, questioning man's fanatical pursuit of material progress. Now, he could only defend Clinton's conduct by praising the material progress that Clinton presided over.

On election night, November 3, 1998, Gore used the progress theme again. Exultant over the fact that the Republicans lost six seats in the House and only broke even in the Senate, the Vice President declared: "Although all the results aren't in yet, Americans had a choice and they chose progress over partisanship. It's a great night for Democrats and a great night for the country."[350] Once again, Al Gore revealed the only bad partisanship in his mind is Republican partisanship.

The election results seemed to signal there would be no impeachment. Clinton and Gore both felt cocky. Gore was relieved by Janet Reno's predictable decision on November 24 not to seek an independent counsel examining his role in the 1996 fundraising scandals. But the Clinton-Gore team misread the resolution of House Republicans. Defying the public opinion polls, which showed Americans opposed to impeachment by an almost 2 to 1 ratio, the House Judiciary Committee Republican majority voted to recommend impeachment of Bill Clinton on four articles of misconduct.

Gore suddenly and belatedly realized the House Republicans were serious about impeachment. He canceled a visit to New Hampshire during the December 14-17 weekend to help Clinton win some wavering House votes. There was another reason for canceling the visit: the Vice President did not want to be seen campaigning in New Hampshire for the 2000 nomination while his boss was being impeached in Washington. Gore told *NBC News*: "I am fighting mad about the way they are carrying out this impeachment matter because everybody knows what the president did was wrong. But everybody knows it's not an impeachable offense, and they're trying to—to make it seem like one, and the best they can do is a straight party line vote. That's wrong. You don't impeach a president over something like this....And they think that people are not going to remember this. Well, I think they may be dead wrong about that, too." [351] Gore claimed the Founding Fathers reserved impeachment for "high crimes and misdemeanors." To Gore, Clinton's perjury and obstruction of justice did not constitute "high crimes and misdemeanors." They were just acts "misleading people in the process." [352]

Gore and Clinton's attempt to stave off impeachment failed. On December 19, 1998, the full House voted to impeach Clinton on two of the four articles: perjury and obstruction of justice. Article I, the perjury before the grand jury count, passed 228 yeas-206 nays. Article III, the obstruction of justice count, passed 221 yeas-212 nays. Immediately after the impeachment vote, many House Democrats repaired to the White House for a pep rally with Clinton and Gore. The Vice President stood up and gave an angry speech assailing the House Republicans' action: "What happened as a result does a great disservice to a man I believe will be regarded in the history books as one of our greatest presidents." [353] Only Al Gore would dare to call the perpetrator of: Whitewater, Travelgate, Filegate, the Somalia fiasco, the 1996 fundraising scandal, and the Lewinsky affair, "one of our greatest Presidents."

After the December 19 impeachment vote, Gore surpassed James Carville and Hillary Clinton as a Clinton defender in public and private. Prince Albert took the lead against Republicans. He buttonholed members of Congress, past Presidents, and other peddlers of influence to help Clinton. When many in the President's inner circle drew away from him, Gore lashed himself even tighter to Clinton's mast.[354]

On January 8, 1999, Gore boasted about his intimacy with Clinton: "I don't have any intention of trying to come up with some artificial political design aimed at separating myself from the President....This has been a Clinton-Gore administration from day one. ...Bill Clinton is a great President and he has made a tremendous positive difference in the lives of Americans. I feel privileged to be a part of his Administration."[355] Did Gore really believe Clinton is a great president ranking with Washington, Lincoln, Franklin Roosevelt, and Ronald Reagan? Apparently he did.

Gore worked with Clinton, the President's many attorneys, James Carville, and the Senate Democratic leadership on a strategy of preventing removal. Gore went along with Clinton's "scorched earth" strategy of using salacious details of the House impeachment managers' and Senate Republicans' personal lives against them. Gore also signed off on Carville's "Round Robin" anti-impeachment strategy. Carville's "Round Robin" strategy emulated the plan used by his fellow Louisianan, Huey Long. While Governor of Louisiana in 1929, Long was impeached by his state House but got more than a third of the state Senate to sign a Round Robin letter guaranteeing they would vote against removal. Long is widely considered America's most successful fascist politician. Being a fascist does not disqualify your utility in the eyes of Bill Clinton, Al Gore, and James Carville.[356] They persuaded Senate Democratic leaders Tom Daschle and Robert Byrd to adopt the same Round Robin strategy against Clinton's removal. So the timid Senate Republicans intimidated by Clinton's "scorched earth" files, opted for a meaningless three-week show trial with no live witnesses.

On February 12, 1999, the Senate mustered only 50 votes for removal. Al Gore called this Senate acquittal "a victory for the Founding Fathers and the Constitution....The Senate has voted, and I agree with the results."[357] While a U.S. Senator, Gore voted against the Supreme Court appointments of both Robert Bork and Clarence Thomas. He feared they wanted to restore the original Constitution of the Founding Fathers. Gore only approved of the original Constitution when its results suited his immediate needs.

The Rape of Juanita Broaddrick

The failure of the Senate to remove Clinton did not relieve Gore of damage control chores for his President. On February 24, twelve days after the vote, *NBC News Dateline* broadcast an interview with Juanita Broaddrick, an Arkansas woman who claimed Bill Clinton raped her back in 1978. Lisa Myers, the highly respected NBC correspondent who conducted the interview, found Mrs. Broaddrick's story to be quite credible. Mrs. Broaddrick supplied Myers with details of the encounter that could be historically checked. Myers and her research staff ran down all leads and found no holes or memory lapses in Mrs. Broaddrick's story.

The deafening silence from the White House supported the validity of Mrs. Broaddrick's accusation. The Clinton rapid response team, for once, did not issue any denials or malign the motives of anyone reporting the story. Hillary Clinton, James Carville, and Al Gore avoided any comment on the story. No one came to Clinton's defense.

Gore offered no comment on the Broaddrick story until December 15, 1999. That day, while campaigning against Bill Bradley in New Hampshire, a woman named Kathleen Prudhomme asked the Vice President about Broaddrick's rape accusation on *Dateline*. Gore claimed: "I didn't see the interview....There have been so many personal allegations and such a non-stop series of attacks. I guess I'm like a lot of people in that I think that enough is enough. I do not know how to evaluate each one of these individual stories. I just don't know."[358] Al Gore, one of the most painstaking and intelligent men to ever serve as Vice President, plead ignorance to a nationally broadcast rape charge about his boss. Imitation is the highest form of flattery. "Just deny it" has become the modus operandi of Al Gore as well as Bill Clinton.

FIFTEEN

The Second Run for the White House in 2000

The Subordinate Beta Male Tries to Become an Aggressive Alpha Male

Al Gore resented Bill Clinton's reckless conduct during the Lewinsky Scandal. Before the scandal and impeachment crisis occurred, the Vice President enjoyed favorable circumstances for a 2000 run to the White House. The economy was booming. Unemployment was only 4.1%. The U.S. reigned unchallenged as the world's only superpower. Clinton's triangulation policy kept the Republicans on the defensive. The President gave his Vice President ample responsibility and credit. As *The Almanac of American Politics, 2000* observed: "More than any other president in American history, he [Clinton] has been campaigning hard for his vice president to succeed him."[359] Clinton also delayed enacting necessary reforms in Social Security and Medicare so Gore could demagogue the Republicans about them in 2000. The only large cloud looming over Gore's 2000 prospects, the 1996 Campaign Finance Scandal, was buried by stonewalling. Janet Reno could be counted on to ignore executive branch crimes. Poll numbers in late 1997 indicated an easy Gore victory in November 2000.

Then Clinton spoiled this roseate prospect with the Lewinsky scandal. For thirteen straight months, Al Gore was compelled to defend indefensible conduct by his boss. Even Gore, a faithful husband and devoted family man, freely admitted Clinton's personal behavior deserved condemnation. The subordinate beta male lost respect just because he was lashed to the mast of the superior alpha male. His poll numbers for winning the Presidency in 2000 plummeted. Al Gore became the only Vice President in history serving under a President impeached by the full House of Representatives. He regarded Clinton with a "primal bitterness"[360] for provoking the impeachment crisis and hurting his own election chances. Gore recognized he still needed Clinton's political sixth sense and awesome fund raising skills.

The Cox Report's Findings

Gore's election prospects were dimmed again in March 1999. That month Congressman Christopher Cox's Committee published its investigation on Chinese nuclear espionage and technology transfer.[361] The Cox Report showed that the People's Republic of China was enabled to steal *all* American nuclear warhead secrets thanks mostly to lax security procedures at Federal research labs enacted by Clinton's Secretary of Energy, Hazel O'Leary. The Committee's report also documented how Loral Space and Communications and Hughes Electronics Corporation, two companies who ranked high among donors to the Clinton-Gore campaigns, supplied China with classified assistance to improve their rocket satellite launches. The Cox Report further documented how the Clinton Administration's permissive policy toward dual use technology (i.e, technology with both civilian and military applications) enabled China to easily acquire supercomputers and satellite technology. Supercomputers and satellite technology make it much easier to develop nuclear weapons, rocket delivery systems, and electronic warfare guidance systems.[362]

Illegal espionage and legal technology transfer thus made it easier for Communist China to cut America's military lead in nuclear weapons and electronic warfare. Gore shared responsibility with Clinton for the Administration's policy toward China, technology transfer, and loosening up security at the Department of Energy. The Clinton-Gore team also had opposed deploying a ballistic missile defense. The Administration was thus doubly guilty of undermining national security. China's acquisition of dual-use technology also reminded voters of the 1996 campaign finance abuses. The White House coffees and the Buddhist Temple scams all traced back to Red China's lust for American high technology.[363]

Gore's 2000 campaign now carried two Chinese burdens: 1) the 1996 campaign finance scandals; and 2) the undermining of American security against nuclear attack.

The Gore 2000 Campaign Staff: Murderer's Row

Gore, as usual, announced his 2000 run for the Presidency standing on the steps of the Smith County courthouse in Carthage. He announced earlier than he preferred, on June 15, 1999, because George W. Bush held such a big lead in the polls.

But the Gore 2000 campaign suffered at first from problems besides Bush. It was unwieldy, wasteful of money, unfocused, and rife with squabbling between subordinates. Clinton enraged Gore by phoning *New York Times* reporter Richard Berke and condescendingly commenting that the Vice President's campaign was still salvageable. Gore took two drastic steps to shake the campaign up. In May he made former Congressman Tony Coelho the campaign's Chairman. In September he moved campaign headquarters from Washington, D.C. to Nashville, Tennessee. Both moves brought order and discipline to Gore's campaign. But Coelho's hiring also brought more scandalous baggage to Gore 2000.

Coelho served as Democratic House Congressional Campaign Chairman in the late 1980s. He became notorious for his cutthroat fundraising methods and intimidating businessmen into coughing up contributions. Coelho sucked up money from sleazy interests such as the formerly corrupt Teamsters Union and convicted junk bond wizard Michael Milken. Cleo tutored able protégés such as Terry McAuliffe, Clinton's crony and leading fundraiser, in his ruthless methods. But Coelho went too far in a slimy 1989 business deal. The resulting publicity compelled him to resign from Congress in disgrace.[364] He went to Wall Street and made a huge fortune. But his insatiable greed kept him in trouble.

While the U.S. Commissioner General for Expo '98 in Lisbon, Portugal, he engaged in shady financial practices.[365] Coelho used his official Ambassadorial status at the Exposition to peddle influence and hustle for his own personal business projects. He hatched an extraordinary number of shady schemes during his stint in Lisbon. One of his projects, Loan Net, an online mortgage-processing scam, involved his shady friend Terry McAuliffe. Loan Net went belly up for its investors, but investigators from the State Department's Inspector General discovered Coelho billed the Federal government for many of Loan Net's long-distance phone calls. Other improper billing and financial irregularities by Coelho in Lisbon are also being investigated for possible criminal violations. Subpoenas are being issued for Coelho's Lisbon financial records. Gore's campaign manager may face a criminal indictment shortly before the 2000 election.[366] Coelho's presence in Gore's campaign ensured that questions would be constantly raised about the Vice President's involvement in fund raising scandals.

Coelho was not the only official of Gore 2000 with a shady past. Al Gore brought his favorite hatchet men, Peter Knight and Carter Eskew, on board. Gore's weepy 1996 convention speech about sister Nancy's death from lung cancer looked retrospectively ridiculous with tobacco industry lobbyist Eskew on board his 2000 campaign. But the Gore campaign's most notorious official was campaign manager Donna Brazile. Gore hired her to win the black primary vote from Bradley. Brazile was a black political consultant who specialized in ruthless race baiting and scandalmongering. She enjoyed a reputation for playing dirty in campaigns as deserved as her fellow Louisianan, James Carville. In October 1988, she smeared George Bush as an adulterer while working for the Dukakis campaign. Dukakis immediately fired her then personally apologized to Bush.[367] In December 1999, Brazile accused General Colin Powell and Congressman J.C. Watts of being "Uncle Toms" for a cruel, racist Republican Party that refused to feed black children. General Powell quickly denounced Gore for employing someone who plays "the polarizing 'race card'"[368] Gore, who pushed for the appointment of Powell's son to the FCC, was unmoved by the General's criticism of Brazile's race baiting.

Gore also hired Bob Shrum, a political consultant renowned for his ruthless tactics. Shrum befriended the young James Carville and taught him many dirty tricks in the 1980s.[369] In the 1998 Maryland race for Governor, Shrum played rougher than Carville ever did. He ran ads against Ellen Sauerbrey, the Republican candidate, accusing her of being a racial bigot opposed to civil rights. Baltimore Mayor Kurt Schmoke, a black Democrat, condemned Shrum's ads and declared: "I will not participate in a campaign to try to persuade people that she [Ellen Sauerbrey] is a racist."[370] Despite Schmoke's condemnation, black voters turned out heavily to reject Sauerbrey, who always had voted for civil rights. In the 1990 Texas Democrat gubernatorial primary, Shrum ran ads against Ann Richards accusing her of using marijuana and cocaine. Richards, a recovering alcoholic, had struggled with alcohol but not with narcotics.[371] Gore had no past association with Shrum; he appreciated his nasty attack ads .

Gore rounded out his "Murderer's Row of political aides" with Tad Devine and Harrison Hickman. Devine once ran ads against Republican Senator Larry Craig of Idaho slandering him as "lying Larry Craig." Devine's own candidate, Democrat Senate nominee Walt Minnick, pulled Devine's ads because they backfired with voters. Harrison Hickman also experienced repudiation by his Democrat candidate because he went too negative. During the 1992 Presidential primary, Hickman played dirty against Bill Clinton by circulating a memo about Slick Willie's draft status. Senator Bob Kerrey, Hickman's employer, criticized Hickman at a press conference by referring to him as "Harrison Hitman."[372] Gore probably hopes Hickman will be even dirtier and more effective against George W. Bush.

Gore's oddest and most valued political consultant does not denounce the Vice President's political opponents. Naomi Wolf's task is much more ambitious than creating attack ads. She has undertaken to humanize Al Gore, the most abstract and robotic figure in American national politics. Wolf became notorious for describing Gore as a subordinate "beta male" who needed to construct a new identity as a dominant "alpha male" to free himself from Bill Clinton's shadow. Naomi Wolf is a radical feminist intellectual who befriended Gore's daughter Karenna. She accurately recognized the Vice President's true love was abstract scientific research, not politics. Gore's close friend and political consultant Bob Squier, observed this about the "beta male." Squier remarked about their respective fathers: "We've talked more about my father than we have about his. Because mine was a scientist."[373] Gore much preferred pursuing the mysteries of the universe to pleasing and understanding people. This truth explained both his arrogance toward his fellow humans and his robotic personality.

Wolf provided a solution to Gore's problematic personality. In a *George* magazine column, "Al's Inner Alien," Wolf wrote: "He [Gore] will have to come to terms with his natural eccentricity....Gore should let his defenses down and allow his inner oddness out....To be that kind of savant when one is a famous senator's son would entail a kind of social death, might breed a formidable inner conflict. It must take a toll to act normal when one doesn't feel normal (which may explain Gore's famously flat public speaking style). An idiosyncratic inner life might also mean knowing one is destined, in some profound way, to be alone inside one's head. But whatever he has suffered personally in the past, Gore should take heart as he 'outs' himself. We have a history of cherishing our loopy visionaries—after we have mocked them hard." [374]

Gore was impressed at Wolf's perceptive grasp of his personality. The young new age feminist did understand what a "loopy visionary" the Vice President was. Wolf also realized how Al Gore needed to escape Bill Clinton's dominating influence. She rightly urged him to ditch his dull blue and gray suits for "reassuring" earth tone colors of green and brown. The earth tone colors enhanced his attractiveness to women voters. The real question is why did Gore need an erratic new age woman his daughter's age to help him understand himself?

When Gore's reliance on Naomi Wolf became public in early November 1999, press attention first focused on Wolf's huge salary, dwarfing that of all his other aides, of $15,000 a month. Donna Brazile's bitter jealousy toward Wolf, her salary, and her standing with Gore were commented upon. Then reporters wondered why he concealed Wolf's role by "funneling her payments through other consulting firms so that her name would not appear on financial reports filed with the Federal Election Commission."[375] The reporters also savored juicy quotes on sexual conduct from Wolf's three books. The quotes urged people to rid themselves of sexual hangups while also resisting sexual exploitation. Wolf's solution to the teen abortion and unplanned pregnancy rate was: "we should teach petting—'sexual gradualism'—and let our kids know that there are many ways of having pleasure and intimacy that don't involve intercourse."[376] Wolf's absurd version of sexual restraint deserved ridicule. But hardly any observer noted the most damning aspect of Wolf's Gore 2000 campaign role: Al Gore, two-term Vice President of the United States, former U.S. Senator and Congressman, husband and father, needed a young, new age feminist to explain to him how to be a man.

The Gore 2000 campaign officials testify to the dehumanized character of their candidate. Like many rich boy heirs, Gore yearns to play hardball to prove he is not a spoiled sissy. This explains his chest pounding bluster in 1991: "You make the decision to run first and then you run with all your heart and soul….You're going to rip the lungs out of anybody else who's in the race, and you're going to do it right."[377] So he surrounds himself with ruthless operators like Nathan Landow, Coelho, Knight, Eskew, Brazile, Shrum, Devine, and Hickman to demonstrate his bullyboy toughness.

Al Gore cannot connect intuitively with voters and articulate their positive aspirations as President Ronald Reagan did. He can only exploit their fears and hatreds. Gore only knows two methods of arousing voter emotions (1) a long, humorless tirade of a speech, or (2) a thirty-second television hate ad.

Bill Bradley's Feeble Challenge

Al Gore aroused base fears and hatreds to dispose of Bill Bradley's challenge for the White House. Bradley, onetime New York Knicks basketball star and former Senator from New Jersey, seemed a formidable rival. He did well at raising money and attracting volunteers. Bradley argued tellingly that polls indicated Gore could not beat Bush in November 2000. The challenger collected some impressive endorsements from heavy hitters such as Senators Daniel Patrick Moynihan and Bob Kerrey.

Al Gore refused to contemplate his own ruin. He seized on Bradley's plans to provide universal health insurance and abolish Medicaid and literally lied about them to Iowa and New Hampshire primary voters. Bradley, obstinately committed to running a positive campaign, refused to respond to Gore's demagoguery. Bradley's failure to respond rapidly to Gore's attacks proved a fatal mistake.

The challenger fell far behind in Iowa, where he lost in January. Bradley changed tactics in New Hampshire, but it was too late. Gore's attack ads worked. Gore's negative campaigning hit a new low in New Hampshire when Bill Shaheen, husband of the state's Governor, a Gore supporter, led a local crowd to humiliate Senator Bob Kerrey, a Bradley supporter. Shaheen's thugs splattered the Congressional Medal of Honor winner, who lost a leg in Vietnam War combat, with mud and called him "a cripple" and "a quitter."[378] When called on to apologize for his supporters' shameful behavior, Gore denied anything untoward happened: "It didn't happen."[379] The rear echelon reporter refused to honor the Navy SEAL Congressional Medal of Honor winner. After all, Kerrey supported his political opponent.

New Hampshire Democratic primary voters who soured on Clinton and Gore crossed over to vote for Republican John McCain. Bradley ended up losing New Hampshire by only two points. Bradley then went on to lose every single primary and caucus the two candidates contested. Bradley withdrew from the race after being trounced on Super Tuesday, March 7, 2000. He endorsed Gore after withdrawing, so many observers suspected the two men cut a deal of some kind.

The Third Term of the Clinton Administration

"Al Gore is too good to waste on Bill Clinton."[380]
Leon Wieseltier

Wieseltier's comment represents a common sentiment among many New Class sympathizers of Al Gore. These people see Al Gore as a pure, uncorrupted Clinton. Our biography shows that the opposite is the case. Clinton certainly has committed more criminal actions and engaged in more corrupt activity than any previous president. But Clinton usually does evil to protect himself from prosecution or to pursue women. He is too lazy and preoccupied to ruthlessly pursue power for its own sake. Clinton is also too cowardly to force change down the throats of people who do not want it. The "don't ask, don't tell" cop-out compromise on gays in the military reflects his usual method of operation. Gore, by contrast, sought to completely overturn the ban on gays and lesbians in the military, even if General Colin Powell opposed him. Gore said he would only appoint members of the Joint Chiefs of Staff who share his absolute views on gay liberation. Clinton would never say anything that direct, forthright, and fanatical on a controversial issue.

Self-pity is the theme of the Clinton Presidency's first two terms. Bill Clinton whined, after causing a needless Constitutional crisis over the Lewinsky scandal, that he was as victimized as Richard Jewell. Self-righteousness will be the theme of the third Clinton term, Al Gore's Presidency. Gore is as fanatical and humorless, as Clinton is frivolous and charming. Clinton will caution Gore in meetings: "You're being a little too abstract here, Al."[381] Clinton's electoral success derives from pleasing a majority, not offending it. In most areas of policy there will be continuity between the three terms of the Clinton-Gore Presidency. But the degree of self-righteousness and fanaticism will be increased in certain controversial areas of policy. Race and affirmative action will be one area where Gore pumps up the volume of discourse.

Al Gore telegraphed his views on race in two encounters. In a 1998 address on Martin Luther King day, Gore slandered the opponents of affirmative action: "They use their color blind [approach to the Constitution and discrimination, based on Justice Harlan's phrase] the way duck hunters use their duck blind. They hide behind the phrase and hope that we, like the ducks, won't be able to see through it."[382] This outrageous analogy implies that Ward Connerly's opposition to racial quotas is equivalent to David Duke's. In February 2000, in order to beat Bradley in the New York primary, Gore met secretly with the Reverend Al Sharpton at his daughter Karenna's apartment. Sharpton is a black racist who foments hatred against whites and blacks who oppose his demagoguery. He is directly responsible for both the Tawana Brawley hoax and the murder of Yankel Rosenbaum in Crown Heights, New York. Gore's favorite magazine, *The New Republic*, condemns Sharpton frequently. Yet Gore met him on bended knee to win a few extra votes.[383]

Al Gore will also genuflect more to the needs of Mother Earth than Clinton. He will certainly issue executive orders to help end the use of the internal combustion engine. Gore will also use executive orders to combat the growth of what he calls "urban sprawl." He outlined his coercive utopian ideas about controlling metropolitan growth by using taxes and zoning laws to favor mass transit over automobiles. Gore plans to use federal planning to control where we live and work.[384]

Al Gore also plans to be more active controlling the outside world than Bill Clinton is. During the last seven years, Gore urged the aggressive use of military force on many occasions when Clinton preferred to wait or not act at all.[385] Look for the United States to become much more militarily involved in the Balkans and Africa under a Gore Administration. Also look for the Joint Chiefs of Staff Generals and Admirals to be even more compliant than Bill Clinton's brasshats.

Al Gore as President will be more arrogant and zealous than he is as Vice President. He will also work much harder to remake the country to his technocratic specifications than lazy, frivolous Bill Clinton. An adviser to Gore commented bitterly: "The son of a bitch thinks he knows everything."[386] President Al Gore will exercise little humility, and will blame the country, not himself, if things go wrong. We hope the voters refuse to allow him the chance to make us all victims of his arrogance.

ENDNOTES

1. ABC News.com, December 23, 1999.

2. Bob Zelnick, Gore: A Political Life (Washington, D.C.: Regnery, 1999.) Unless otherwise indicated, Zelnick's biography is the main source for this chapter.

3. Frederick W. Marks III, Wind Over Sand: The Diplomacy of Franklin D. Roosevelt (Athens, GA: University of Georgia Press, 1989; "Albert A. Gore, Sr." in Current Biography, 1952, pp. 213-215; Press conference by VP Gore.

4. Id.

5. Albert Gore in Current Biography, 1952 pp. 213-215.

6. David Maraniss & Ellen Nakashima, "Tennessee Roots" *Washington Post* October 3, 1999, page A20.

7. Frederick W. Marks III, Wind Over Sand: The Diplomacy of Franklin D. Roosevelt (Athens, GA: University of Georgia Press, 1989; "Albert A. Gore, Sr." in Current Biography, 1952, pp. 213-215; Press conference by VP Gore, 1994; Gore Vidal, "Blood and Gore" GQ, December 1998.

8. Gore Vidal Palimpsest (New York, Random House, 1995), pp. 43-65; Monroe Billington, Senator Thomas Gore of Oklahoma (Lawrence: Kansas, 1967); Richard Lowitt "Thomas P. Gore" in American National Biography Vol. IX, (1998), pp. 299-300.

9. Vidal, Palimpsest, op.cit.

10. Gore Vidal, Palimpsest, pp. 223-224; 322; Vidal, "Blood and Gore" GQ December 1998; and comments on C-Span, January, 1999.

11. Ibid.

12. Zelnick Gore pp. 13-16; "Albert Gore" Current Biography 1952 pp. 213-215. These are the sources for Section A of Chapter 2.

13. Zelnick, page 16.

14. Michael Barone & Grant Ujifusa, Almanac of American Politics, 2000, page 53.

15. John Lukacs, Outgrowing Democracy (New York: Doubleday, 1983).

16. Quoted in Zelnick, op. cit., pp. 20-21.

17. Current Biography, op,cit. , page 215.

18. Edward Jay Epstein, Dossier.

19. Stephen J. Randall, "Armand Hammer" in *American National Biography* Vol. IX, (New York: Oxford University Press, 1999), pp. 941-942; Charles Lewis, et.al The Buying of the President, 2000 (New York: Avon Books, 2000), pp. 144, 149-150; Edward Jay Epstein, The Dossier (New York: Carroll & Graf, 1995).

20. Ibid., pp. 144, 149-150.

21. Id.

22. Bill Turque, Inventing Al Gore (Boston: Houghton, Mifflin, 2000), page 17-18.

23. Charles Fontenay, Estes Kefauver (Knoxville: University of Tennessee Press, 1980).

24. See Robert Caro's and Robert Dallek's biographies of LBJ.

25. Numan V. Bartley, The New South, 1945-1980 (Baton Rouge: Louisiana State University Press, 1995), page 406.

26. Bartley's cronies include Court TV anchorman Fred Graham, his two historian brothers Otis and Hugh, and Vanderbilt historian Dewey Grantham, who is Bartley's mentor. All five men are southern liberal Democrats personally close to the Gores.

27. Albert Gore, Sr., Let the Glory Out: My South and Its Politics (New York: Viking, 1972), page 77.

28. Maraniss & Nakashima, pp. A20-21.

29. Fontentay, op. cit.; Rubin quoted in Zelnick, page 37.

30. Albert Gore, Sr. interview quoted in Alex Jones, "Al Gore's Double Life" *The New York Times*, October 25, 1992.

31. Edward Jay Epstein, Dossier: The Secret History of Armand Hammer (New York: Random House, 1993).

32. Zelnick, page 23; Epstein, Dossier.

33. Zelnick, page 23; Lewis, op. cit., page 150.

34. Quoted in Maraniss & Nakashima, *Washington Post*, December 26, 1999, page A25.

35. Zelnick, Chapter 4; Alex Jones, op. cit.; Turque, pp. 13-15.

36. Epstein, Dossier.

37. See Epstein Dossier.

38. Noel Fisher, War at Every Door: Partisan Politics and Guerilla Violence in East Tennessee, 1860-1869 (Chapel Hill: University of North Carolina Press, 1997); Gordon McKinney, Southern Mountain Republicans, 1865-1900 (Chapel Hill: University of North Carolina Press, 1978).

39. See Albert Gore, Sr., Let the Glory Out, *The Boston Globe*, October 2, 1999; The Florida Times Union, December 8, 1999.

40. Turque, pp. 18, 392; *Williamson Leader*, September 24, 1992.

41. Ibid.; Zelnick, Chapter Two.

42. Alex Jones, op. cit.

43. Quoted in Turque, page 29.

44. Tipper Gore quoted in Michael Kelly, "Al Gore" *The Baltimore Sun*, December 13, 1987.

45. Quoted in Zelnick, page 38.

46. Maraniss & Nakashima, *Washington Post* October 10, 1999, page A26.

47. Ibid. , page A27.

48. Id.

49. Zelnick, page 41.

50. Zelnick, page 42; Maraniss & Nakashima, Oct. 10, 1999, page A26.

51. All these quotes are from Marjorie Williams, "The Chosen One," *Vanity Fair*, February 1998.

52. Zelnick, page 43.

53. *Time*, December 15, 1997; Interview with *Des Moines Register*, December 15, 1997.

54. Turque.

55. Zelnick, page 57; Maraniss & Nakashima, *Washington Post*, December 26, 1999, page A22.

56. William Chafe, Never Stop Running (New York: 1994).

57. See Turque, pp. 51, 61, 67; Zelnick, Chapter 3.

58. Article on Peretz in Capital Style, September 1998.

59. John Ellis, "Why Peretz fired his editor," *Boston Globe*, September 20, 1997.

60. Howard Kurtz, two articles in The Washington Post, September 29, 1999, and October 18, 1999; personal conversation with *New Republic* staffers.

61. Lloyd Grove, *Washington Post*, January 20, 1993; Jonathan Broder "Another one bites the dust," *Salon*, September 9, 1997; *Capital Style*, October 1998; Gail Sheehy, "Gore: The Son Also Rises," *Vanity Fair*, March 1988. Information from confidential source to authors.

62. Zelnick, Gore, pp. 56-57, 256-62.

63. Turque, pp. 275, 300-301; Paul Starobin, "The Liberal Hawk Soars" *National Journal*, May 15, 1999.

64. Quoted in *Boston Globe*, August 18, 1995.

65. Henry James, The Bostonians (New York, 1886).

66. Ibid., pp. 47-48.

67. Id.

68. Turque, pp. 100-101; Maraniss & Nakashima, December 27, 1999; Zelnick, page 51.

69. Letter quoted in Peter Boyer, "Gore's Dilemma," *The New Yorker*, November 28, 1994.

70. Bill Clinton letter to Colonel Eugene Holmes, U.S. Army ROTC, December 5, 1969.

71. Maraniss & Nakashima, *Washington Post*, December 29, 1999, page A16.

72. Id.

73. Ibid. ; Zelnick, pp. 57-61.

74. Maraniss & Nakashima, *Washington Post*, December 29, 1999.

75. Turque, pp. 67-70.

76. Maraniss & Nakashima, *Washington Post*, December 30, 1999, page A20.

77. Maraniss & Nakashima, pp. A20-21.

78. Maraniss & Nakashima, *Washington Post,*December 31, 1999; Zelnick, pp. 67-77.

79. Id.

80. Turque, pp. 82-83.

81. Id.

82. Id.

83. Zelnick, page 92.

84. Ibid., page 95; *Columbia Journalism Review*, January 1993; *Nashville Tennessean*, October 4, 1987.

85. Turque, pp. 109-110.

86. Turque, pp. 100-101.

87. Interview of John Warnecke by Adam Smith, *The Week Online.com* January 20, 2000; Turque, pp. 100-101.

88. Id.

89. Id.; Matt Labash, "Al Gore and Drugs" *The Weekly Standard* February 7, 2000, pp. 18-20; *The National Star* February, 8, 2000, pp. 4-5.

90. Id.

91. Id.

92. Floyd Brown, Slick Willie (Washington, D.C.: Eagle, 1992).

93. Charles Babcock, "Gore getting mineral rights for $20,000 A Year on Farm," *Washington Post*, August 15, 1992; Zelnick, pp. 87-89; Turque, pp. 105-106.

94. Turque, page 112.

95. Zelnick, page 96.

96. Gail Sheehy, op.cit.

97. Zelnick, page 97; Maraniss & Nakashima, *Washington Post* December 30, 1999.

98. Zelnick, page 98.

99. Current Biography, 1987, page 212; Turque, Chapter 8.

100. Day quote in Maraniss & Nakashima, *Washington Post*, October 10, 1999.

101. Marjorie Williams, "The Chosen One," *Vanity Fair*, February 1998.

102. Gail Sheehy, op. cit.

103. Lyons quoted in Turque, pp. 124-125.

104. Quoted in Turque, page 126.

105. Turque, pp. 125-126.

106. Turque, page 167.

107. Ibid., page 107; Current Biography, 1987, page 213.

108. Turque, pp. 138-139, 144.

109. Turque, pp. 123, 130; Zelnick, page 114.

110. Turque, page 144.

111. Turque, page 109.

112. Lewis, op. cit., page 165; Zelnick, pp. 114-115, 230, 311-317

113. Turque, pp. 134-136; Zelnick, pp. 101-107.

114. Quoted in Marjorie Williams, op. cit.

115. Ibid., pp. 107-108.

116. Al Gore & Sandra Peram, Biotechnology (Washington, D.C.: Brookings Institution, 1985).

117. Turque, page 137.

118. Almanac of American Politics, 1994 page 930; *The New York Times*, December 01, and 10, 1999.

119. Ibid., pp. 110-111.

120. Ibid., page 111.

121. National Right to Life Committee release, September 14, 1992; Congressional Quarterly roll call votes: # 466, 8/2/77; #584, 8/9/78; #417, 8/20/80; #334, 9/22/83; #247, 06/27/84; #242, 6/26/84.

122. Id.

123. Turque, page 122.

124. World Almanac, 1992; Almanac of American Politics, 1992; Current Biography, 1987; Debate between Gore, Ashe, and McAteer, October, 1984.

125. Zelnick, pp. 125-126.

126. Peter Rodman, More Precious than Peace: The Cold War and the Struggle for the Third World (New York: Scribner's, 1994); Robert W. Kagan, A Twilight Struggle (New York: The Free Press, 1995).

127. See the issues of *The New Republic* between 1982-1990; Peretz's quoted comments in Walter Kirn, "The Editor as Gap Model," *The New York Times Sunday Magazine*, March 7, 1993; Conversations with Mr. Leiken and Dr. Falcoff during the 1980s.

128. Zelnick, page 115.

129. National Public Policy Forum "Second Thoughts Conference Proceedings" Published in November, 1987; Observations of the authors.

130. Lloyd Grove, "Pop Goes the Wieseltier" *Vanity Fair*, March 1995.

131. Lloyd Grove, op. cit.

132. Senate vote # 1136, July 20, 1989.

133. Senate vote # 1119, June 11, 1985.

134. Zelnick, page 117; Turque, pp. 141-142.

135. Walter McDougall, The Heavens and the Earth: A Political History of the Space Age (New York: Basic Books, 1985); Marc Trachtenberg, History and Strategy (Princeton, N.J.: Princeton University Press, 1991); and Patrick Glynn, Closing Pandora's Box: Arms Races, Arms Control, and the End of the Cold War (New York: Basic Books, 1992).

136. Glynn, Ibid.

137. Gore told the anecdote on himself; MSNBC Equal Time, February 2, 2000.

138. Interview with Senator Gore, UPI, February 14, 1985.

139. Interview with Senator Gore, *San Diego Union Tribune*, October 22, 1986.

140. Congressional Quarterly Votes # 100, 101, and 102, 06/04/85.

141. Congressional Quarterly Vote # 136, 05/13/88; Vote # 101, 08/05/88.

142. Zelnick, pp. 145-147.

143. *Washington Post*, January 26, 1978.

144. Id.

145. Id.

146. Id.

147. *National Review*, June 24, 1991.

148. *The New Republic*, April 22, 1985.

149. *Los Angeles Times*, May 3, 1987.

150. *The New Yorker*, November 28, 1994.

151. *Baltimore Sun*, April 13, 1987.

152. *Newsweek* March 23, 1998; *Washington Post*, January 30, 1999.

153. Zelnick, pp. 145-147.

154. Ibid., page 149.

155. Ibid., pp. 149-150.

156. Ibid., pp. 148-149.

157. *CBS News.com*, January 30, 2000.

158. Id.

159. *Los Angeles Times*, August 23, 1987.

160. CBS News.com, January 30, 2000.

161. Ibid., page 156.

162. Peretz quote in Zelnick, page 156; Wieseltier quote in *The New Yorker*, November 28, 1994.

163. Ibid., pp. 151, 157.

164. Quoted in *Newsday*, February 26, 1988.

165. *The Washington Post*, August 30, 1996; CNN's "Inside Politics," March 19, 1999.

166. Lewis, Buying of the President, 2000, page 145.

167. Michael Barone & Grant Ujifusa, The Almanac of American Politics, 1990.

168. Zelnick, page 163.

169. Zelnick, pp. 161-164.

170. Zelnick, pp. 164-165; *Washington Post*, April 10, 1988.

171. Turque, pp. 210-211.

172. Zelnick, page 165.

173. Ibid. pp. 166-168.

174. Charles Lewis The Selling of the President, 2000 (New York: Avon, 2000), pp. 167-168; Zelnick, pp. 287-288; *Dave Bossie Special Report* "The Chinese Fund Raising and Espionage Scandals" 2000; FBI FD 302 Transcript of Interviews with John Huang, December 2, 1998.

175. Zelnick, page 170.

176. Lloyd Grove, "Pop Goes the Wieseltier" *Vanity Fair*, March 1995; Sam Tanenhaus, "Wayward Intellectual Finds God" *The New York Times Sunday Magazine*, January 24, 1999.

177. Andrew Sullivan, (ed.) Same Sex Marriage (New York: Vintage Books, 1997; Sullivan, Virtually Normal: An Argument About Homosexuality (New York: Knopf, 1996); Sullivan, (ed.) The New Republic Guide to the Candidates, 1996 (New York: Basic Books, 1996); Walter Kirn, "The Editor as Gap Model," *The New York Times Magazine*, March 7, 1993.

178. *CQ Weekly Report*, July 11, 1992; Gore on Meet the Press, September 6, 1992.

179. Gore on Meet the Press, September 6, 1992.

180. Congressman Don Edwards at NARAL press conference, January 22, 1990.

181. RNC briefing book, Albert Arnold Gore, Jr.: On the Issues, (Washington, D.C.: RNC, April 1999), page 145.

182. Jeffrey J. Clarke, Advice and Support, 1965-1973: The U.S. Army in Vietnam (Washington, D.C., GPO, 1986.)

183. Michael Barone & Grant Ujifusa, The Almanac of American Politics, 1992 (National Journal, 1991).

184. See *The New Republic*'s coverage August 1990-March 1991.

185. *The New York Times*, July 25, 1992.

186. Matthew Rees, "The Real Al Gore" *Weekly Standard* May 19, 1997.

187. The New York Times, July 25, 1992.

188. Michael Barone & Grant Ujifusa, The Almanac of American Politics, 1992 (National Journal, 1991).

189. Al Gore, *Congressional Record,* January 30, 1991.

190. Boston Globe, April 13, 1991.

191. Al Gore to the Associated Press, July 17, 1991.

192. Al Gore on *ABC's Nightline,* July 24, 1991.

193. Albert Gore, Jr. Earth in the Balance, page 15.

194. The Williamson Leader, September 24, 1992.

195. Id., *The Washington Times,* October 29, 1992.

196. Michael Barone & Grant Ujifusa, The Almanac of American Poltics, 1992 (Washington, D.C.: National Journal, 1991).

197. Albert Gore, Jr. Earth in the Balance (1992), page 269.

198. Julian Simon, The Ultimate Resource (Princeton, 1981); P.T. Bauer, Dissent About Development (Harvard, 1971) Reality and Rhetoric (Harvard, 1984); Nicholas Eberstadt, The Tyranny of Numbers (AEI, 1994).

199. Albert Gore, Jr., Earth in the Balance (1992), page 42.

200. Ibid., page 49.

201. Ibid., pp. 49, 177.

202. Ibid., page 294.

203. Gregg Easterbrook, Review of Earth in the Balance, *Newsweek* June 1, 1992.

204. Easterbrook, "Green Cassandras" *The New Republic,* July 6, 1992.

205. Earth in the Balance, pp. 40, 73.

206. Roger Revelle quoted in George Will column, *The Washington Post,* September 8, 1992.

207. Revelle, Singer, and Starr, First issue of Cosmos, 1991.

208. Turque, pp. 235-236, 237.

209. Zelnick, pp. 190-194.

210. Earth in the Balance, pp. 297, 300-301, 304; transcript of Quayle-Gore debate, October, 1992, RNC Working Document, October 14, 1992.

211. Earth in the Balance, page 213.

212. Ibid. pp. 325, 326.

213. Statistics compiled by National Automobile Manufacturers Association, 1992.

214. Gore comment to *The Washington Post,* September 4, 1992.

215. Reported in The Washington Times, May 31, 1996.

216. Earth in the Balance, page 26; Senate Public Financial Disclosure Report of Sen. Al Gore, 1991, page 6.

217. Earth in the Balance, page 144; Gore interview, *The New York Times*, January 27, 1988.

218. Earth in the Balance, page 114.

219. Quoted in the *Nashville Tennessean*, September 21, 1992; Turque, pp. 199-202;

220. All quotes, *Washington Times*, October 29, 1992.

221. See UPI "Tiny Mussel Delays $216 Million Columbia Dam, November 28, 1983; H.R. 5879, March 31, 1977; Letter from Senator Gore to James Pulliam, Regional Director, U.S. Dept. of Interior, August 4, 1986; "Endangered Species Endanger Dam" Washington Post, February 11, 1977; UPI, "Senate kills amendment to Endangered Species Act," October 23, 1990.

222. Boston Globe, August 16, 1992; Gore's financial disclosure forms and FEC disclosure forms.

223. Zelnick, page 206.

224. He admitted it to Monica Lewinsky, See Starr Report, (Washington, D.C.: GPO, 1998).

225. Floyd Brown, Slick Willie (Annapolis Publishing Company, 1992), Page 133, Appendix A.

226. Zelnick, pp. 208-210.

227. 1991 Congressional Quarterly Almanac

228. Lewis, The Selling of the President, 2000 pp. 154-158.

229. Washington Post, January 24, 1988; The New York Times, July 31, 1992; CQ Vote # 49, March 13, 1992; CQ Vote #179, July 4, 1981; Earth in the Balance (1992).

230. Average of Annual ADA rankings in Albert Arnold Gore, Jr. *On the Issues* (Washington: D.C.: RNC, April 1999), page 142-143.

231. Al Gore on NBC *Today*, April 16, 1993; Newsweek, October 31, 1994.

232. Peretz interview quoted in Turque, page 247.

233. Votes for gender-racial quotas: 1990, CQ, 108, 138, 158, 159, 161, 275, 276.; 1991, CQ, 110,187.

234. Michael Barone & Grant Ujifusa, Almanac of American Politics, 1994.

235. Quotation in Turque, page 21.

236. James Carville & Mary Matalin, with Peter Knobler All's Fair (New York: Random House, 1994).

237. Zelnick, page 218.

238. Zelnick, pp. 219-223.

239. Ibid., pp. 223-228.

240. Mary McGrory column, *Washington Post* June 10, 1993.

241. NBC Today April 16, 1993.

242. Quoted in the *Tennessean*, July 25, 1976.

243. Quoted in the *Tennessean*, October 17, 1984.

244. Quoted in *United Press International*, October 13, 1987.

245. Congressional Record, March 18, 1993.

246. Gore quoted in Bob Woodward, The Agenda (New York: Random House, 1994).

247. Turque, pp. 270-271.

248. HJ Res. 350 in Congress and the Nation, 1981-1984; 1992 Senate Votes, 72, 135, and 136, Congressional Quarterly.

249. 1986 Senate Vote 45, Congressional Quarterly.

250. Al Gore quoted in *National Journal*, April 2, 1988.

251. Zelnick, pp. 267-268.

252. *Washington Times*, May 9, 1995.

253. *U.S. News and World Report*, June 26, 1995; *London Financial Times*, January 29, 1996.

254. James O. Finckenhauer & Elin T. Waring, The Russian Mafia in America: Immigration, Culture, and Crime (Boston: Northeastern University Press, 1998).

255. New York Times, November 23, 1998.

256. *The Moscow Times*, November 25, 1998.

257. Jacob Heilbrunn, "Tomorrow Never Dies" *New Republic* March 2, 1998, page 45.

258. David Reminick, *Foreign Affairs*, January/February 1997.

259. *The New York Times*, May 5, 1999.

260. Lewis, The Buying of the President, 2000, pp. 152-153.

261. Ibid., pp. 153-154.

262. Id.

263. Audrey Hudson, "Report: Clinton aides, environmentalists ally," *Washington Times* February 22, 2000.

264. Turque, pp. 294-296; oil rigs number from Oliver North, "U.S. over a barrel," *The Washington Times*, March 12, 2000.

265. Turque, pp. 333-336; Zelnick, pp. 319-334.

266. "Accomplishments," National Partnership for Reinventing Government website, March 2, 1999.

267. Andrew J. Bacevich, Schulze lecture reprinted in *Marine Corps Gazette*, November 1998.

268. *The Washington Times*, September 8, 1998.

269. Robert J. Samuelson column, *The Washington Post*, September 25, 1996.

270. *The Washington Post*, March 3, 1998.

271. *The Arkansas Democrat Gazette,* February 9, 1998.

272. Quoted in *The Washington Post*, November 6, 1997.

273. CNN's *Late Edition* with Wolf Blitzer, March 9, 1999.

274. Almanac of American Poltics, 2000, page 53.

275. Tucker Carlson, "Follow the Money" *Talk*, March 2000.

276. Carlson, op.cit.; Lewis, op.cit.

277. Id.

278. Id.

279. Id.

280. Radio Communications Report, March 23, 1998.

281. Ibid., pp. 156-157.

282. Lewis, page 157.

283. Lloyd Grove, "The Reliable Source," *The Washington Post*, March 1, 2000.

284. Gore at Democratic Convention, August 28, 1956.

285. House Republican Policy Committee, *Policy Perspective*, October 28, 1996.

286. *The Los Angeles Times*, October 6, 1996.

287. *The Wall Street Journal*, November, 3, 1998.

288. David Carr, "There's Something About Terry" *Washington City Paper* October 1-7, 1999.

289. *The Dave Bossie Investigative Report* , December 1999.

290. Tim Russert on *Meet the Press*, December 19, 1999.

291. Bossie, op.cit.; Lewis, op.cit. pp. 167-168.

292. Bob Woodward, *The Washington Post*, March 2, 1997.

293. Michael Barone & Grant Ujifusa, The Almanac of American Politics, 1998.

294. Quoted in Cal Thomas column, *Newsday*, April 1, 1997.

295. Quoted in *The Wall Street Journal*, January 26, 2000.

296. *Universal Gates Monthly (*May 1996) translated by Becky Chang for House Gov. Affairs Comt., quoted in Turque, page 315.

297. See *Dave Bossie Investigative Report* on Campaign Fund Raising Scandals and Chinese Espionage; Zelnick, pp. 293-295; RNC document, 11 Reasons Why Al Gore Should Have Known the Buddhist Temple Event Was a Fundraiser.

298. *The Washington Post*, February 15, 1997.

299. Gore quoted in *The New York Times*, March 12, 2000.

300. Pete Yost, "Dems Fund Raiser Hsia Found Guilty" *Associated Press* March 2, 2000; Neil A. Lewis, "Gore Fund-Raiser Convicted for Arranging Illegal Gifts" *The New York Times*, March 3, 2000.

301. Id.

302. Gore on audio tape released by the White House in Memphis Commercial Appeal, October 17, 1997.

303. *Los Angeles Times*, March 10, 2000, page 1.

304. Zelnick, pp. 250-251.

305. FBI Interview, August 8, 1998; Memo by David Strauss, November 21, 1995.

306. Al Gore, White House Press Conference, March 3, 1997; *The Washington Times*, March 4, 1997.

307. *The New York Times*, August 27, 1997; *The Washington Times*, August 27, 1997.

308. *The Washington Times*, August 27, 1997.

309. See *Dave Bossie's Special Report* : The Rajin' Cajun James Carville— Bill Clinton's Untethered Attack Dog (Washington, D.C.: National Media Enterprises, 1999).

310. Albert Hunt column, *The Wall Street Journal*, March 13, 1997.

311. Id.

312. Landow letter to the editor, *The Wall Street Journal*, March 20, 1997.

313. Albert Hunt column, *The Wall Street Journal*, March 19, 1998.

314. Lewis, The Selling of the President, 2000, page 165.

315. Quoted in *The Washington Times*, March 18, 1998.

316. Quoted in The Starr Report (Washington, D.C.: Government Printing Office, 1998).

317. Quoted in *The Washington Times*, March 18, 1998.

318. Lewis, Selling of the President, 2000, page 165.

319. Id.

320. Matthew Rees, *The Weekly Standard*, March 30, 1998.

321. *Newsweek*, March 23, 1998.

322. Id.

323. *The Washington Post*, January 30, 1999.

324. Id.

325. Quoted in *Arkansas Democrat Gazette*, February 1, 1999.

326. Matthew Rees, *The Weekly Standard*, March 30, 1998.

327. Lewis, Selling of the President, 2000, page 172.

328. Id.

329. Zelnick, page 313.

330. Lewis, pp. 172-173.

331. Lewis, page 172; *Time*, June 9, 1997; *The Washington Times*, November 6, 1997.

332. Lewis, pp. 172-173; *The Washington Times*, November 6, 1997.

333. Quoted in Lewis, page 173.

334. Id.

335. Quoted in *The Washington Post*, January 23, 1998.

336. *The Sacramento Bee.*

337. Quoted in *The Washington Times*, July 31, 1998.

338. *Los Angeles Times*, August 18, 1998.

339. Id.

340. Turque, pp. 350-356.

341. Quoted in *The New York Times*, September 13, 1998.

342. Quoted in *Gannett News Service*, September 26, 1998.

343. Quoted in *The New York Times*, September 23, 1998.

344. Quoted in *The Associated Press*, September 28, 1998.

345. Quoted in *the Associated Press*, September 30, 1998.

346. Quoted in *The Baltimore Sun*, October 2, 1998.

347. Quoted in *The Washington Post*, October 7, 1998.

348. Quoted in *The Washington Post*, October 14, 1998.

349. Quoted in *The Saint Louis Post Dispa*tch, October 17, 1998.

350. Quoted in *The Washington Times*, November 4, 1998; *Star Tribune*, November 5, 1998.

351. Gore interview with *NBC News*, December 18, 1998.

352. Gore interview on *Both Sides with Jesse Jackson*, December 27, 1998.

353. Quoted in *The Washington Post.*

354. *The Washington Post*, December 23, 1998.

355. Quoted in *The Associated Press*, January 8, 1999.

356. See *Dave Bossie Special Report* "The Rajin' Cajun James Carville" (Washington, D.C.: National Media Enterprises, 1999; T. Harry Williams, Huey Long (New York: Alfred A. Knopf, 1969), Chapters 14, 15.

357. Quotes from *Gannett News Service*, February 12, 1999.

358. Quoted in *News Max Com*, December 15, 1999.

359. Michael Barone & Grant Ujifusa, The Almanac of American Politics, 2000, page 51.

360. Michael Duffy & Karen Tumulty, "Gore's Secret Guru" *Time* November 8, 1999.

361. See *Dave Bossie Special Report*, Chinese Espionage and Technology Transfer.

362. Ibid.

363. Ibid.

364. Brooks Jackson, Honest Graft (New York: 1990).

365. See Bill Hogan, "The Coelho Case," *National Journal* March 23, 2000. Center for Public Integrity web site, www.public-.org, October 1, 1999; *Associated Press*, October 4, 1999.

366. Id.

367. *The Washington Post*, October 22, 1988; Newsday, October 26, 1988.

368. Powell letter to Al Gore, January 6, 2000.

369. *Dave Bossie Special Report*, "The Ragin' Cajun James Carville," page 6-7.

370. Schmoke quoted in *The Washington Post*, November 2, 1998.

371. *St. Petersburg Times*, A

372. *The Associated Press*, February 16, 1992.

373. Marjorie Williams, op.cit.

374. Quoted from *George*, June 1998.

375. *The Washington Post*, November 1, 1999.

376. Naomi Wolf, Promiscuities (New York: Random House, 1997).

377. Gore quoted in *Tennessean*, July 1, 1991.

378. Ellen Warren & Terry Armour, *Chicago Tribune*, February 2, 2000.

379. Gore on MSNBC *Equal Time*, February 2, 2000.

380. Peter Boyer, "Gore's Dilemma" *The New Yorker* November 28, 1994.

381. Marjorie Williams, op. cit.

382. Quoted in Turque, page 342.

383. *The New York Post* and *The New York Times*, both February 16, 2000.

384. Speech to the Brookings Institution, September 2, 1998.

385. See Turque and Gore, op. cit.

386. Marjorie Williams, op. cit.